a+u

Architecture and Urbanism
Forthcoming June, 2020
Special Issue
建築と都市　2020年6月号臨時増刊

エー・アンド・ユー
2020年6月臨時増刊
発売：2020年5月28日
予価：2,200円（税込
発行：（株）エー・アン

infraordinary 東京 Tokyo, the Rights to the City

June 2020 special *a+u* research issue edited by Darko Radović

In May 2020, *a+u* will release a special issue featuring "Tokyo".
With Professor Darko Radović from Keio University as a guest editor and a
word by Georges Perec, "infra-ordinary" (Perec, "Approaches to What?", 1973)
as a keyword, this issue will introduce multiple "infra" layers underneath the
"ordinary" Tokyo.
Professor Radović who studied architecture and urbanism in Europe,
Australia, and various Asian countries, has been living in Tokyo for more
than a decade. His skilled "outsider's" eyes and real "lived" (Lefebvre, 1974)
experiences will be the underlying structure of the issue. And we will invite
more than 20 experts in architecture, urbanism, and sociology to introduce
research-based discussion from various perspectives.
This issue will demonstrate Professor Radović's fractal understandings of
Tokyo in-between architecture and urbanism.

2020年5月、『a+u』臨時増刊号で「東京」を特集する。
ゲスト・エディターに慶應義塾大学のダルコ・ラドヴィッチ教授を迎え、ジョルジュ・ペ
レックの言葉「infra-ordinary（並－以下のもの）」(Perec, "Approaches to What?",
1973) をキーワードに、ふだん見なれた（ordinary）都市を掘り下げる（infra-）という意
図で、新たな「東京」を多層的に紹介する。
欧豪そしてアジア各国で建築・都市を研究し、過去十数年東京に在住しているラドヴィ
ッチ氏の、熟練した「外からの」視点と、実際に「生きられた」(Lefebvre, 1974) 東京の
場所々々が本号の軸である。その中で国内外からの20名以上の建築家・都市計画家・社
会学者などに様々な目線から東京をリサーチ・ベースで語っていただいた。
「建築」と「都市」のはざまで東京をとらえるラドヴィッチ氏のフラクタルな思考の一端を
紹介する。

Drawing by Davisi Boomtharm

Architecture and Urbanism

2020:04　No.595

発行者・編集長
吉田信之

デザイン・コンサルタント
マッシモ・ヴィネリ

副編集長
横山圭
シルビア・チェン

編集スタッフ
グレイス・ホン
小野寺諒朔
佐藤綾子
キャメロン・コルテズ

レイアウト制作
安藤聡(pickles design)

海外事業担当
ヌル・ロスマワティ

表紙：モジュール式壁の組立て構造から、骨片やDNAハイドロゲルにわたる検討を行った、ポリブリック1.0から3.0までのポリブリック・シリーズの発展形態。
裏表紙：モルフェウス・ホテルの自由形状構造外骨格のディテール。

©建築と都市　595号　令和2年3月27日発行
毎月1回27日発行
昭和46年3月3日第三種郵便物認可
定価：2,852円(本体2,593円)
年間購読料34,224円(年12冊／税・送料込み)
発行：株式会社エー・アンド・ユー
〒100-6017　東京都千代田区霞が関三丁目2番5号霞が関ビルディング17階
電話：(03)6205-4384　FAX：(03)6205-4387
青山ハウス
〒107-0062　東京都港区南青山二丁目19番14号
電話：(03)6455-5597　FAX：(03)6455-5583
E-mail: au@japan-architect.co.jp
URL: https://shinkenchiku.online
振替：00130-5-98119
印刷：大日本印刷株式会社
取次店＝トーハン・日販・中央社・鍬谷・西村・楽天ブックスネットワーク

特集：
コンピュテーショナル・デザインの展開

Architecture and Urbanism
2020:04   No.595

Publisher/Editor:
Nobuyuki Yoshida

Design Consultant:
Massimo Vignelli

Senior Editor:
Kei Yokoyama
Sylvia Chen

Editorial Staff:
Grace Hong
Ryosaku Onodera
Ayako Sato
Cameron Cortez

Layout Design:
Satoshi Ando (pickles design)

**International Business
Development:**
Nur Rosmawati

Distributor:
Shinkenchiku-sha Co., Ltd.

*Front Cover: The evolving morphologies of the
PolyBrick series, from PolyBrick 1.0 to 3.0,
with considerations ranging from modular
wall assemblies, to bone fragments, to DNA
hydrogels. Courtesy of the Sabin Lab.
Back Cover: Detail of the Morpheus Hotel's
free-form structural exoskeleton. Photo by Ivan
Dupont, courtesy of Zaha Hadid Architects.*

©A+U Publishing Co., Ltd. 2020
Printed in Japan
Published by A+U Publishing Co., Ltd.
Kasumigaseki Building 17F, 3-2-5,
Kasumigaseki, Chiyoda-ku, Tokyo
100-6017, Japan
Tel: +81-3-6205-4384 Fax: +81-3-6205-4387
Aoyama House
2-19-14 Minamiaoyama, Minato-ku, Tokyo
107-0062, Japan
Tel: +81-3-6455-5597 Fax: +81-3-6455-5583
E-mail: au@japan-architect.co.jp
URL: https://au-magazine.com

ISBN 978-4-9002-1249-7
a+u = Architecture and Urbanism is handled
exclusively
by Shinkenchiku-sha Co., Ltd.:
Kasumigaseki Building 17F, 3-2-5,
Kasumigaseki, Chiyoda-ku, Tokyo
100-6017, Japan
Tel: +81-3-6205-4380 Fax: +81-3-6205-4386
E-mail : ja-business@japan-architect.co.jp
Subscription rate for 2019 outside Japan
¥42,000 (Airmail – Asia), ¥45,000 (Airmail –
Europe, North America, Oceania, & Middle
East), ¥49,000 (Airmail – South America &
Africa)
U.S.Dollars, Euro, and Sterling Pounds
equivalent to the above Japanese Yen prices
are acceptable. Your remittance should be
converted at the current exchange rate when
you remit us.

Feature:
Computational Discourses

ナル・デザインの展開

Morpheus Tower
Zaha Hadid Architects

10^6

+u examines the application of computational
ital fabrication across a spectrum of scales – from
gh-rise exoskeleton, to bio-mimetic wearables
o the printed structure of a nonstandard brick –
eptual cues from Charles and Ray Eames' 1977
f Ten. Selected here are 14 projects by individuals
orking in cross-disciplinary ways, that suggest
g digitally" can do with the means of our present

e issue's projects, the shaping and organizing
erials, via computational methods, serve as
ints. Supporting them are texts by Jenny E.
chumacher, and Achim Menges. Through the
rawn from this iterative collection of work, we
the unfamiliar more familiar, and to provoke
t the relationship between natural systems, digital
d the shaping of the material environment.   *(a+u)*

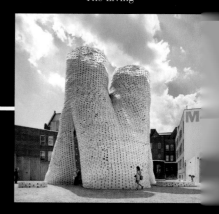

Hy-Fi
The Living

ーショナル・デザインとデジタル・マニファクチュアの応用を特集
レイ・イームズによる短編映画『パワーズ・オブ・テン』(1977) に
を横断して──高くそびえる自由形態の外骨格から、ウェアラブル、
された非標準煉瓦まで──プロジェクトを並べた。いま現在利用でき
「デジタル思考」によって何が可能となったのか、という問いに答える
個人や団体による14作品を紹介する。

ル手法を用いて多様な素材にどうかたちを与えていくのか。この点
紹介する際の出発点となる。その理解を深めるためジェニー・E・セ
・シューマッハ、アヒム・メンゲスらによる論考を収録した。これ
紹介することで導かれてくる関係性を手がかりに、得体の知れない
みをもたせ、自然の体系、デジタル技術、物質界にかたちを与える
れるべく関係について、その魅力の一端が垣間見えるのではないだ
（編）

Silk Pavilion
Neri Oxman and The Mediated Matter
Group, Massachusetts Institute of
Technology (MIT)

Minima | Maxima
MARC FORNES / THEVERYMANY

Ada
Jenny Sabin Studio

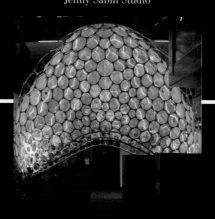

One Thousand Museum
Zaha Hadid Architects

Kolon One & Only Tower
Morphosis

Embodied Computation Lab
The Living

BUGA Fiber Pavilion
University of Stuttgart
Institute for Computational Design
and Construction (ICD)

BUGA Wood Pavilion
University of Stuttgart
Institute for Computational Design
and Construction (ICD)

ICD/ITKE Research Pavilion
University of Stuttgart
Institute for Computational Design
and Construction (ICD)

Aguahoja
Neri Oxman and The Mediated Matter
Group, Massachusetts Institute of
Technology (MIT)

Wanderers
Neri Oxman and The Mediated Matter
Group, Massachusetts Institute of
Technology (MIT)

PolyBrick Series
Sabin Lab, Department of Architecture,
Cornell University

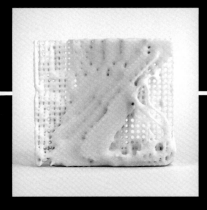

10^{-6}

Essay Contributors

エッセイ寄稿者

Portrait by Jesse Winter

Jenny E. Sabin is an architectural designer whose work is at the forefront of a new direction for 21st-century architectural practice – one that investigates the **intersections of architecture and science** and **applies insights and theories from biology and mathematics to the design of responsive material structures and adaptive architecture**. Sabin is the Arthur L. and Isabel B. Wiesenberger Professor in Architecture and Associate Dean for Design at Cornell College of Architecture, Art, and Planning, where she established a new advanced research degree in Matter Design Computation. She is the principal of Jenny Sabin Studio, an experimental architectural design studio based in Ithaca and Director of the Sabin Lab at Cornell AAP. Sabin holds degrees in ceramics and interdisciplinary visual art from the University of Washington and a Master of Architecture from the University of Pennsylvania. She was awarded a Pew Fellowship in the Arts 2010 and was named a USA Knight Fellow in Architecture. In 2014, she was awarded the prestigious Architectural League Prize. Her work has been exhibited internationally, including at the FRAC Centre, Cooper Hewitt Design Triennial, MoMA, and most recently as part of Imprimer Le Monde at the Pompidou. Her book *LabStudio: Design Research Between Architecture and Biology*, co-authored with Peter Lloyd Jones, was published in 2017. Sabin won MoMA & MoMA PS1's Young Architects Program with her submission Lumen in 2017.

ジェニー・E・セイビンは、21世紀における建築実践の新たな方向の最前線に立つ建築家であり、**建築と科学の交差点**について研究し、**生物学と数学からの洞察や理論を応答性材料構造のデザインとアダプティブ・アーキテクチュアに応用**する。コーネル大学建築・芸術・計画学部（AAP）アーサー・L＆イザベル・B・ヴィーゼンベルガー建築教授、およびデザイン副学部長であり、物質設計計算の新しい先端研究学位を設立。イサカに拠点を置く実験的な建築デザイン・スタジオであるジェニー・セイビン・スタジオのプリンシパルであり、コーネル大学AAPセイビン・ラボのディレクターである。ワシントン大学でセラミックと多分野視覚芸術の学位を取得、またペンシルベニア大学で建築学の修士号を取得。2010年芸術のピュー・フェローシップを受賞し、建築の米国ナイト・フェローに任命された。2014年に名誉あるアーキテクチュラル・リーグ・プライズを受賞した。セイビンの作品は、FRACセンター、クーパー・ヒューイット・デザイン・トリエンナーレ、ニューヨーク近代美術館（MoMA）、またごく最近ではポンピドゥー・センターの「変化・創造／世界をプリントする」など、世界で展示されている。ピーター・ロイド・ジョーンズとの共著である『LabStudio：建築と生物学の間のデザイン・リサーチ』は2017年に出版された。セイビンは、2017年のMoMA & MoMA PS1のヤング・アーキテクツ・プログラムに「ルーメン」を応募し、勝利した。　　　　　　（松本晴子訳）

See pp. 8–9 for the essay ／ エッセイは 8 〜 9 頁掲載

Portrait courtesy of ZHA

Portrait courtesy of ICD

Patrik Schumacher is the principal of Zaha Hadid Architects (ZHA). He joined ZHA in 1988 and was seminal in developing ZHA to become a global architecture and design brand. Patrik Schumacher studied philosophy, mathematics, and architecture in Bonn, Stuttgart, and London. He received his Diploma in Architecture in 1990. He has been a partner at ZHA since 2003 and a co-author on all projects. In 2010, Patrik Schumacher won the Royal Institute of British Architects' Stirling Prize, together with Zaha Hadid. In 1996, he founded the Design Research Laboratory at the Architectural Association in London where he continues to teach. In 1999, he completed his Ph.D. at the Institute for Cultural Science, Klagenfurt University. Over the last 20 years, he has contributed over 100 articles to architectural journals and anthologies. In 2008, he coined the phrase **Parametricism** and has since published a series of manifestos promoting Parametricism as the new epochal style for the 21st century. In 2010/2012, he published his two-volume theoretical opus, *The Autopoiesis of Architecture*. Patrik Schumacher is widely recognized as one of the most prominent thought leaders within the fields of architecture, urbanism, and design.

Achim Menges is a registered architect in Frankfurt and professor at Stuttgart University, where he is the founding director of the Institute for Computational Design and Construction (ICD) and the director of the Cluster of Excellence on Integrative Computational Design and Construction for Architecture (IntCDC). In addition, he has been Visiting Professor in Architecture at Harvard University's Graduate School of Design and held multiple other visiting professorships in Europe and the United States. He graduated with honors from the Architectural Association (AA), where he subsequently taught in the AA Diploma and Graduate School.

The focus of Achim Menges' practice and research is on the **development of integrative design at the intersection of computational design methods, robotic manufacturing, and construction**, as well as **advanced material and building systems**. He has published more than 15 books on this work and related fields of design research, and he is the author/co-author of more than 175 scientific papers and numerous articles. His projects and design works have received many international awards, have been published and exhibited worldwide, and form parts of several renowned museum collections, including the permanent collection of the Centre Pompidou in Paris and the Victoria and Albert Museum in London.

パトリック・シューマッハはザハ・ハディド・アーキテクツ（ZHA）の代表を務める。シューマッハは1988年にザハ・ハディッドに加わり、ZHAを世界的な建築デザイン・ブランドに発展させる主要な役割を担った。ボン、シュトゥットガルト、ロンドンで哲学、数学、建築を学ぶ。建築学の学位を取得したのは1990年である。2003年からパートナーとなり、すべてのプロジェクトを共同で考案。2010年にザハ・ハディッドと共に英国王立建築家協会スターリング賞を受賞。1996年にロンドンのAAスクールにデザイン研究所を設立し、現在まで教鞭をとっている。999年にクラーゲンフルト大学文化科学研究所で博士課程を修了。過去20年にわたり、建築雑誌や論考集に100件を超える記事を寄稿。2008年にパ**ラメトリシズム**という造語を考案し、爾来、パラメトリシズムを21世紀の新しい画期的なスタイルとして推進する一連のマニフェストを発表している。2010〜2012年に、2巻にわたる理論的著作『建築のオートポイエーシス』を発表した。建築、都市化、デザインの分野で最も著名な思想的リーダーの一人として広く認知される。

（松本晴子訳）

アヒム・メンゲスはフランクフルトの登録建築家であり、シュトゥットガルト大学の常勤教授、計算設計建設研究所（ICD）の設立時からのディレクター、建築統合計算設計建設（IntCDC）クラスター・オブ・エクセレンスのディレクターを務める。またハーヴァード大学デザイン大学院で建築学客員教授を務めており、さらに欧州と米国の複数の大学で客員教授を務めてきた。メンゲスはAAスクールを優秀な成績で卒業し、その後AAディプロマと大学院で教鞭をとった。

メンゲスは、**コンピューテーショナル・デザイン・メソッド、ロボット製造・建設、先端材料と建築システムの交差点において、統合デザインの開発**に実践と研究の焦点を置く。こうした研究とデザイン研究の関連分野で15冊以上の著作を出版し、単著、共著を含めて175以上の科学的論文と多数の記事を発表してきた。メンゲスのプロジェクトとデザイン作品は、多数の国際的な賞を受賞し、世界中で公開、展示されており、いくつかの著名な美術館に収蔵され、とりわけパリのポンピドゥー・センターやロンドンのヴィクトリア＆アルバート美術館の常設コレクションの一部を形成している。

（松本晴子訳）

See pp. 40–47 for the essay ／ **エッセイは40〜47頁掲載**

See pp. 112–119 for the essay ／ **エッセイは112〜119頁掲載**

Introduction:
Generative Architecture: Making a Critical Practice
Jenny E. Sabin, Founder of Jenny Sabin Studio and Sabin Lab

イントロダクション：
生成的建築：批評的実践の習慣化
ジェニー・E・セイビン（ジェニー・セイビン・スタジオ、セイビン・ラボ創設者）
松本晴子訳

A comprehensive history of generative architecture has yet to be written, but many of the featured designers and architects in this issue of *a+u* have made substantial contributions to its more recent history over the last 20 years. Has a critical project around generative architecture emerged? In his book, *The Alphabet and the Algorithm*, Mario Carpo unfolds how digital technology has altered the role of authorship in architecture and, in turn, how this has opened up existing notation systems – our tools for drawing – through parametric functions and the possibility of variability. As Carpo points out, the pioneering thinkers at the onset of digital architecture in the 1990s focused primarily upon variation as afforded through simple manipulations of parametric functions and animation software.[1] One of the more interesting early practices at the forefront of form and algorithm and computer-aided manufacturing was led by structural engineer and pioneer, Cecil Balmond and his Advanced Geometry Group (AGU) at Arup in London, U.K. Through collaborations with architects such as Toyo Ito, the AGU broke new ground in the integration of complex geometries generated through sophisticated scripts and digital tools with new trajectories in digital fabrication, construction logics, and advanced engineering. For a number of years at the turn of the 21st century in schools of architecture and emerging practices, digital techniques took over in favor of developing digital dexterity and a facility with the tools, thus overriding any coherent critical project and discourse around computational design and digital architecture. Perhaps this investment of time and technological navel-gazing was absolutely essential to progress. However, there were costs. I think about economist, architect, designer, and writer Bernard Cache, who very purposefully "left the conversation" because he was so frustrated by where early innovators in digital fabrication took things. What happened?

In the 1990s, Cache coined terms that are now commonplace, 'the non-standard', which formed the foundation for his workshop, Objectile, and subsequently generated a critical and political practice around computational design and digital fabrication. Cache discusses variation and variable curvature through his concept objectile and the difference between concavity and convexity, or, in other words, an inflection.[2] Carpo points to Cache's contribution to digital discourse in the following statement, "…the objectile is not an object but an algorithm – a parametric function which may determine an infinite variety of objects, all different (one for each set of parameters) yet all similar (as the underlying function is the same for all)."[3] Cache was interested in the inherent democratization that mass-customization through computer-aided manufacturing promised: Design and making for all. He was the first person to implement a methodology and web interface for file-to-factory production through mass-customized CNC machining of plywood panels and other wood materials. So, when he saw his famous panels in every other boutique hotel, it is not a stretch to understand why he may have been discouraged by the commodification of the non-standard and the making of digital architecture. The mainstreaming of what previously had been experimental and innovative had something to do with the technology itself and the bloodlines of digital tools that quickly became stylized and consumed. Where are things now?

Recent advances in computation, visualization, material intelligence, and fabrication technologies have begun to alter fundamentally our theoretical understanding of general design principles as well as our practical approach towards architecture and research. This renewed interest in broadening the discipline has offered alternative methods for investigating the interrelationships of parts to their wholes, and emergent self-organized material systems at multiple scales and applications. The advantages of researching and deploying such methodologies in the field of architecture are immense as they impact aspects of material systems, bio-informed and adaptive architecture, fabrication and circular construction logics, sustainable and ecological design, optimization, and formal aesthetics. The non-standard is now standard as we grapple with the complexity of the physical world of making through direct correspondence with digital fabrication machines. The work presented in this issue brings variation and the non-standard, into the realm of dynamic reciprocity through honed and diverse critical practices; what I and fellow collaborator and cell and molecular biologist, Peter Lloyd Jones, call Matrix Architecture, what Matthias Kohler calls Computational Contextualism, what Achim Menges calls Material Computation, and what Neri Oxman calls Material Ecology. Through protocols and emerging technologies that span and link disciplines, matter and form are in communication with context and the complexity of the physical and natural world. Generative techniques in fabrication emerge alongside new understandings in the organization of material through its properties and potential for assemblage, where the architect as the 21st century maker links matter, context, and form in the pursuit of meaningful, resilient, and purposeful applications in our built environment.

生成的建築（ジェネラティブ・アーキテクチュア）の包括的な歴史はまだ書かれていないものの、今号の『a+u』でとりあげられたデザイナーや建築家の多くは、過去20年間の直近の歴史に多大な貢献を果たしてきた。それでは生成的建築について、決定的なプロジェクトは出現しただろうか。マリオ・カルポは、著書『アルファベットとアルゴリズム（The Alphabet and the Algorithm）』の中で、デジタル技術が建築における作者の役割をいかに変化させたか、また一方で、それがパラメトリック関数と変異可能性を通じて、既存のノーテーション（表記）システム——私たちが描画に使うツール——をどのように開放したか、明らかにしている。カルポが指摘するように、1990年代のデジタル・アーキテクチュアの最初期の先駆的思想家たちは、この変異性をおもにパラメトリック関数とアニメーション・ソフトウェアの簡単な操作により与えられるものとして扱った[1]。形態・アルゴリズム・コンピュータ支援の製造過程を扱った、さらに興味深い最初期の実践としては、英国ロンドンを拠点とするArupでの構造エンジニア・パイオニアであるセシル・バルモンドと、バルモンド率いるアドヴァンスド・ゲオメトリー・グループ（AGU）によるものが挙げられる。AGUは、伊東豊雄をはじめとする建築家たちとのコラボレーションを通じて、洗練されたスクリプトとデジタル、ツールで生成された複雑な幾何学とデジタル・ファブリケーション、構築ロジック、高度なエンジニアリングなどの新基軸との統合に、新たな地平を切りひらいた。21世紀への変わり目、多くの建築学校や新興の設計事務所では、デジタル技術を用いてデジタルの巧緻性と道具の便宜性を向上させることにたくさんの年月が費やされた。結果、コンピュテーショナル・デザインやデジタル建築に関連する、一貫した重要なプロジェクトや議論は後回しにされることとなった。おそらく、時間や技術的な自己省察にこのように時間を費やすことは、進歩のために絶対に不可欠であったかもしれない。しかしそこには犠牲がともなった。私の脳裏に浮かぶのは、経済学者・建築家・デザイナー・著述家のベルナール・カッシュである。彼は非常に意図的に「会話から離れた」が、それはデジタル・ファブリケーションの初期の革新者たちがとりくむ場所へすこぶる不満を募らせていたためであった。一体何が起こったのか。

カッシュは1990年代に、今では決まり文句となった「非・標準（ノン・スタンダード）」という用語を考案し、「オブジェクティル」と呼ばれるワークショップの基盤を築き、その後、コンピュテーショナル・デザインとデジタル・ファブリケーションに関する政治的かつ重要な実践を行った。カッシュは、「オブジェクティル」という概念、そして凹面と凸面の違い——変曲とも——を通して曲率の変化とその変数を考察する[2]。カルポはデジタル関連の議論へのカッシュの貢献を指摘し、以下のように述べている。「…オブジェクティルは、オブジェクトではなくアルゴリズムである。このパラメトリック関数は無限にオブジェクトをつくりだすことができ、これらオブジェクトはすべて異なるが（パラメータ1組につき一つ）、すべて似通っている（基本となる関数は同じであるため）。」[3]。カッシュは、コンピュータ支援製造によるマス・カスタマイゼーションに必ず付随するであろう民主化、つまりすべての人のためのデザインと製造に関心を抱いていた。カッシュは、マス・カスタマイズされたCNC機械加工により、合板パネルやその他の木材材料を加工する、ファイル・トゥ・ファクトリー生産のための方法論とWebインター

フェイスを実装した最初の人物であった。したがってカッシュが、どこのデザイナーズ・ホテルでも自分の有名なパネルが使われているのを見て、ノン・スタンダードとデジタル・アーキテクチュア製作の商品化に落胆していただろうと理解するのは間違いではない。以前は実験的で革新的だったものが主流化することは、テクノロジーそのものと、急速に様式化され消費されるデジタル・ツールの血統と関係がある。現在はそうしたものはどこにあるのか。

コンピュテーション、視覚化、知的材料、および製造技術の最近の進歩により、一般的なデザイン原理の理論的理解と、建築や研究にたいする実践的なアプローチは根底から変化しはじめている。規範を拡大することへのこうした新たな関心は、部分と全体の相互関係を調査するための代替的な方法や、複数のスケールと応用における新興の自己組織化材料システムを提供してきた。建築の分野でこのような方法論を研究、展開する利点は、材料システム、生物情報・順応型の建築、製造循環構造ロジック、持続可能性および生態学的デザイン、最適化、および形態美学の側面に影響を与えるため、計りしれない。ノン・スタンダードは今ではスタンダードとなり、デジタル製造機械との直接的なやりとりを通じて作成する物理的な世界の複雑さを扱う。今号で紹介された作品は、研ぎすまされた多様な批判的実践を通じ、変化とノン・スタンダードを、ダイナミックな相互主義の領域にもちこむ。私と、同僚の共同研究者で細胞分子生物学者であるピーター・ロイド・ジョーンズはそれをマトリックス・アーキテクチュアと呼び、マティアス・ケーラーはコンピュテーショナル・コンテキスト主義と呼び、アヒム・メンゲスはマテリアル・コンピューティングと呼び、ネリ・オックスマンはマテリアル・エコロジーと呼ぶ。物質と形態は、専門分野を横断するプロトコルと新しいテクノロジーを通じ、物理的世界や自然界の文脈や複雑さとつながっている。製造における生成的技術は、材料の特性と集合の可能性を通じた材料の組織化における新たな理解とともに出現するが、そこでは21世紀の建築家が、つくり手として、私たちの構築環境において、意味深く、強靭で、目的のある応用を追求するために、物質、文脈、形態を結びつける。

Notes:
1. Mario Carpo, *The Alphabet and the Algorithm* (Cambridge, MA: MIT Press, 2011) 39. See Carpo's discussion on the discourse of digital variability in his first chapter titled, "Variable, Identical, Differential."
2. Bernard Cache and Michael Speaks, *"Décrochement,"* in *Earth Moves: The Furnishing of Territories* (Cambridge, MA: MIT Press, 1995).
3. Ibid., 40.

原註
1.～3. 英文参照

Commentary:
Zaha Hadid Architects

コメンタリー：
ザハ・ハディド・アーキテクツ

a+u spoke to Shajay Bhooshan, Senior Associate of Zaha Hadid Architects and co-founder of ZHA's computational design research group (ZH CODE).

a+u: *Generally speaking, how do you use computational design?*
Shajay Bhooshan: At ZH CODE, we seek a co-evolution of research and practice. Our research spans computational geometry, the wisdom of traditional building cultures and the modern discipline of computational design and robotic fabrication and manufacturing. In parallel, we apply such project-independent disciplinary knowledge with project-based opportunities, constraints and problems.

We have contributed to over 100 projects spanning from early-design to design development stages across a variety of building types – institutional to residential. We develop:
- several tool-kits to aid the creation and manipulation of shape. These tool-kits enable novel aesthetic expressions, optioneering and design evolution. We develop relationships and workflow-integration with manufacturers & suppliers for novel supply chain and delivery.
- bespoke interfaces for early design tools with Building Information Modeling (BIM) teams and workflows.

a+u: *How are you expanding upon what you have done?*
Shajay Bhooshan: We believe our accrued expertise and experience can contribute strongly and positively in the following architectural tasks and associated business value:
- High value, unique buildings that demonstrate the spatial, structural and ecological benefits of computational design with an increasing focus on timber.
- High volume residential developments including rapid deployment and factory-made housing.

On the research side, we aim to expand our existing efforts in both scientific and design-research in the so-called field of Architectural Geometry – specific shapes that integrate structural and manufacturing constraints, robotic and digital fabrication opportunities, etc.

We are particularly interested in near-field robotic construction technologies such as large-format 3D printing, along with the application of machine learning and artificial intelligence technologies within the domain of Architectural Geometry.

10

Photograph by Archmospheres.

a+uは、ザハ・ハディド・アーキテクツ（ZHA）のシニア・アソシエイトであり、ZHAのコンピュテーショナル・デザイン研究グループ（ZH CODE）の共同設立者であるシャジェ・ブーシャンに話を聞いた。

a+u: コンピュテーショナル・デザインをどのように利用しているのか、概要を教えてください。

シャジェ・ブーシャン（SB）: ZH CODEでは、研究と実践の共進化を追求している。私たちの研究は、コンピュテーショナル幾何学から伝統的な建築文化の知恵、コンピュテーショナル・デザインとロボットによる製作・製造に関する近代学問にまで及ぶ。並行して、こうしたプロジェクトに依存しない学問的知識を、プロジェクト基盤の機会、制約、および問題に応用する。

私たちは、施設設計から住宅設計まで、様々な建物の初期設計から設計開発段階に及ぶ100以上のプロジェクトに貢献してきた。とり組んできた開発は以下の通りである:

・ 形態の創造と操作を支援するツールキット。これらのツールキットにより、斬新な美的表現、選択肢の増加、デザイン的進化が可能となる。私たちは、新しいサプライチェーン（供給連鎖管理）とデリバリー（供給）のために、メー

カー・サプライヤー間の関係とワークフロー統合を進めている。

・ ビルディング・インフォメーション・モデリング（BIM）チームとワークフローを備えた初期設計ツール用の特注インターフェイス。

a+u: これまでの活動をいかに展開していきますか。

SB: 蓄積された専門知識と経験は、以下の建築のタスクと関連ビジネスの価値に大きく前向きに貢献できると考えている:

・ コンピュテーショナル・デザインにおいて木材を重点化した際の空間的、構造的、生態学的な利点を示す、高価値のユニークな建物。

・ 迅速な設置や工場生産などを備えた大規模な住宅開発。

研究面では、いわゆる建築幾何学の分野——構造および製造上の制約、ロボット工学、デジタル製造の機会などを統合する特定の形態——における科学研究とデザイン研究の既存とり組みの拡大を目指している。

私たちは、近距離ロボット構築テクノロジー（大規模な3Dプリンティングなど）に加えて、建築幾何学の領域内における機械学習および人工知能技術の応用に特に興味を抱いている。

（松本晴子訳）

Zaha Hadid Architects
Morpheus Hotel at City of Dreams
Macau, China 2013–2018

サハ・ハディド・アーキテクツ
モルフェウス・ホテル・シティ・オブ・ドリームス
中国、マカオ 2013〜2018

Conceived as a vertical extrusion of its rectangular footprint, a series of voids is carved through its centre to create an urban window connecting the hotel's interior communal spaces with the city and generating the sculptural forms that define the hotel's public spaces.

Linked at ground level with the surrounding three-storey podium of the City of Dreams resort, the Morpheus houses 770 guest rooms, suites and sky villas, and includes civic spaces, meeting and event facilities, gaming rooms, lobby atrium, restaurants, spa and rooftop pool, as well as extensive back-of-house areas and ancillary facilities.

The design resolves the hotel's many complex programs within a single cohesive envelope. Zaha Hadid Architects (ZHA) was commissioned to build the hotel in 2012. At that time, foundations were already in place of a condominium tower that did not progress. ZHA designed the Morpheus as a simple extrusion of the existing abandoned foundations; using this rectangular footprint to define a 40-storey building of two internal vertical circulation cores connected at podium and roof levels where the many guest amenities were required.

This extrusion generated a monolithic block making best use its development envelope that is restricted to a 160 m height by local planning codes. This block was then 'carved' with voids. The underlying diagram of the hotel's design is a pair of towers connected at ground and roof levels. The central atrium in-between these towers runs the height of the hotel and is traversed by external voids that connect the north and south facades. These voids create the urban window that links the hotel's interior communal spaces with the city.

Three horizontal vortices generate the voids through the building and define the hotel's dramatic internal public spaces, creating unique corner suites with spectacular views of both the atrium and the city. This arrangement maximises the number of hotel rooms with external views and guarantees an equal room distribution on either side of the building. In-between the free-form voids that traverse the atrium, a series of bridges create unique spaces for the hotel's restaurants, bars and guest lounges by renowned chefs including Alain Ducasse and Pierre Hermé.

The atrium's twelve glass elevators provide guests with remarkable views of the hotel's interior and exterior as they travel between the voids of the building. As one of the world's leading hotels, the Morpheus' interior spaces necessitated a high degree of adaptability to accommodate the many varying requirements of its guest amenities. The building's exoskeleton optimizes the interiors by creating spaces that are uninterrupted by supporting walls or columns. The world's first free-form high-rise exoskeleton, its rich pattern of structural members at lower levels progresses upwards to a less-dense grid of lighter members at its summit.

Morpheus draws on a ZHA's 40 years of research into the integration of interior and exterior, civic and private, solid and void, Cartesian and Einsteinian. Space is woven within structure to tie disparate programs together and constantly make connections.

モルフェウスのデザインは、翡翠彫刻という中国の豊饒な伝統における流体的な形態にもとづき、劇的な公共空間とゆったりとしたゲストルームを、革新的なエンジニアリングと形態的な凝集力によって合体させる。連続する空隙は、長方形の土地への接地面を垂直方向に押しだしたものとして構想され、中心を貫くように彫りこまれており、ホテル内部の共同空間と都市をつなぐアーバン・ウィンドウを創出し、ホテルの公共空間を定義づける彫刻的な形態を生成する。

モルフェウスは、シティ・オブ・ドリームス・リゾート周辺の3層のポディウムと地上階で接続しており、770室の客室、スイート、スカイ・ヴィラを擁し、また市民のための空間、会議室、イベント施設、ゲーム室、アトリウム・ロビー、レストラン、スパ、屋上プール、そして広大なバックヤードと補助施設を含む。

このデザインは、ホテルの多くの複雑なプログラムを、一つのまとまった外被で解決している。ザハ・ハディド・アーキテクツ（ZHA）は、2012年にこのホテルの建設を依頼された。当時、建設は止まっていたが、タワーマンションの建物の基礎工事はすでになされていた。ZHAは、モルフェウスを、放置状態であった既存の基礎部分をシンプルに押しだすデザインとして活用した。こうした長方形の接地面を利用し、この40階建ての建物が定義された。鉛直循環流型の2つのコアはポディウムおよび屋根レヴェルで接続され、ここに多くのゲスト用設備が設置された。押しだし部分は、地元の計画規範で160mの高さに制限された開発限度を最大限に活用した一枚岩のようなブロックを生成した。そしてブロックに空隙が「彫刻された」。

ホテルのデザインのもととなったダイアグラムは、地上と屋根のレヴェルで接続した一対のタワーである。2本のタワーの間にある中央アトリウムは、ホテルの高さ全体に走り、南北のファサードをつなげる外部の空隙に横切られる。これらの空隙は、ホテル内部の共同空間と都市をつなぐアーバン・ウィンドウとして機能する。

3つの水平な渦が建物全体に空隙を生み、ホテル内部にドラマティックな公共空間をつくりだす。そしてコーナー・スイートからはアトリウムと都市への唯一無二の壮観を臨むことができる。こうした配置により、最大限の屋外眺望を備えたホテルの居室を確保でき、建物の両側に均等配分できるようになった。アトリウムを横切るフリーフォームの空隙の間にはブリッジが架かり、ここにアラン・

デュカスやピエール・エルメら、有名シェフたちによるホテルのレストラン、バー、ゲストラウンジなど、ユニークな空間が創出される。アトリウムのガラスのエレヴェータは12基あり、ゲストは建物の空隙の間を移動する際に、ホテルの内部、外部空間に広がる素晴らしい景色を楽しめる。

モルフェウスは、世界をリードするホテルの一つであり、その内部空間は多種多様なゲスト用設備の要件に対応するため、高度な適応性を要した。建物の外骨格は、壁や柱といった支持体に中断されない空間をつくりあげ、内部空間は最適化される。世界初のフリーフォームの高層外骨格であり、構造部材が織りなす豊饒なパターンは、低層階から頂部に向かうにつれ、より軽量な部材でできたより低密度のグリッドへと上昇していく。

モルフェウスは、内部空間と外部空間、市民生活とプライヴェートな暮らし、固体と空隙、デカルトとアインシュタインの統合を目指してきたZHAの40年にわたる研究にもとづいてる。空間は構造内に織りこまれ、ばらばらのプログラムを一つに結びつけ、たえず連結をつくっている。

（松本晴子訳）

pp. 12–13: Detail of the Morpheus Hotel's free-form structural exoskeleton. Opposite: The project's steel exoskeleton works in union with two concrete cores, which operate as the main horizontal and vertical load-bearing systems. Photos by Ivan Dupont, courtesy of Zaha Hadid Architects.

12〜13頁：モルフェウス・ホテルの自由形状構造外骨格のディテール。左頁：このプロジェクトの鋼鉄製の外骨格は、主要な水平・垂直耐力システムとして機能する2つのコンクリート製コアと連動して機能する。

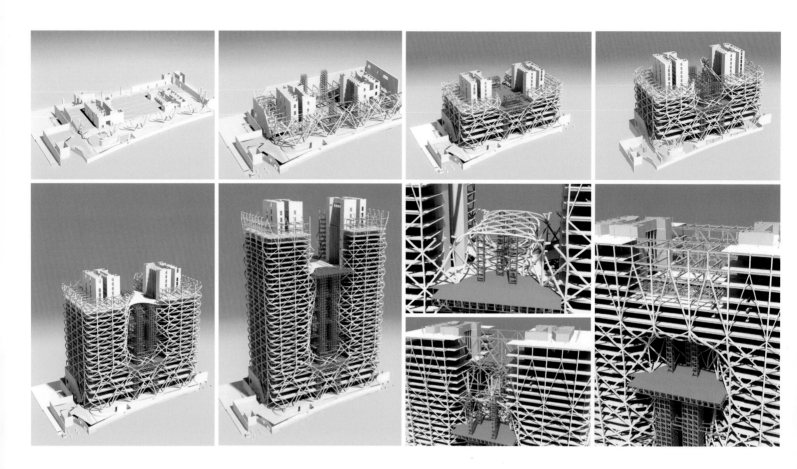

This page: Detailed construction sequence, showing the temporary structure in the center and the bottom-up methodology used in flanking areas. The exoskeleton and temporary structure were constructed in tandem, and were critical path items in determining the construction sequence. Opposite: Temporary construction access to the free-form exoskeleton and central voids. All courtesy of Zaha Hadid Architects.

本頁：中央部の仮設構造と、その両側のエリアで用いたボトムアップ工法を示した施工シークエンスの詳細。施工シークエンスを決定する上でのクリティカル・パス項目であった外骨格と仮設構造は、同時に施工された。右頁：自由形状外骨格と中央ヴォイドへの仮設構造物によるアクセス。

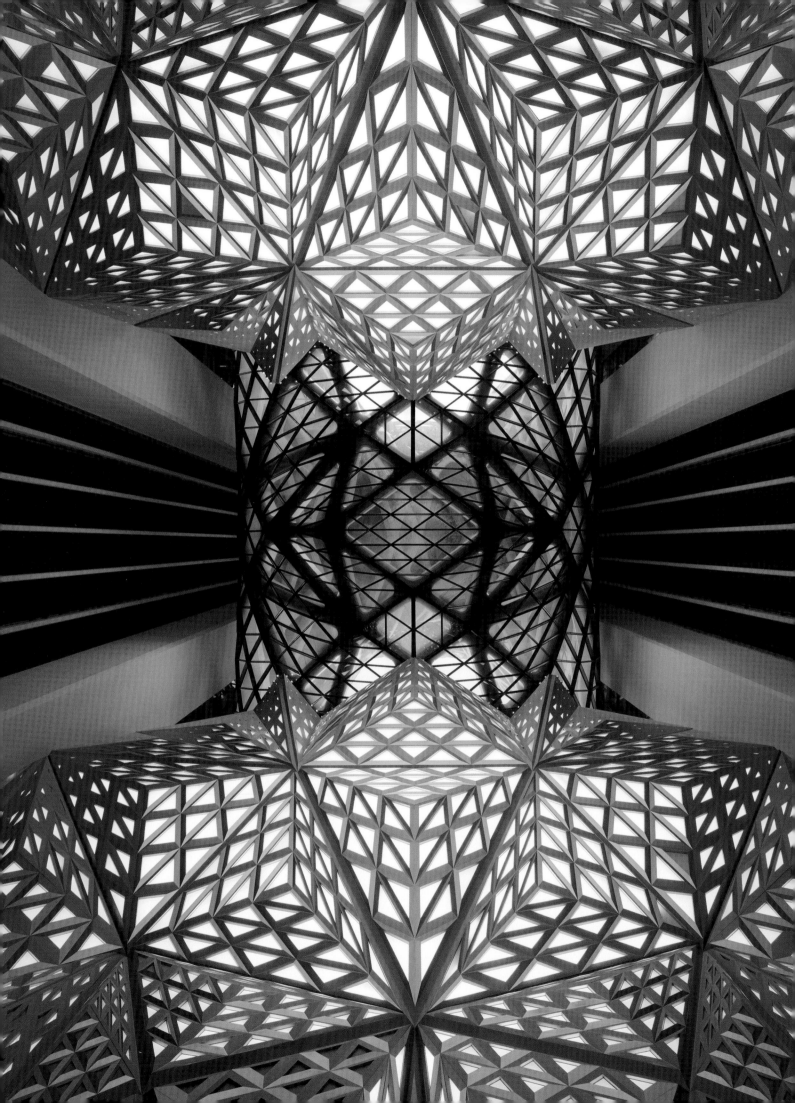

pp. 18–19: View toward the triangulated facade from the L23 Art Space. pp. 20–21: View of the L21 restaurant from the lifts. Opposite: View of the upper atrium, from the lobby. Passengers in the panoramic lifts enjoy views of alternating and interlocking internal and external spaces. This page: L01 entrance lobby with faceted front, patterned feature wall, and panoramic lifts. All photos by Virgile Simon Bertrand, courtesy of Zaha Hadid Architects.

18〜19頁：L23アート・スペースから眺めた三角形状のファサード。20〜21頁：エレヴェータから眺めたL21レストラン。左頁：ロビーから上部吹抜けを見上げる。エレヴェータの乗客は、内部と外部の空間が交互に組み合わさるパノラマビューを楽しむことができる。本頁：L01エントランスロビー。多面体で構成されたフロント、パターン状のフィーチャー・ウォールおよびパノラマビューを楽しめるエレヴェータが特徴的。

The Architectural Concept／建築コンセプト

Initial concept modeling／初期コンセプト・モデリング

Overall Elements

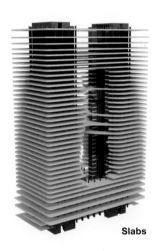

Slabs

Facade Glazing

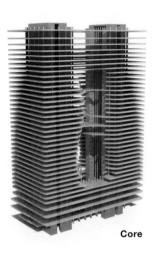

Core

Principal building components／主要構成要素

The Structural Frame／構造フレーム

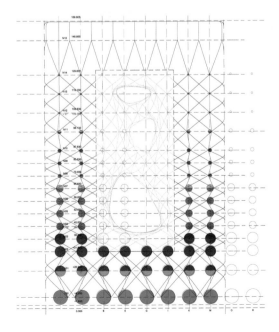

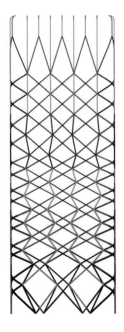

E8_350 mm	■
A7_300 mm	■
A9_406 mm	■
E7_350 mm	■
E6_400 mm	■
A6_400 mm	■
B6_368 mm	■
B7_406 mm	■
B5_406 mm	■
A5_550 mm	■
E5_450 mm	■
B4_406 mm	■
A4_600 mm	■
E4_500 mm	■
E1_700 mm	■
A1_700 mm	■
B1_600 mm	■
B3_550 mm	■
B2_550 mm	■
A3_700 mm	■
A2_700 mm	■
E2_650 mm	■
E3_650 mm	■
D1_350 mm	■
B8_406 mm	■
D2_500 mm	■
D3_700 mm	■

Colour coded diagram of exoskeleton nodes families
外骨格グループのカラー・コード・ダイアグラム

Colour coded diagram of exoskeleton member sizing
部材サイズのカラー・コード・ダイアグラム

Installation of brackets assembly on pre-welded cleats in progress on free-form exoskeleton／先に溶接されたくさび形部材にブラケットを設置する。施行中の自由形態外骨格。

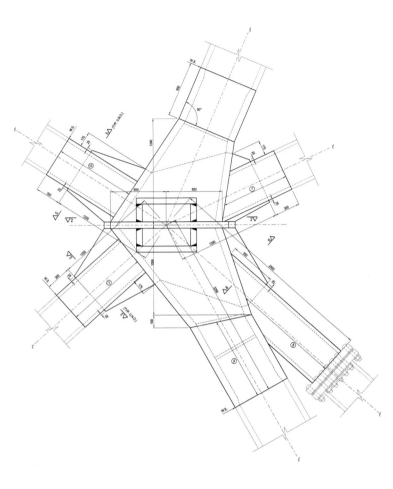

Shop drawing of steel connection／接続部施工図

This spread: A sequence of digital inputs and outputs was created to develop the project. Put generally, a reference surface was first generated in Rhinoceros, approximating the glass envelope, using custom scripts. An algorithm was then used to generate a topological mesh to define the exoskeleton. After, a wire frame that established node points, member axes, and mean planes was sent to the project's structural engineer. In parallel, a second model was produced that defined exoskeleton cladding. These models were used by engineering teams to develop the structure and construction method, in their scope, and iteratively sent back to the architects to resolve inconsistencies.

本頁：このプロジェクトを展開するにあたり、デジタル入出力のシークエンスが作成された。概して言うと、最初にRhinocerosで基準となるサーフェスを生成し、カスタム設定のスクリプトを用いてガラスの外殻の概形を得た。次にアルゴリズムを用いて、外骨格を決定するトポロジカルなメッシュを生成した。その後、プロジェクトの構造技術者に節点・構成部材軸・平均平面を規定するワイヤーフレームのデータが送られた。これと並行して、外骨格のクラッディングを決定する2つ目のモデルが作成された。エンジニアチームはこれらのモデルを使用して自身の作業範囲内で構造と施工方法を開発し、建築家に送り返して矛盾点を解決するということを繰り返した。

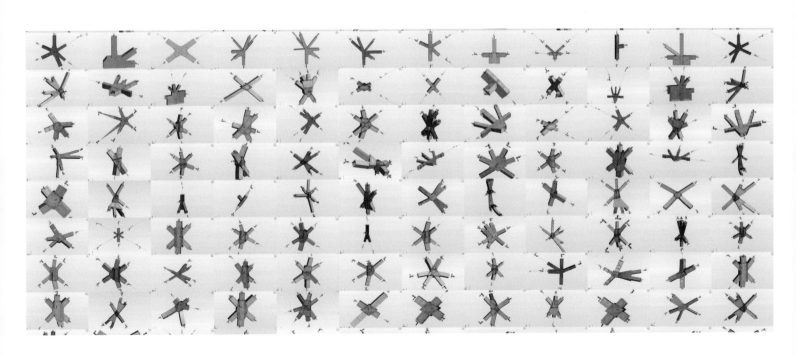

Connection types study／接続タイプのスタディ

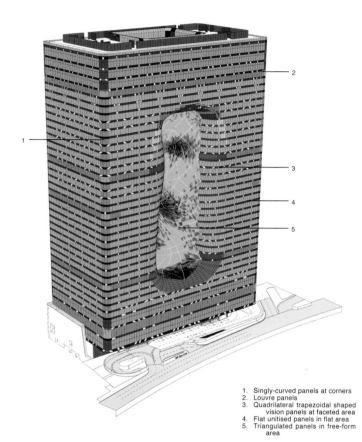

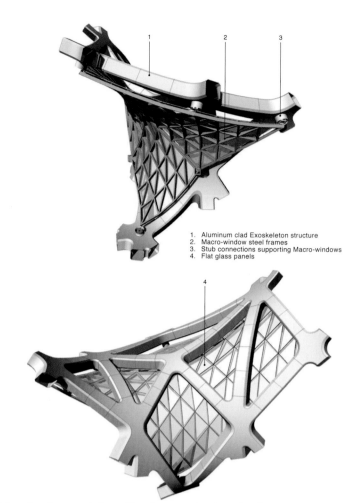

1. Aluminum clad Exoskeleton structure
2. Macro-window steel frames
3. Stub connections supporting Macro-windows
4. Flat glass panels

1. Singly-curved panels at corners
2. Louvre panels
3. Quadrilateral trapezoidal shaped vision panels at faceted area
4. Flat unitised panels in flat area
5. Triangulated panels in free-form area

Colour coded axonometric view of glazing types
施釉タイプのカラー・コード・アクソノメトリック

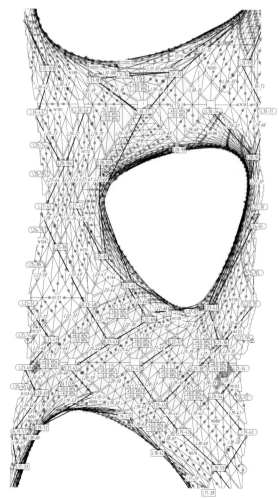

Internal and external view of facade system in triangulated area
三角部分のファサード・システム

Triangulated panels in free-form area／自由形態部の三角パネル

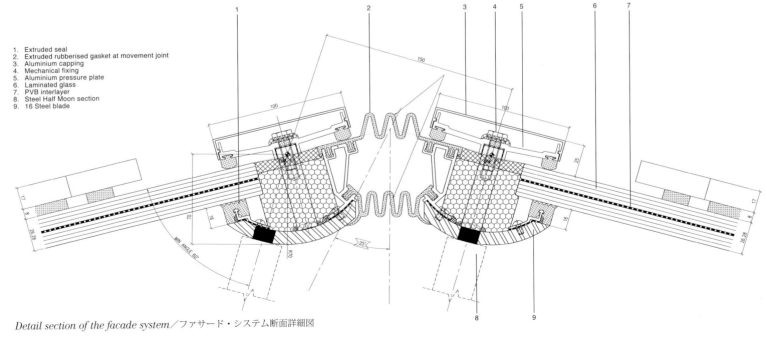

1. Extruded seal
2. Extruded rubberised gasket at movement joint
3. Aluminium capping
4. Mechanical fixing
5. Aluminium pressure plate
6. Laminated glass
7. PVB interlayer
8. Steel Half Moon section
9. 16 Steel blade

Detail section of the facade system／ファサード・システム断面詳細図

Cladding the Exoskeleton／外骨格の外装

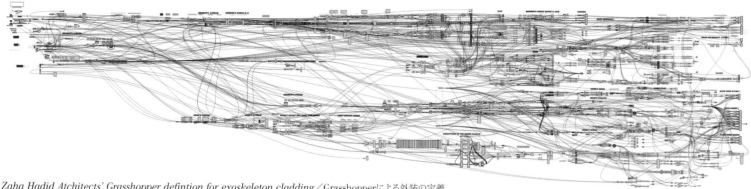

Zaha Hadid Atchitects' Grasshopper defintion for exoskeleton cladding／Grasshopperによる外装の定義

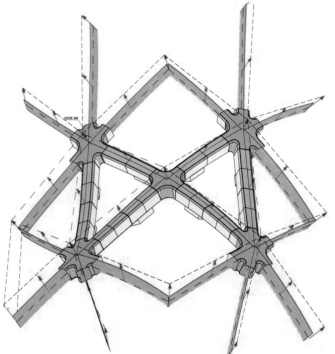

3D model assembly of the structural node's cladding sub-structure
外装のサブストラクチュアの3Dモデルによる組み立て図

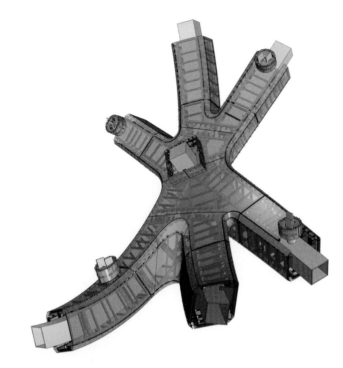

Exoskeleton cladding geometrical setout／外装の幾何学的装備図

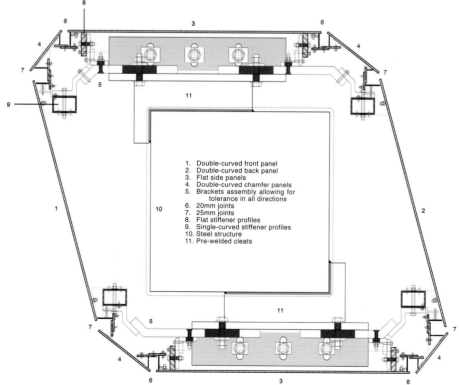

1. Double-curved front panel
2. Double-curved back panel
3. Flat side panels
4. Double-curved chamfer panels
5. Brackets assembly allowing for
   tolerance in all directions
6. 20mm joints
7. 25mm joints
8. Flat stiffener profiles
9. Single-curved stiffener profiles
10. Steel structure
11. Pre-welded cleats

Typical free-form cladding section／外装部材断面図

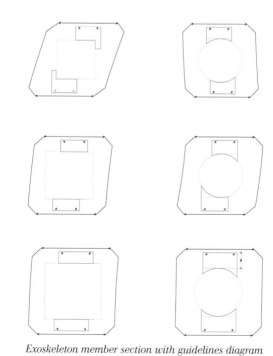

Exoskeleton member section with guidelines diagram for typical conditions above
ガイドとなるダイアグラムつきの外骨格部材断面図

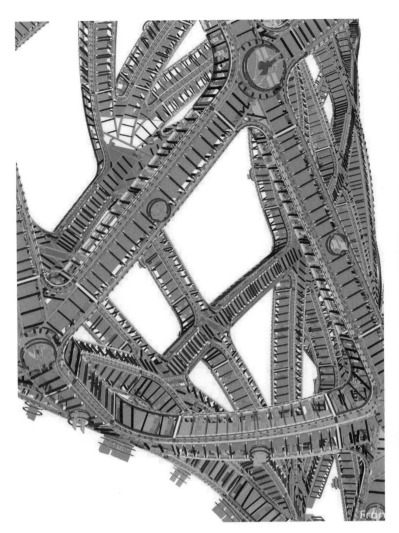

This spread: Rationalized 3D models and generative scripts, that controlled relations between the cladding components, were provided to facade engineers and fabricators, who would iteratively send back data to the architects to be remodeled. Every component, down to the scale of the bolts, was numbered and digitally positioned in space. All courtesy of Zaha Hadid Architects. p. 30: View of the "Sky Pool" at L40. Photo by Virgile Simon Bertrand, courtesy of Zaha Hadid Architects.

本頁：外装の構成部材間の関係を制御する合理化された3Dモデルと生成スクリプトがファサード技術者と製作業者に提供され、建築家にデータを送り返してモデルを修正することを繰り返す。ボルトのスケールにいたるまですべての構成部材に番号が付与され、空間内にデジタル的に配置される。30頁：L40における「スカイプール」の眺め。

Credits and Data

Project title: Morpheus Hotel at City of Dreams
Client: Melco Resorts and Entertainment
Location: Macau, China
Design: 2013
Completion: 2018
Architect: Zaha Hadid Architects (ZHA)
Designers: Zaha Hadid, Patrik Schumacher
Project team: Viviana Muscettola, Michele Pasca di Magliano (ZHA Project Directors); Paolo Matteuzzi (ZHA Facade Director); Michele Salvi, Bianca Cheung, Maria Loreto Flores, Clara Martins (ZHA Project Architects); Miron Mutyaba, Milind Khade, Pierandrea Angius, Massimo Napoleoni, Stefano Iacopini, Davide Del Giudice, Luciano Letteriello, Luis Migue Samanez, Cyril Manyara, Alvin Triestanto, Muhammed Shameel, Goswin Rothenthal, Santiago Fernandez- Achury, Vahid Eshraghi, Melika Aljukic (ZHA Project Team); Daniel Fiser, Thomas Sonder, Daniel Coley, Yooyeon Noh, Jinqi Huang, Mirta Bilos, Alexander Kuroda, Gaganjit Singh, Marina Martinez, Shajay Bhooshan, Henry Louth, Filippo Nassetti, David Reeves, Marko Gligorov, Neil Rigden, Milica Pihler-Mirjanic, Grace Chung, Mario Mattia,
Mariagrazia Lanza (ZHA Interior Team); Viviana Muscettola, Tiago Correia, Clara Martins, Maria Loreto Flores, Victor Orive, Danilo Arsic, Ines Fontoura, Fabiano Costinanza, Rafael Gonzalez, Muhammed Shameel (ZHA Concept Team)
Consultants: Leigh & Orange, Hong Kong (Executive Architect); CAA City Planning & Engineering Consultants, Macau (Local Architect); Buro Happold International, London/ Hong Kong (Structural Engineering); J. Roger Preston (M&E Engineering); Buro Happold International, Hong Kong (Facade Engineering); Rolf Jensen & Associates (Third-party reviewer); Remedios Studio, Hong Kong (Guestrooms, L01 VIP lobby, L03 Spa and Gym, L40 Pool deck and pool villas), Westar Architects International (L02 Gaming areas and Li Ying Restaurant, L42 Gaming Salons), Jouin Manku (L03 Alain Ducasse Restaurant), MC Design (L30 Executive Lounge), Leigh & Orange, Macau (BOH Areas) (Other interior designers); WT Partnership, Hong Kong (Quantity Surveyor); Isometrix, London/Hong Kong (Lighting Design); Arup, Hong Kong (Fire Engineering); Shen Milson and Wilke, Hong Kong (Acoustic Consultant); MVA Hong Kong (Traffic Engineer)
Project area: 147,860 m²

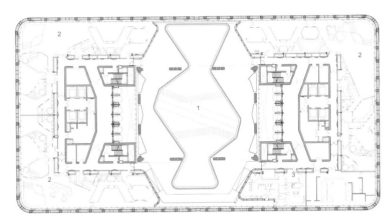

40th floor plan／40階平面図

1. Infinity pool
2. Pool villas
3. Changing rooms

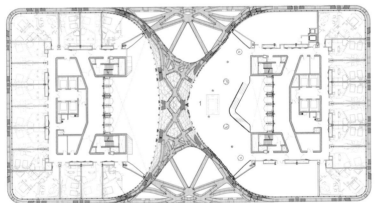

23rd floor plan／23階平面図

1. Gallery Space

21st floor plan (scale: 1/1,000)／21階平面図（縮尺：1/1,000）

1. Main restaurant
2. Private dining rooms
3. Private club
4. Male restroom
5. Female restroom
6. Kitchen

Section (scale: 1/750)／断面図（縮尺：1/750）

Zaha Hadid Architects
One Thousand Museum
Miami, U.S.A. 2012–2020

ザハ・ハディド・アーキテクツ
ワンサウザンド・ミュージアム
米国、マイアミ　2012〜2020

One Thousand Museum is a 62-storey residential tower opposite Museum Park in Miami. With views across Biscayne Bay, this popular 30-acre park was redeveloped in 2013 as one of downtown Miami's primary public spaces and includes the city's new art and science museums.

The tower's design continues Zaha Hadid Architects' research into high-rise construction that defines a fluid architectural expression consistent with the engineering for the entire height of a structure. One Thousand Museum's concrete exoskeleton structures its perimeter in a web of flowing lines that integrates lateral bracing with structural support. Reading from top to bottom as one continuous frame, columns at its base fan out as the tower rises to meet at the corners, forming a rigid tube highly resistant to Miami's demanding wind loads; its curved supports create hurricane-resistant diagonal bracketing.

"The design expresses a fluidity that is both structural and architectural," explains Zaha Hadid Architects' project director Chris Lepine. "The structure gets thicker and thinner as required, bringing a continuity between the architecture and engineering."

One Thousand Museum incorporates glass fibre-reinforced concrete form-work, which remains in place as construction progresses up the tower. This permanent concrete formwork also provides the architectural finish that requires minimal maintenance. Behind the exoskeleton, the faceted, crystal-like facade contrasts with the solidity of the structure. With its frame at the perimeter, the tower's interior floor plates are almost column free; the exoskeleton's curvature creates slightly different plans on each floor. On the lower floors, terraces cantilever from the corners, while on the upper floors, the terraces are incorporated behind the structure. The top floors of the tower feature an aquatic center, lounge and event space. Landscaped gardens, terraces and pools are located above the lobby and residents' parking.

ワンサウザンド・ミュージアムは62階建てのタワー型コンドミニアムであり、マイアミのミュージアム・パークの向かいに建つ。ビスケーン湾を一望できる広さ30エーカー（約12万1,406m2）の人気の公園は、2013年にマイアミの商業地区における主要な公共スペースの一つとして再開発が行われ、市内の新しい美術館や科学博物館が含まれている。

タワーのデザインは、ザハ・ハディド・アーキテクツの高層建築研究を継続するものであり、構造物の全高のエンジニアリングと首尾一貫した流線型の建築表現を定義づける。ワンサウザンド・ミュージアムのコンクリートの外骨格は周辺構造となり、横方向の筋かいと構造的支持体を統合する流線状の網目を構成する。頂上部から基底部までを一つの連続したフレームとして読み解くのなら、タワーが立ちあがりコーナーに至って基礎部分の柱が扇状に広がり、マイアミの厳しい風荷重にたいして高度な耐性をもつ基礎部分の柱は剛性チューブを形成し、曲線状の支持体はハリケーンに耐えうる斜めブラケットを創出する。

ザハ・ハディド・アーキテクツのプロジェクト・ディレクターであるクリス・レピーヌは、「このデザインは構造的かつ建築的な流動性を表現しており」「構造は必要に応じて場所により厚みを変え、建築とエンジニアリングの連続性をもたらす」と説明している。

ワンサウザンド・ミュージアムには、ガラス繊維補強コンクリートの型枠が組みこまれており、タワー上方の工事に有効である。この打込みコンクリート型枠は最小限のメンテナンスで十分な建築的仕上げとな

る。外骨格の背後の結晶のような多面体の外観は、堅固な構造と対照をなす。周囲にフレームを設置することで、タワー内部のフロアプレートは柱からほぼ解放され、外骨格の曲率により各階のプランはフロアごとにヴァリエーションに富む。下層階にはコーナーのキャンチレヴァーのテラスがある一方で、上層階では構造の背後にテラスが設置されている。タワーの最上階の目玉となるのはアクアティクス・センター、ラウンジ、イベント・スペースである。手入れのゆきとどいた庭園、テラス、プールは、ロビーと居住者用駐車場の上に設置されている。

（松本晴子訳）

Opposite: Detail of the exoskeleton, an in-situ hybrid concrete system cast using a GFRC permanent formwork solution. Photo by Hufton+Crow, courtesy of Zaha Hadid Architects.

右頁：外骨格のディテール。GFRC（ガラス繊維強化セメント複合材料）の永久型枠工法を用いた、現場打設のハイブリッド・コンクリート・システム。

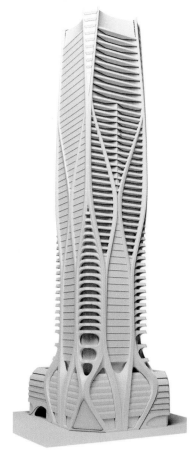

This page, top: Digital technology enabled the architecture, structure, exterior facade, and interior finish to be synthesised through an innovation in construction. The architectural, curving "x-braces" were employed as a bracing system and joined at "nodes." In this configuration, the braces work in unison with the shear walls so that they are thinner and more efficient. Balconies appear to scallop from the exoskeleton at each *corner through the lower levels of the tower, and are essential structural brackets supporting balcony slabs that cantilever over 35 feet. Bottom: Factory-finished panels are positioned, clamped together, filled with structural concrete and then remain in place to become the exterior and interior finish. Opposite, top: Implementation of the GFRC permanent formwork at the tower's base. All courtesy of Zaha Hadid Architects.*

本頁、上：デジタル・テクノロジーによって可能となった建築、構造、ファサード、内装仕上げは、建設的なイノヴェーションを通じて統合された。構造補強システムとして採用された曲線的な「Xブレース」が「ノード」で交差している。この構成においてはブレースがせん断壁と一体的な挙動を示すため、せん断壁はより薄く効果的なものとなった。バルコニーはタワーの低層レベルにおいて外骨格の各コーナーからせりだしており、10m超のキャンチ・レヴァーによるバルコニー・スラブを支持する重要

な構造ブラケットとなっている。本頁、下：工場で仕上げられたパネルが設置・固定され、構造コンクリートで充填される。その後、そのままの状態で外観とインテリアの仕上げとなる。右頁：タワー基礎部分におけるGFRC永久型枠の施工。

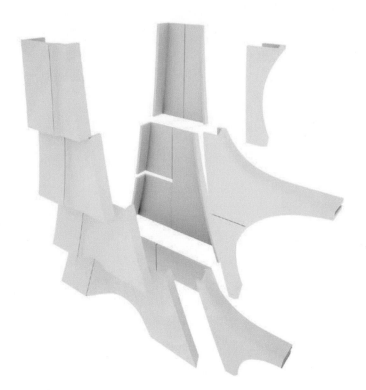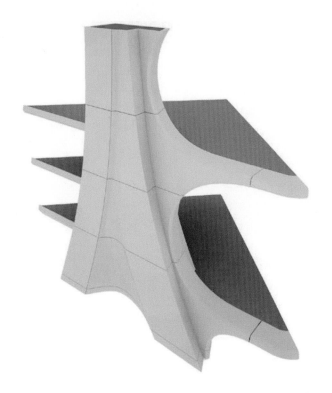

Reinforcement bar erected
鉄筋の立ち上がり

Panels placed into position
パネルの設置

Concrete poured into braced panels
固定されたパネル内にコンクリートを注ぐ

Credits and Data
Project title: One Thousand Museum
Client: 1000 Biscayne Tower, LLC
Location: Miami, U.S.A.
Design: 2012
Completion: 2020
Architect: Zaha Hadid Architects
Design: Zaha Hadid and Patrik Schumacher
Project Director: Chris Lepine
Project Team: Alessio Constantino, Martin Pfleger, Oliver Bray, Theodor Wender,
    Irena Predalic, Celina Auterio, Carlota Boyer
Competition Team: Sam Saffarian, Eva Tiedemann, Brandon Gehrke, Cynthia
    Du, Grace Chung, Aurora Santana, Olga Yatsyuk
Consultants: O'Donnell Dannwolf Partners (Local Architect); DeSimone
    Consulting Engineers (Structural); HNGS Consulting Engineers (MEP); Terra
    Civil Engineering (Civil); Enea Garden Design (Landscape); SLS Consulting Inc
    (Fire Protection); Lerch Bates Inc (Vertical Transportation); RWDI Consulting
    Engineers & Scientists (Wind Tunnel Consultant)
Project area: 84,637 m²

*pp. 36–37: View toward the One
Thousand Museum from the recently
re-developed Museum Park. Opposite:
The tower's base, seen from the street.
This page: Parametric design was used
to generate many of the 3D patterns
that give the design its character, such
as the perforation pattern across the
geometrically-complex parking garage
cladding. All photos by Hufton+Crow,
courtesy of Zaha Hadid Architects.*

36〜37頁：近年再開発されたミュージア
ム・パークから見るワンサウザンド・ミュー
ジアム。左頁：ストリートからタワーの基
礎部分を見る。本頁：特徴的なデザインと
なるよう、パラメトリック・デザインによっ
て多くの3Dパターンが生成された。駐車
場外装材部の幾何学的に複雑な穿孔パター
ンなどがその例。

Parametricism: The Next Decade
Patrik Schumacher, Partner at Zaha Hadid Architects (ZHA)

エッセイ：
パラメトリシズム：ザ・ネクスト・ディケード
パトリック・シューマッハ（ザハ・ハディド・アーキテクツ・パートナー）
中田雅章訳

Parametricism is architecture's answer to contemporary, computationally empowered civilization. Parametricism is the only style that can take full advantage of the computational revolution that drives contemporary civilization. More specifically it is the only style congenial to recent advances in structural and environmental engineering capacities based on computational analytics and optimization techniques. All other styles are incapable of working with the efficiencies of the adaptive structural and tectonic differentiations that issue from the new engineering intelligence, i.e. they force its adherents to waste this opportunity and thus to waste resources. So, once contemporary architects take those performance conditions seriously they are nearly inevitably led to Parametricism and the geometric transcoding of parameter variations into differentiated geometries. This much pertains to Parametricism's obvious superiority in terms of the built environment's technical functionality. What is perhaps less obvious but by no means less compelling is Parametricism's superiority with respect to the advancement of the built environment's social functionality. Due to its versatile formal and spatio-organisational repertoire Parametricism is the only contemporary style that can adequately address the new societal tasks posed to architecture by the new social dynamics engendered by the information age. Accordingly, Parametricism is by now addressing all major urban building tasks, on all scales.

However, these facts are only rarely appreciated. The functionality of Parametricism – whether technical or social – is usually seen as suspect. Indeed the works of Parametricism are not even presumed to aim at functionality, they are misunderstood as expressions of artistic or technophil exuberance, or as esoteric design process fetishism. This misunderstanding is unfortunate, but perhaps excusable, since on the one hand, the functionality of many projects remains indeed suspect and, on the other hand, the discourse of parametric design movement has not placed enough emphasis on the discussion and explication of the practical advantages of Parametricism, especially in the domain of social functionality. This is an aspect of the movement's avant-garde character where artistic and technophil exuberance (as well as "esoteric" internal design process orientation) must initially indeed play a part. But this aspect must recede now as the movement matures, goes mainstream and wants to be taken seriously as a contender for global best practice.

However, the 2008 economic crisis and subsequent great recession has slowed down Parametricism's expansion into the mainstream. Moreover, the misleading assessment of

Parametricism turned into outright hostility during the last few years of economic stagnation when the investment into spatial and formal complexity was regarded to be an indefensible self-indulgence in the face of general austerity. Parametricism – associated with the unsustainable profligacy of the boom years – therefore experiences a crisis of legitimacy.

In order to succeed in its ambitious quest for unifying the discipline's fragmented efforts under its banner, in the coming decade, Parametricism has to shift its focus from foregrounding formal principles and design processes to the foregrounding of functional principles and societal purposes (while taking the new formal options and design processes of parametricism for granted). Design research continues but becomes more strategic, applied and performance-oriented, with a strong emphasis on social performativity[1]. This emphasis on social performativity, in the face of increasing societal complexity, must be supported by a new methodology and tool set. The author is developing this enhanced capacity via the development of semiologically empowered life-process simulations[2], further introduced towards the end of this paper.

History
The author started to promote 'Parametricism' in early 2008, at the Smart Geometry Conference in Munich, and later that year at the Venice Architecture Biennale where the 'Parametricist Manifesto' was launched and published. The concept is both retrospective and prospective. The intention was to mark out, recognize and galvanize the important innovative work of a whole generation of young architects that had not only charted a new path for architecture on the basis of new computational design tools but that had forged a coherent movement where research, knowledge and values had been building up cumulatively over the previous decade. A year later, in 2009, the author published the article 'Parametricism: A New Global Style for Architecture and Urban Design'[3] in *AD* (*Architectural Design*).

To talk about a new emerging epochal style seemed in order. It was clear that the movement identified by the proposed name had already outgrown, in size and significance, a precursor movement that had 20 years earlier been hailed under the banner of 'Deconstructivism'. Parametricism emerged within the ambit of the protagonists of deconstructivism, via a new generation of protagonists within the design studios of Peter Eisenman, Zaha Hadid, Frank Gehry, Rem Koolhaas and Wolf Prix. Young protagonists like Greg Lynn a.o. within these studios, that were all hotbeds of avant-gardism in the early 1990s, started to invest in computational design processes

パラメトリシズムは、コンピュータによって力を得た現代文明にたいする、建築からの答えである。パラメトリシズムは、現代文明の原動力であるコンピュータ革命の恩恵を、余すところなく活かすことができる、唯一のスタイルである。さらに言うならばそれは、コンピュータによる分析と最適化技術にもとづく、構造エンジニアリングと環境エンジニアリングの近年の技術力の向上に適合する、唯一のスタイルである。それ以外のスタイルはいずれも、新たなエンジニアリングの知見がもたらす、アダプティヴな構造とテクトニックの細分化に対応することができない。パラメトリシズム以前のスタイルは、そこに安住する人々にこの好機を無にすることを強い、結果的にそのリソースを無にすることを強いているのである。したがって、ひとたびこうした実務環境を真正面から受け止めたならば、現代の建築家はほぼ必然的に、パラメトリシズムへと、そしてパラメータの変化が細分化された形態に変換される、幾何学的なトランスコーディングへと導かれる。これは建築の技術的な機能の面での、パラメトリシズムの明らかな優位性と深くかかわっている。そしておそらく、さほど明確ではないものの決して無視できない点は、建築の社会的な機能の向上に関しての、パラメトリシズムの優位性である。その変幻自在な形態と空間構成のレパートリーのゆえに、パラメトリシズムは情報化の時代に生まれた新たな社会のダイナミクスが建築に突きつけた、これまでにない社会的なタスクに適切に対処できる、現代の唯一のスタイルとなっている。したがって今では、パラメトリシズムが都市を構築する主要なタスクのすべてに、あらゆるスケールで対応しているのである。

しかしこうした現実は、ほとんど理解されていない。技術的なものであれ、社会的なものであれ、パラメトリシズムの有効性は疑念をもって受け止められることが多い。実際パラメトリシズムの作品は、機能の実現を目指していると受け止められることなく、アーティスティックな表現やテクノマニアの好奇心の発露、あるいは難解なデザイン・プロセスへのフェティシズムと誤解されている。この誤解は残念なことであるが、ある意味では無理からぬものでもある。というのも、多くのプロジェクトの有効性が実際に疑問の余地を残しており、またパラメトリック・デザインのムーブメントをめぐる対話が、特にその社会的な機能の面で、パラメトリシズムの実利的な側面についての議論と丁寧な説明に、十分に力を尽くしてこなかったからである。これは、初期にはアーティスティックな表現やテクノマニアの好奇心（さらには「難解な」内的なデザイン・プロセスへの志向）が確かに果たすべき役割をもっていた、アヴァンギャルドな性格をもつムーブメントの一側面である。しかしムーブメントが成熟し、主流となり、世界的なベスト・プラクティスの候補として真剣に受け入れられることが期待される今、こうした側面は後退していかなければならない。

ところが、2008年の経済危機とそれに続く大不況が、パラメトリシズムが主流の座に着くことを遅れさせた。そればかりか、ここ数年経済が停滞する中で、空間や形態の複雑さに資金を費やすことは何であれ贅沢とみなされる全般的な緊縮ムードに包まれ、パラメトリシズムにたいする誤解を招くような評価が、明確な敵意へと変わってきた。その結果、好況だった時代の持続不能な浪費と結びつけられたパラメトリシズムは、その存在の正統性の危機に直面している。

パラメトリシズムが、分断された活動を自らの旗印の下に一つに集めるという野心的な探求を成功させるためには、これからの10年、その焦点を（パラメトリシズムがもたらす新たな形態の選択肢とデザイン・プロセスを当然のこととしつつ）、形態的な原理とデザイン・プロセスを重視することから、機能的な原理と社会的な目的を重視することにシフトしていかなければならない。デザインの探求は続くが、それは社会的な役割を果たすことをこれまで以上に強調しつつ、より戦略的で、実用的で、パフォーマンスを志向したもの[1]となる。ますます高まる社会の複雑さに向き合い、社会的な役割を重視していくためには、新たな方法論とツール・セットに支えられることが不可欠である。筆者は、本稿の後半で紹介する記号論（セミオロジー）によって強化されたライフ・プロセス・シミュレーション[2]の開発を通して、パラメトリシズムの拡張された能力をさらに発展させている。

歴史

筆者は、2008年のはじめにミュンヘンで開催されたスマート・ジオメトリー・カンファレンス、そして同じ年に開催され、「パラメトリシスト・マニュフェスト」が発表、出版されたヴェネチア・ビエンナーレ国際建築展において、「パラメトリシズム」の普及・啓発にとり組みはじめた。そのコンセプトはレトロスペクティブであり、プロスペクティブでもある。その目的は、新たなコンピューテーショナル・デザインのツールをもとに建築の新たな道筋を描くだけでなく、それまでの10年の間に系統的なムーヴメントをつくり上げ、研究、知識、成果を着実に積み上げてきた一群の若手建築家の世代の重要で革新的な業績を世に示し、その価値を認め、後押しすることであった。翌2009年、筆者はAD（アーキテクチュラル・デザイン）誌から、『パラメトリシズム：ニュー・グローバル・スタイル・フォー・アーキテクチュア・アンド・アーバン・デザイン』[3]を出版した。

はじめに、新たに姿を現しつつある、画期的なスタイルをとり上げることが適切であろう。その名称によって他から区別されるこのムーヴメントはすでに、その規模と重要性という面で、20年前に「デコンストラクティヴィズム」の旗印の下で盛んに議論され、実践されていた先駆的なムーヴメントをしのぐものとなっていることは明らかである。パラメトリシズムは、ピーター・アイゼンマン、ザハ・ハディド、フランク・ゲーリー、レム・コールハース、ヴォルフ・プリックスのデザイン・スタジオに籍を置いていた新たな世代の主導者を通して、デコンストラクティヴィズムの主要メンバーの足もとから姿を現してきた。これらのスタジオはいずれも、1990年代初頭のアヴァンギャルドの中心地で、そこで働いていたグレッグ・リンなどの若き主導者は、デコンストラクティヴィズムのスタジオで熱心に模索されていたこれまでにないレヴェルの幾何学的な複雑さに対応するた

to cope with the new level of geometric complexity aspired to within these deconstructivist studios. The new tools, in turn, impacted the further development of the work. A new movement started to emerge under the banner of "Folding in Architecture", proclaimed in an eponymous issue of *AD* in 1993. This emerging movement was also supported by schools of architecture like New York's Columbia University, lead by deconstructivist Bernard Tschumi, and London's Architectural Association where Jeff Kipnis made an impact at that time. In 1994 Columbia University made its commitment to the digital era by setting up its so-called "paperless studio", empowered by Silicon Graphics machines that were more than state-of-the-art at that time. The author, who was, with Zaha Hadid, teaching 'Folding' at Columbia University in 1993 and 1998, at Harvard University in 1994, and then at the Architectural Association since 1996, has always implicitly considered 'Folding' as the beginning of 'Parametricism'. More recently this was made explicit by charting the stages of Parametricism, in terms of subsidiary styles, as follows: Foldism, Blobism, Swarmism and finally Tectonism[4], the latest, most mature and sophisticated substyle within the epochal paradigm of Parametricism.

The aspirations of Tectonism began to emerge when the designs of Foldism and Blobism started to be implemented at scale and the protagonists of the movement shifted their attention and discourse increasingly from conceptual and formal questions to the problems of engineering, fabrication and construction. At this point the congeniality of Parametricism in architecture with the new analytical, computationally-empowered capacities of the engineering disciplines, i.e. structural and environmental engineering, became evident and the respective digital tools, like finite element analysis and sun exposure maps, were eagerly appropriated by the Parametricist architects. These tools could take in complex parametric forms and allowed a parametric feedback and rationalisation loop to be established. Another factor in the emergence of Tectonism was the rediscovery and wholehearted embrace of the work of Frei Otto and his research group.

Tectonism

In recent years structural engineering science radically transformed its ontology and methodology from a typological to a topological paradigm. This implies a radical reset of the categories that guide engineering practice. The modern forms of engineering rationality based on system types are now exposed as inefficient. We now witness the proliferation of radically new forms that the new paradigm makes possible. This radical expansion of structural possibilities – mirroring the endless forms of nature – is congenial with the requirements of contemporary architectural design where a much higher degree of versatility is required to meet the challenges of a much more complex society.

In contrast with the modern typological approach based on discrete system types, contemporary engineering has become topological and can thus better serve the new architectural style that aims to create spaces which are morphing different spatial sections into a seamlessly differentiated continuum that resists any decomposition into discrete spaces that could be conveniently structured by discrete structural systems. In traditional structures the ability to analyze and calculate the behaviour of the structure is premised upon the purity of structural type and the severing of all redundant connections. However, conceptually distinct structural system types – beam

vs arch etc. – are disappearing from engineering due to the new modeling techniques like Finite Element Analysis. We thus witness a radical conceptual shift – a paradigm shift – within engineering. This is also an ontological shift as it revolutionizes the most basic entities that constitute a structure. We might call this shift the shift from typology to topology. It is at the same time a conceptual shift from parts to particles with respect to the mode of decomposition for calculation. While this shift in structural engineering has not been triggered by the new architectural style, this style is surely uniquely congenial to these engineering advances. These advances follow from the internal logic of structural science in the pursuit of structural optimization, in combination with the computational empowerment that makes this pursuit feasible. The re-tooled engineer allows the structural forces to flow freely through the surfaces provided by the architect. This is the era of structural fluidity. It thus becomes evident that the architectural style of Parametricism is congenial with the most advanced engineering thinking, and indeed that Parametricism is the only style that fully utilizes the new engineering intelligence. This explicit and congenial utilization engenders the latest stage of Parametricism: Tectonism.

Tectonism implies the stylistic heightening of engineering- and fabrication-based form-finding and optimization processes. To be clear, despite its dependency on engineering logics, 'Tectonism' is an architectural style. In fact, the concept of style(s) is a category that only makes sense within the discipline of architecture, as it necessarily refers to recognizable visual characteristics as the designer's concern. In contrast to engineering, all design is communication. Since the engineering and fabrication methods that Tectonism utilizes are inherently plural and open ended, this additional rigour comes along with additional tectonic variety and thereby offers a new reservoir of morphological physiognomies. This empowers designers to give a particular, recognisable identity to each of their projects, or to avoid monotonous repetition in their larger projects by differentiating their tectonic articulation. Tectonism thus delivers much more expressive variety than Foldism or Blobism, without descending into arbitrary form invention.

Parametricism has the formal repertoires to shape and fit buildings so as to meet these complex requirements in ways that can also maintain legibility in the face of these unprecedented complexities. Tectonism achieves this while simultaneously meeting structural and environmental optimization criteria. Furthermore, the morphologies that result from this pursuit gain – as if by serendipitous coincidence – additional visual legibility advantages. It is the very rigor of the engineering logics that ruthlessly impose their selection criteria at every point across the overall form and that thus not only sponsor a formal unity across the project but also ensure that the morphological variations are rule-based and thus predictable and legible despite their complexity.

Spatial Communication as Architecture's Core Competency

Parametricism in general, as well as Tectonism in particular, are well-suited styles to elaborate architectures with an enhanced communication capacity. Where, as is the case within the parametric design paradigm, every design action engenders a number of design reactions within the overall composition, where every rule-based visible feature allows an inference back to its cause or motivation and where further all rule-based

めに、コンピューテーショナル・デザインにとり組みはじめた。この新たなツール
は逆に、作品のさらなる展開にインパクトを及ぼした。新たなムーヴメントは、
1993年にAD誌の特集号がその名の由来となった、「フォールディング・イン・
アーキテクチュア」の旗印の下で姿を現しはじめた。そして登場しつつあったこの
ムーヴメントは、デコンストラクティヴィストのバーナード・チュミが率いてい
たニューヨークのコロンビア大学や、当時ジェフェリー・キプニスが影響力をもっ
ていたロンドンのアーキテクチュラル・アソシエーション（AA）といった、建築
の教育機関からの後押しを得た。1994年、コロンビア大学は当時、最先端以上の
存在であったシリコン・グラフィックス社の装置を導入したいわゆる「ペーパーレ
ス・スタジオ」を開設し、デジタル時代へのとり組みに乗りだした。ザハ・ハディ
ドとともに活動し、1993年と98年にコロンビア大学、94年にハーヴァード大学、
96年にAAで「フォールディング」を教えていた筆者は、その当時から「フォール
ディング」は明らかに「パラメトリシズム」の始まりであると考えていた。近年に
なってこのことは、パラメトリシズムの段階を次のような補助的なスタイルに整理
することで明確になっている。それは、フォールディズム、ブロビズム、スワー
ミズム、そして最後に、パラメトリシズムの画期的なパラダイムの中でも最も新
しく、最も成熟し、洗練されたサブスタイルである、テクトニズム[4]である。

テクトニズムへの志向は、フォールディズムとブロビズムのデザインが実際に建
設されはじめ、ムーブメントの主導者が彼らの意識と対話をコンセプトと形態の
問題から、エンジニアリング、ファブリケーション（製作）、そしてコンストラクショ
ン（建設）の問題へと徐々にシフトしていった時に姿を現しはじめた。この頃には、
建築におけるパラメトリシズムが、構造エンジニアリングや環境エンジニアリン
グなどのエンジニアリングの世界の、分析的でコンピュータによって強化された
新たな技術に適合していることが明らかになり、そうした技術に対応した有限要
素解析や日照分布図などのデジタル・ツールが、パラメトリシズムの建築家によっ
て積極的に活用された。これらのツールは複雑な変数のフォームをとり込み、パ
ラメトリックなフィードバックと合理化のループの確立を可能にしている。テク
トニズムが姿を現してくる段階でのもう一つのファクターは、フライ・オットー
と彼の研究グループによる業績の再発見と積極的な受け入れであった。

テクトニズム

近年、構造エンジニアリングは、そのオントロジー（実態論）とメソドロジー（方
法論）を、タイポロジー（類型論）の世界からトポロジー（形態論）の世界へと急
激に移行している。このことが暗示しているのは、エンジニアリングの実践をガイ
ドするカテゴリーの劇的な再編である。システムの形式にもとづいたエンジニ
アリングの合理性という近代のあり方は、現在では非効率なものとして批評され
ている。我々は今、新たなパラダイムが可能にする、きわめて斬新な形態の爆発
的な増加を目の当たりにしている。構造的な可能性——自然の無限の形態を反映
した——の劇的な拡張は、これまでよりもはるかに複雑な社会的な課題に対応す
るために、より高度な多様性が必要とされる現代の建築デザインに適合している。

特定のシステム形式にもとづく近代のタイポロジー的なアプローチとは対照的に、
現代のエンジニアリングはトポロジカルなものとなり、そしてその本領は、特定
の構造システムによって容易に構造が決定される特定の空間に分解されることに
断固として抵抗し、それぞれの空間断面がシームレスに細分化された連続体に変
容される空間をつくりだしていく、新たな建築のスタイルにおいて最大限に発揮
される。伝統的な構造では、構造の動きの分析と計算は、構造形式の純粋さとす
べての冗長な接合を分離することを前提としている。しかし、梁やアーチといっ
たコンセプトにもとづいて区分される構造システムの形式は、有限要素解析など
の新たなモデリング技術によって、エンジニアリングの世界から姿を消しつつあ
る。かくして我々は、エンジニアリング内部での劇的なコンセプト・シフト——パ
ラダイム・シフトを目撃している。それは構造を構成する最も基本的な要素に大

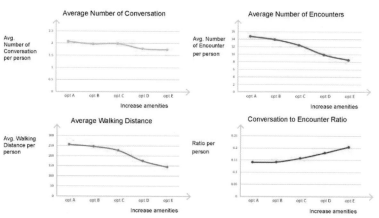

Average Number of Conversation

Avg. Number of Conversation per person

Increase amenities

Average Number of Encounters

Avg. Number of Encounter per person

Increase amenities

Average Walking Distance

Avg. Walking Distance per person

Increase amenities

Conversation to Encounter Ratio

Ratio per person

Increase amenities

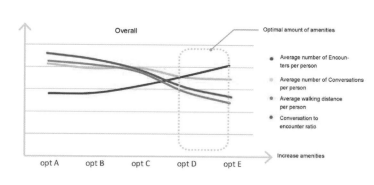

Overall

Optimal amount of amenities

opt A   opt B   opt C   opt D   opt E

Increase amenities

- Average number of Encounters per person
- Average number of Conversations per person
- Average walking distance per person
- Conversation to encounter ratio

Opt D Analysis Maps

History Map of Conversation

Encounter Map
Бессловесные встречи

Agent Trail Data Points

Views of the Amenity Space

p. 43, from top: Foldism – Guang Zhou Opera House (2003–2010); Blobism – Soho Galaxy, Beijing (2008–2012); Tectonism, utilizing structural engineering logic – One Thousand Museum, Residential Tower, Miami (2012–2020). This page: Life-process Simulation by Zaha Hadid Architects, AI Research Group for Sberbank Technopark, Moscow (2016 – TBC). Photographs on pp. 43–44, courtesy of Zaha Hadid Architects.

43頁、上から：フォールディズム：ザハ・ハディド・アーキテクツ、広州オペラハウス、2003〜10年。ブロビズム：ザハ・ハディド・アーキテクツ、ギャラクシー SOHO、北京、2008〜12年。構造エンジニアリングのロジックを用いたテクトニズム：ザハ・ハディド・アーキテクツ、ワンサウザンド・ミュージアム、レジデンシャル・タワー、マイアミ、2012〜20年。 本頁：ライフ・プロセス・シミュレーション：ザハ・ハディド・アーキテクツ、ズベルバンク・テクノパーク、モスクワ、2016年〜。

きな変革をもたらすことから、オントロジカルなシフトでもある。我々はこのシフトを、タイポロジーからトポロジーへのシフトと呼ぶこともできるだろう。それは同時に、計算のための分解のモードの、パーツからパーティクルへのコンセプト・シフトでもある。構造エンジニアリングにおけるこのシフトは、新たな建築のスタイルによって引き起こされたものではなく、エンジニアリングの進化と、明確に一意的に合致している。これらの進化は、この探究を可能にしたコンピュータの力と一体となった、構造を最適化するための構造解析の内的なロジックに従っている。新たなツールを得たエンジニアは、建築家が描く形態の上を構造の応力が自由に流れることを可能にしている。構造が流動する時代である。このように、パラメトリシズムという建築のスタイルは、最先端のエンジニアリングの考えに適合しており、そしてパラメトリシズムこそが、新たなエンジニアリングの知見を完全に活かすことができる唯一のスタイルであることは明らかである。この明確で適合したエンジニアリングの活用が、パラメトリシズムの最も新しい段階、テクトニズムを生みだしている。

テクトニズムは、エンジニアリング、そしてファブリケーションにもとづく形態発見と最適化のプロセスにおける、スタイル的な側面の高まりを暗示している。より端的に言うならば、「テクトニズム」はエンジニアリングのロジックに依存しているにもかかわらず、建築の一つのスタイルなのである。実際にはスタイルという概念は、デザイナーが考える認識可能な視覚上の独自性に必然的にかかわるものであることから、建築の世界でのみ意味をもつカテゴリーである。エンジニアリングとは対照的に、すべてのデザインはコミュニケーションである。テクトニズムが用いるエンジニアリングとファブリケーションの手法は本質的に複層的でオープン・エンドなものであることから、新たにつけ加えられるこの厳格さはさらなるテクトニックの変化をともない、それによって形態表現の新たな引きだしを提供している。これは、テクトニックな表現を細分化することによって、それぞれのプロジェクトに固有の認識可能なアイデンティティをもたらす力、あるいは大規模なプロジェクトにおいて単調な反復から逃れる力をデザイナーに与えている。かくしてテクトニズムは、恣意的な形態の創造に陥ることなく、フォールディズムあるいはブロビズムよりもはるかに豊かな表現上の多様性をもたらしている。

パラメトリシズムは、これまでにない複雑さに直面する中で、わかりやすさを保ちながらそれらの複雑な要求に対応する建物をかたちづくり、フィットさせていく形態のレパートリーを有している。テクトニズムはこれを、構造と環境の最適化の要件を同時に満たしながら実現している。さらにこの探究からもたらされたモルフォロジーは、——あたかも幸運な偶然の一致のごとく——さらなる視覚上のわかりやすさを獲得している。エンジニアリングのロジックの厳格さにそのものよって、全体的な形態のすべてのポイントにエンジニアリングにもとづく選択基準が徹底的に適応されていく。それによって、プロジェクト全体の形態的な統一性が保証されるだけでなく、形態の変化がルールにもとづくものとなり、結果的にその形態が、複雑でありながらも、予測可能で読みとり可能なものとなることが担保されている。

建築のコア・コンピテンシーとしての空間コミュニケーション
パラメトリシズム全般、中でも特にテクトニズムは、拡張されたコミュニケーション能力で建築をより豊かなものとしていくことに非常に適したスタイルである。パラメトリック・デザインのパラダイムに見られるケースと同じように、そこではデザイン行為のすべてが全体のコンポジションに様々なデザイン上のリアクションを引き起こし、ルールにもとづく視覚的な特徴のすべてがその原因あるいは誘因に立ち戻る推論を可能にし、さらにルールにもとづいて細分化されたサブシステムのすべてが互いに関連し、呼応している。そこには、豊かな情報を備え、表現力のある建築的なコミュニケーションのための条件が十分に整えられている。

建築とエンジニアリングの区分は、人工的な環境の中で、社会的な機能を技術的な機能から弁別することによっている。建築の社会的な機能は、社会的なプロセスの順序づけである。これは空間構成を通じて実現される。しかし建物はこの構成の中で、利用者が目的地までの経路と互いを見つけだす助けとなることによってのみ機能する。すなわち建物は、秩序立て、誘導するコミュニケーションの枠組みとして機能しなければならず、そしてそれは、見え方とわかりやすさによって機能している。結果として建築のコア・コンピテンシーは、構成に加え、表現の面での重要なタスクで構成されることになる。わかりやすさは2つの側面に関係している。認識上の明快さと意味情報の伝達である。したがって表現の全般的なタスクは、現象学的な表現と記号論的な表現の2つに分けられる。いずれの側面も、新たなエンジニアリングとファブリケーションの手法がもたらす、選択肢が激増していく状況の中で、デザイナーの意志決定のプロセスを導いていく必要がある。

構造的な形態発見の手法を使うことは、表現上のタスク、すなわち体系的な空間言語をより豊かなものにしていくタスクに有利なやり方で、空間のモルフォロジーをルールにもとづくものとしている。これによって記号論的な表現は、形態の違いがプログラムの違いを示すものとなるように、重要なプログラム上の差異を明らかな形態上の差異に関連づけていくことができる。すなわち建築のタスクは、考えられるすべての構造的なモルフォロジーのセットからサブセットを選びだし、それらを意味のある言語として組織立てるデザインされた視覚的なコードを介して、エンジニアリングのロジックに語らせることである。この言語はナビゲーションの補助として利用者を導き、彼らにその場所で利用可能な社会的な機会を伝えている。建物の形態はその構造的なパフォーマンス(それは利用者にはまったく興味のないことである)について語るのではなく、その社会的な目的について語り、そしてこのコミュニケーションがその目的そのものを前進させていく。コミュニケーションのこの目的が、記号論的なプロジェクトを、あらゆる主要な建築プロジェクトの中心に位置するものとしている。記号論的なプロジェクトは、拡張された社会的な機能を果たしていくうえでの建築の能力を、決定的に強化している。記号論的に明快で、情報が豊かな環境は、すべての利用者に直感的に引きだすことができる情報と知識をもたらすのである。

エージェント・ベースト・ライフ・プロセス・モデリング
建築の記号論は、その社会的な機能を検証し、予測するための普遍的な手段となる、新たなデザイン・シミュレーションを介して利用可能なものとなる。このツールは今のところ実現されていないが、ザハ・ハディド・アーキテクツのリサーチ・プロジェクトのテーマである。実現が待たれるこのエージェント・ベースト・ライフ・プロセス・モデリングによる記号論的なプロジェクトの拡張はやがて、我々がプロジェクトの社会的な機能の向上を検証し、確認することを可能にするであろう。つまり、記号論的に強化されたデザインがもたらす運用効率の向上は、シミュレーションを通じて明確なものとなるのである。[5]

エージェント・ベースト・ライフ・プロセス・モデリングは、建築のコア・コンピテンシーに焦点を合わせた、新たな鍵となる実務上の方法論である。「エージェント・ベースト・パラメトリック・セミオロジー」の研究テーマのもとで開発されたシミュレーションの手法は、現時点では避難、動線処理能力、ボトルネックや混雑区域の同定などのために交通コンサルタントやエンジニアリング・コンサルタントが利用する群衆シミュレーションの、汎用化と必要に応じた改良として考えられている。リサーチ・グループがとり組んでいる革新の概要は以下の通りで、それらは一般化され記号論的に有効なライフ・プロセス・モデリングによって実現される必要がある。

1.　行動／振る舞いのレパートリーの拡張

subsystem differentiations are correlated and thus resonate with each other, there the conditions for an information-rich, eloquent architectural communication are well prepared.

The demarcation between architecture and engineering rests on the distinction of the built environment's social functioning from its technical functioning. The social function of architecture is the ordering of social processes. This is achieved via spatial organization. However, buildings function only by empowering users to find their way and each other within this organization, i.e. the building must function as ordering and guiding communicative frame, and is thus functioning via its appearance and legibility. The core competency of architecture comprises thus, besides organization, the crucial task of articulation. Legibility involves two aspects: the perceptual palpability and the semantic-informational charge. Accordingly, the general task of articulation bifurcates into the two specific tasks of phenomenological articulation and semiological articulation. Both aspects need to guide the designer's decision-making process in the context of the proliferating options that emerge from the new engineering and fabrication methods.

The use of structural form-finding methods disciplines the spatial morphologies in ways that are advantageous for the task of articulation, i.e. the task of elaborating a systematic spatial language. Semiological articulation can then map significant programmatic distinctions onto conspicuous morphological distinctions so that morphological differences indicate programmatic differences. The architectural task is thus to make engineering logics speak, via a designed visual code that selects a subset from the set of all conceivable structural morphologies and orchestrates these into a telling language. This language orients users as a navigation aid and tells them about the social offerings at hand. The built forms are not speaking about their structural performance (which is of no interest to users) but about their social purposes, and this communication facilitates these very purposes. This aim of communication establishes the semiological project as central aspect of any non-trivial architectural project. The semiological project delivers a decisive augmentation of architecture's capacity to deliver an enhanced social functionality. A semiologically cohered, information-rich environment gives every user more intuitively retrievable information and awareness.

Agent-based Life-process Modelling
Architectural semiology can be operationalized via a new design simulation tool that is bound to become a pervasive medium to test and anticipate architecture's social functionality. This tool is not yet available but the subject of a research project within ZHA. The augmentation of the semiological project by means of this prospective agent-based life-process modeling will soon enable us to test and ascertain the enhancement of the project's social functionality, i.e. the gains in operational efficiency delivered by the semiologically augmented design should become manifest via simulation.[5]

Agent-based life-process modeling is a new key working methodology that focuses in on architecture's core competency. The simulation methodology developed under the research agenda 'Agent-based Parametric Semiology' is conceived as a generalization and corresponding upgrade of the kind of crowd simulations currently offered by traffic and engineering consultants concerned with evacuation, circulatory throughput, the identification of bottlenecks and zones of congestion, etc.

Here is the summary list of innovations that the research group is working on and that must be delivered by a generalized and semiologically informed life-process modeling:

1. expansion of action/behaviour repertoire
2. differentiation of agent population
3. designation dependency of behaviours
4. information empowered, language competent agents
5. agent decisions via dynamic utility functions
6. focus on social interactions and event scenarios
7. domain tailoring and client customization

The meaning of architecture, the prospective life processes it frames and sustains, is modeled and assessed within the design process, thus becoming a direct object of creative speculation and cumulative design elaboration. This allows for the elaboration and successive refinement of the design with respect to its ultimate criteria of success, in the relevant terms of the life and communication processes to be facilitated: footfall, dwell time, encounter frequency, encounter diversity, can be quantified and the quality of interaction scenarios can be intuitively appraised by observing the simulation.

We should thus expect that the generalized life process modeling envisioned here will be compelling to both architects and clients, and soon become architecture's new best practice standard. A drawing or model that does not include interacting agents can no longer count as architectural drawing or model.

2. エージェント集団の細分化

3. 振る舞いの指示依存性

4. 情報によって強化された言語的能力をもつエージェント

5. ダイナミックな効用関数を介したエージェントの決断

6. 社会的な交流とイベントのシナリオの重視

7. 領域への最適化とクライアント・カスタマイゼーション

建築の意味、建築がもたらし、持続させると予測されるライフ・プロセスは、デザイン・プロセスにおけるモデル化と評価を経て、創造的な思索と積み重ねによるデザインの深化の直接的な対象となる。これによって、生活とコミュニケーション・プロセスの促進に適した条件の中で、その最終的な成功の判断基準に照らしたデザインの深化と継続的な洗練が可能になっていく。来場者数、滞留時間、遭遇頻度、遭遇の多様性は数値化することが可能で、相互作用のシナリオの質的な側面は、シミュレーションを観察することで直感的に評価することができる。

かくして、ここに紹介した一般化されたライフ・プロセス・モデリングは、建築家とクライアント双方にとって注目すべきものとなり、やがて建築家の新たなベスト・プラクティスのスタンダードとなることが期待される。相互に作用するエージェントを含まないドローイングやモデルは、もはや建築のドローイングあるいはモデルとして認められることはないのである。

Notes:

1. Patrik Schumacher, "Social Performativity: Architecture's Contribution to Societal Progress", Published in: *The Routledge Companion to Paradigms of Performativity in Design and Architecture*, Ed. Mitra Kanaani, Routledge, Taylor & Francis Group, New York & London 2020.

2. Patrik Schumacher, "Parametric Order – Architectural Order via an Agent Based Parametric Semiology", Published in: *Adaptive Ecologies – Correlated Systems of Living by Theodore Spyropoulos*, AA Publications, London 2013.

3. Patrik Schumacher, "Parametricism - A New Global Style for Architecture and Urban Design", Published in: *AD Architectural Design – Digital Cities*, Vol. 79, No 4, July/August 2009, Guest-edited by Neil Leach.

4. Patrik Schumacher, "Tectonism in Architecture, Design and Fashion – Innovations in Digital Fabrication as Stylistic Drivers", Published in: *AD 3D-Printed Body Architecture*, guest-edited by Neil Leach & Behnaz Farahi, Architectural Design, Profile No. 250, November/December 2017, 06/Vol. 87/2017.

5. Patrik Schumacher, "Advancing Social Functionality via Agent Based Parametric Semiology", Published in: *AD Parametricism 2.0 – Rethinking Architecture's Agenda for the 21st Century*, Guest-edited by Patrik Schumacher, AD Profile #240, March/April 2016.

原註

1.～5. 英文参照

Commentary:
Morphosis

コメンタリー：
モーフォシス

a+u spoke to Kerenza Harris, Morphosis' Director of Design Technology, and Thom Mayne, Morphosis' Founding Partner.

a+u: *Generally speaking, how do you use computational design?*
Kerenza Harris, Director of Design Technology: We think of computational design mostly as a connector between tools and processes, an ever-present background to design and facilitator for our concepts. We are pushing to not only realize complex assemblies and design ideas, but also to maintain control over the process by developing a high level of expertise and flexibility. Overall the workflow in our office is very much process driven; we utilize a multitude of "tools" and mediums (e.g. hand sketching, digital modeling, simulation, prototyping, physical modeling, analysis) during a project. Computational design is like the glue that keeps it all working together, enabling interoperability and information retention, and expanding the utility of our digital models in a way that allows process to remain at the forefront of our workflow.

a+u: *How are you expanding upon what you have done?*
Kerenza Harris: The landscape and use of computational design are always evolving. Once computational tools became the core of how we make architecture, we leaned on it as a conduit and platform for exploring new technologies, new processes, and innovations in architecture and other related fields. We also think about it as a way to advance or retool existing processes to better fit our goals. It's cyclical – a design problem engenders the development or adoption of a new computational tool, and the use of that tool might lead to unexpected options and discoveries that inform and impact design ideas.

a+u: *How would you describe the mess in your workplace?*
Thom Mayne, Founding Partner: Studio 'mess': the conscious, purposeful organizational structure that advances randomness, chance, and the unexpected, which is the basis of creativity… a collective Fingerspitzengefühl…

a+uは、モーフォシスのデザイン技術部門のディレクターであるケレンザ・ハリスと、モーフォシスの創設パートナーであるトム・メインに話を聞いた。

a+u：コンピュテーショナル・デザインをどのように利用しているのか、概要を教えてください。

ケレンザ・ハリス（KH、デザイン技術部門ディレクター）：コンピュテーショナル・デザインを、おもにツールとプロセスを繋げるものととらえている。絶えず存在するデザインの背景にあり、コンセプトを促進するものであると考えている。複雑なアセンブリとデザインのアイディアを実現するだけでなく、高度な専門知識と柔軟性を開発することで、プロセスの制御を維持することも進めている。全体的に、私たちのオフィスのワークフローはプロセスにより駆動される部分が大きく、プロジェクト中に多数の「ツール」とメディア（手描きスケッチ、デジタルモデリング、シミュレーション、プロトタイピング、物理モデリング、分析など）を利用している。コンピュテーショナル・デザインは接着剤のようなものであり、すべてを連携させ、相互運用性と情報保持を可能にし、私たちのデジタル・モデルの有用性を拡大し、プロセスがワークフローの先頭にとどまるよう保つ機能を果たす。

a+u：これまでの活動をいかに拡大させますか。

KH：コンピュテーショナル・デザインの景観と使用は常に進化している。一度コンピュータ・ツールが建築をつくりあげるコアとなると、我々は建築やその他の関連分野における新しいテクノロジー、新しいプロセス、イノヴェーションを探求するための管路とプラットフォームとしてそれに依拠するようになった。また、目標に合わせた調整を行うため、既存のプロセスを前進、改良するための方法としてもとらえられる。循環的であり、デザイン上の問題によって、新しいコンピュテーショナル・ツールの開発と採用が発生し、そうしたツールの使用は、デザインのアイディアのもととなる予期しないオプションや発見につながる可能性がある。

a+u：仕事場の混沌とした状況をどのように表現しますか。

トム・メイン（設立パートナー）：スタジオの「混沌」、それは意識的かつ意図的な組織構造である。無作為性、偶然性、予期せぬ出来事を促進し、創造性──集合的なフィンガーシュピッツェンゲフュール（指先感覚、本能）──の基盤となる。

（松本晴子訳）

Morphosis
Kolon One & Only Tower
Seoul, Korea 2013–2018

モーフォシス
コーロン・ワン・アンド・オンリー・タワー
韓国、ソウル　2013〜2018

The Kolon Group, based in Seoul, is a diverse corporation whose activities range from textiles, chemicals, and sustainable technologies, to original clothing lines in the athletic and ready-to-wear fashion markets. Between the group's 38 divisions, Kolon covers research, primary material manufacture, and product construction – a unique configuration that enables the company to capitalize on its own resources and advances, and to forge innovative collaborations between divisions. Supporting this collaborative model was a primary goal behind the design of Kolon's new flagship research and development facility, the Kolon One & Only Tower. Bringing researchers, leadership, and designers together in one location, the building combines flexible laboratory facilities with executive offices and active social spaces that encourage greater interaction and exchange across the company.

The R&D facility is located in the Magok district, an emerging hub for technology and light industry that is revitalizing the Han-River area in south-eastern Seoul. Fostered by the Seoul Metropolitan Government, the Magok district is conceived to function as an "industrial ecosystem" where a range of tech and information fields will co-locate to spawn new intersecting markets. Kolon is one of the first firms moving their research and development operations to Magok, and the new building will set the standard for performance and design in the district. The four-acre project site sits adjacent to Magok's central park – a prominent location for what will be the district's first major completed building.

The building folds towards the park, providing passive shading to the lower floors. Bridging the three extending laboratory wings, this folding volume contains conference rooms and social spaces, augmented by flagship retail and exhibition galleries at the street level to communicate the brand's vision to the public. A transparent ground plane extends the landscape into the interior, drawing light and movement towards an open pedestrian lane-way and grand entry. At 30m tall and 100m long, the expansive multi-story atrium serves as the building's social center. Movement is revealed on all floors through the atrium's transparent liner system, which is comprised of massive, 8m 'stretchers' that allow for a changing display of Kolon's own fabrics.

The performance of the building was approached as a holistic concept encompassing energy efficiency, resource conservation, and environmental stewardship, working in concert with education and employee health and well-being. Along with goals for LEED Gold and the most rigorous sustainability certification in Korea, the project focuses on the quality of the work environment through roof terraces, courtyards, and other measures that increase access to natural light and air for employees. Other sustainable measures include green roofs; recycled materials; and utilizing a bubble deck slab that reduces the amount of concrete used by 30%. The distinctive brise-soleil system on the western facwade is both a performative and symbolic feature of the building; the façade units have been parametrically shaped to balance shading and views, and are made from a GFRP formulation that uses one of Kolon's own high-tech fabrics, Aramid, to dramatically increase the material's tensile strength. Together, the building's siting, spatial qualities, and technological innovations express Kolon's investment in and commitment to sustainability.

Site plan／配置図

pp. 50–51: The bespoke curtain wall system is comprised of steel mullions with extruded aluminum closures, cassette insulating glass unit panels, and external FRP sunshades. Photos by Jasmine Park, Courtesy of Morphosis. Opposite: Detail of the FRP sunshades, within a modeled facade section. Courtesy of Morphosis. This page, left to right: Integrated parametric design and BIM performance modeling drove CNC (computer numeric control) tooling of the GFRP sunshades. The fabrication and installation of these sunshades is shown. All photos courtesy of Morphosis.

50〜51頁：特注のカーテン・ウォール・システムは、押出しアルミニウム製のキャップを備えたスチール製のマリオン、はめ込み式断熱ガラスユニットパネル、および屋外用のFRP製サンシェードで構成されている。左頁：ファサードモデルの断面とFRP製サンシェードのディテール。本頁、左から右：統合されたパラメトリックデザインとBIM性能モデリングにより、GFRP製サンシェードのCNCツールを操作した。これらのサンシェードの製作と設置を示す。

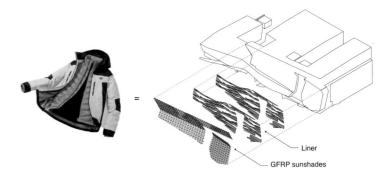

Axonometric diagram of the facade／ファサードのアクソノメトリック・ダイアグラム

コーロン・グループは、ソウル市に拠点を置き、繊維、化学薬品、持続可能なテクノロジーから、スポーツ分野や既製服市場におけるオリジナルの衣料品ラインまで、多岐に渡る範囲で活動する企業体である。コーロン・グループの38部門間で、研究、原材料の製造、製品製造を網羅している。こうしたユニークな構成により、会社は独自の資源と進歩を活用し、部門間の革新的なコラボレーションが可能となっている。こうしたコラボレーション・モデルをサポートすることが、コーロン社の新しい最高研究開発施設である、コーロン・ワン・アンド・オンリー・タワーのデザインのおもな目標であった。この建物は、研究者、管理職、デザイナーを一つの場所に集め、フレキシブルな実験施設、エグゼクティブ・オフィス、そして会社全体での交流促進する活動的な共用空間を合体させた。

この研究開発施設はマゴク地区に位置するが、この地区はソウル南東部の漢江地域を活性化するテクノロジー業界、軽工業の新たなハブとなっている。ソウル市政府が育てたマゴク地区には、様々な技術分野と情報分野が共に設置され、新興の複合マーケットを生みだす「産業エコシステム」として機能するよう構想されている。研究開発業務をマゴクに移転した最初の企業の一つとして、コーロン社の新たな施設は、当地区における性能とデザインの標準となるだろう。4エーカー（約16187.4㎡）に及ぶプロジェクトの敷地は、マゴクの中央公園に隣接しており、この地区に最初に完成した主要建築が建つのにふさわしい傑出した場所である。

建物は公園に向かって屈曲し、低層階にたいするパッシヴ・シェーディングの役割を果たす。3つに延伸する実験棟をつなぐこの折りたたまれたヴォリュームには、会議室と共有スペース空間が入り、さらにはブラ

ンドのヴィジョンを一般に伝えるために通りに面した旗艦店やギャラリーが入居している。透明な地上階は、ランドスケープを空間内部まで拡張し、開放的な歩行者レーンと大きなエントランスにたいして光と動きを引きこむ。高さ30m、長さ100mの広大な多層アトリウムは、建物内の社会活動の中心として機能する。アトリウムの透明な線形システムを通じてすべてのフロアに動きが表出するが、このシステムは、コーロン社独自の繊維を利用した可変式ディスプレイを可能にする8mの頑丈な「ストレッチャー」で構成されている。

建物の性能は、教育、従業員の健康と幸福と連携し、エネルギー効率、資源保護、環境管理を包含する、全体的なコンセプトとしてとらえられている。このプロジェクトは、LEEDゴールドの目標と韓国でもっとも厳格なサステイナビリティ認証に加えて、従業員により多くの自然光と新鮮な空気を与える環境である屋上テラス、中庭、およびその他の手段を通じて、作業環境の品質に焦点を置いている。その他の持続可能性を高める手段として、グリーンルーフ、リサイクル素材、コンクリートの使用量を30％削減するバブル・デッキ・スラブが含まれる。西側のファサードで使われた独特のブリーズ＝ソレイユの日除けは、建物の性能や象徴性の両面を特徴づける。ファサードのユニットは、日除けと視界のバランス調整用のパラメーターとしてつくられており、コーロン社独自のハイテク繊維の一つであるアラミド繊維を使用し、素材の抗張力を劇的に高めるガラス繊維強化プラスチック（GFRP）が配合されている。建物の立地、空間的特性、技術革新により、コーロン社の持続可能性にたいする投資とコミットメントが表現されている。

（松本晴子訳）

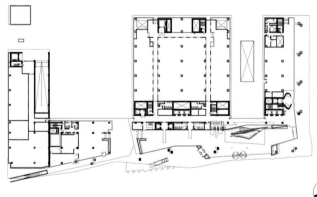

Ground floor plan (scale: 1/2,000)／地上階平面図（縮尺：1/2,000）

Credits and Data
Project title: Kolon One & Only Tower
Client: Kolon Industries, Inc.
Location: Seoul, Korea
Design: 2013–2015
Completion: 2018
Design team (Morphosis): Thom Mayne (Design Director); Eui-Sung Yi (Project Principal); Sung Lim (Project Manager); Ji-Young Jon, Sung-Soo Lim, Zach Pauls, Aaron Ragan (MEP Engineer); Daniel Pruske, Natalia Traverso-Caruana (Project Designers); Ilaria Campi, Yoon Her, Meari Kim, Sarah Kott, Michelle Siu Lee, Jung Jae Park, Go-Woon Seo, Pablo Zunzunegui (Project Team); Cory Brugger, Kerenza Harris, Stan Su, Atsushi Sugiuchi (Advanced Technology); Natalie Abbott, Viola Ago, Lily Bakhshi Sheppard, Paul Cambon, Jessica Chang, Tom Day, Kabalan Fares, Stuart Franks, Fredy Gomez, Marie Goodstein, Parham Hakimi, Maria Herrero, James Janke, Dongil Kim, OneJea Lee, Seo Joo Lee, Katie MacDonald, Eric Meyer, Nicole Meyer, Elizabeth Miller, Carolyn Ng, Liana Nourafshan, Brian Richter, Ahmed Shokir, Ari Sogin, Colton Stevenson, Henry Svendsen, Derrick Whitmire, Jamie Z. Wu, Eda Yetim, Helena Yun (Project Assistants); Jasmine Park, Sam Tannenbaum (Visualization)
Consultants: Haeahn Architecture (Local Architect, Landscape Architect, Signage / Graphics, Code / Life Safety, Waterproofing, Specifications); Buro Happold, SSEN (Structural Engineer, Interiors); Arup, HiMec, Nara (MEP Engineer); Arup, Transsolar, HiMec, Eco-Lead (Sustainability / LEED); ACE ALL (Civil Engineer); Horton Lees Brogden Lighting Design, Alto Lighting (Lighting); Kolon (Audiovisual / IT); Arup, FACO, POSCO (Façade); Arup, KF UBIS (Fire Protection); Kolon (Security); Kolon (Cost Estimator); Kidea (Interiors)
Construction team: Kolon Global Corp. (Construction Manager, General Contractor); Korea Carbon (GFRP), Korea Tech-Wall (GFRC), Han Glass (Curtain Wall), Steel Life (Interior Liner) (Façade Construction); Morphosis Architects, DTCON Architecture, Trimble-Gehry Technologies (BIM)
Project area: 2.02 hectares (site area), 76,300 gross m² (size)

This page: View of the west facade. The GFRP sunshades' forms were derived using solar path diagrams to identify angles of solar incidence, greatly reducing heat gain while preserving interior views. Photo by Roland Halbe, Courtesy of Morphosis.

本頁：西側ファサード。FRP製サンシェードの形状は、太陽光の入射角を特定するために用いた太陽経路ダイアグラムから得られたもので、屋内からの眺望を保持しつつ、熱取得を大幅に削減している。

1. Lobby
2. Grand stair
3. Multi-purpose hall
4. Research lab
5. Daycare center
6. Garden cafe
7. Lounge
8. Pilot
9. Office
10. Lecture room
11. Meeting room
12. Reception room
13. Idea room
14. Break room
15. Bridge
16. Gym
17. Changing room
18. Kitchen
19. Cafeteria
20. Parking
21. Mechanical room
22. Storage

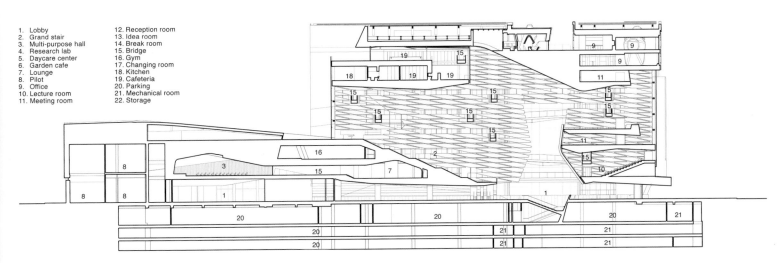

Long section (scale: 1/1,000)/長手断面図（縮尺：1/1,000）

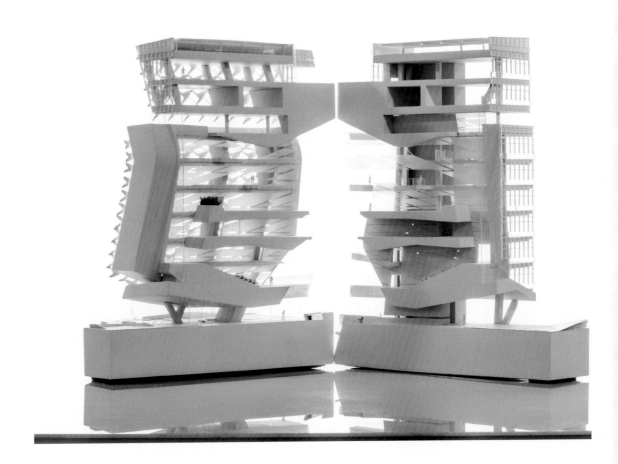

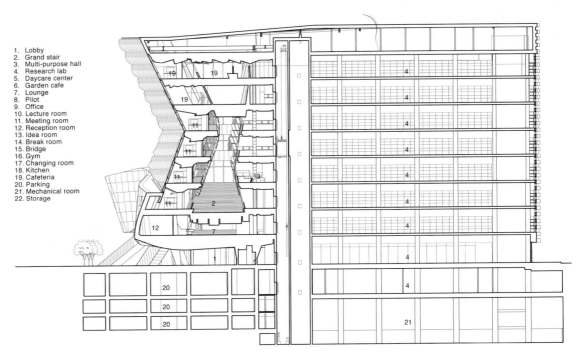

1. Lobby
2. Grand stair
3. Multi-purpose hall
4. Research lab
5. Daycare center
6. Garden cafe
7. Lounge
8. Pilot
9. Office
10. Lecture room
11. Meeting room
12. Reception room
13. Idea room
14. Break room
15. Bridge
16. Gym
17. Changing room
18. Kitchen
19. Cafeteria
20. Parking
21. Mechanical room
22. Storage

Opposite: The multi-story atrium contains conference rooms and a series of social spaces, functioning as a public extension of the laboratory wings. Photo by Jasmine Park, Courtesy of Morphosis. This page: A section model showing the atrium's circulation. Courtesy of Morphosis.

左頁：複数階層にわたる吹き抜けには会議室や一連の社交スペースが含まれ、実験室棟を拡張した公共空間として機能する。本頁：吹き抜けの動線を示す断面模型。

Short section (scale: 1/750)／短手断面図（縮尺：1/750）

The Living
Embodied Computation Lab
Princeton, U.S.A. 2014–2017

ザ・リヴィング
エンボディド・コンピュテーション・ラボ
米国、プリンストン 2014〜2017

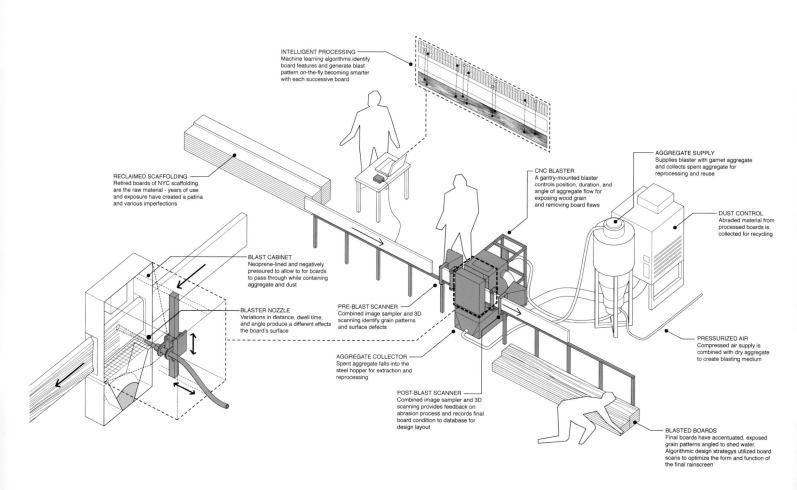

INTELLIGENT PROCESSING
Machine learning algorithms identify board features and generate blast pattern on-the-fly becoming smarter with each successive board

RECLAIMED SCAFFOLDING
Retired boards of NYC scaffolding are the raw material - years of use and exposure have created a patina and various imperfections

BLAST CABINET
Neoprene-lined and negatively pressured to allow to for boards to pass through while containing aggregate and dust

BLASTER NOZZLE
Variations in distance, dwell time, and angle produce a different effects the board's surface

PRE-BLAST SCANNER
Combined image sampler and 3D scanning identify grain patterns and surface defects

AGGREGATE COLLECTOR
Spent aggregate falls into the steel hopper for extraction and reprocessing

POST-BLAST SCANNER
Combined image sampler and 3D scanning provides feedback on abrasion process and records final board condition to database for design layout

CNC BLASTER
A gantry-mounted blaster controls position, duration, and angle of aggregate flow for exposing wood grain and removing board flaws

AGGREGATE SUPPLY
Supplies blaster with garnet aggregate and collects spent aggregate for reprocessing and reuse

DUST CONTROL
Abraded material from processed boards is collected for recycling

PRESSURIZED AIR
Compressed air supply is combined with dry aggregate to create blasting medium

BLASTED BOARDS
Final boards have accentuated, exposed grain patterns angled to shed water. Algorithmic design strategys utilized board scans to optimize the form and function of the final rainscreen

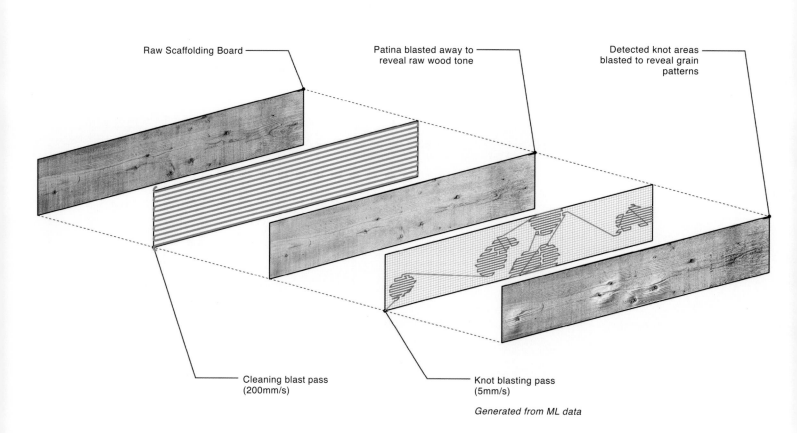

Raw Scaffolding Board

Patina blasted away to reveal raw wood tone

Detected knot areas blasted to reveal grain patterns

Cleaning blast pass
(200mm/s)

Knot blasting pass
(5mm/s)

Generated from ML data

pp. 58–59: Detail of the 900 reclaimed boards constituting the facade. Targeted thermal insulation is based on micro-contours. Photo courtesy of The Living. Opposite: The sand-blasting process used custom machine learning tools to detect and expose contours located at knots. This page, from the top, left to right: The boards were gathered from New York City construction sites; The boards were then photographed and digitally analyzed; A CNC sand-blaster was customized to contour the boards based on knot analysis; View into the fabrication space, looking toward the CNC sand blaster; The boards were then sorted and trimmed based on their contours, tone, and the solar analysis for the project; Detail of the micro-contours, after blasting. All courtesy of The Living.

58〜59頁：ファサードを形成する900枚の再生板材のディテール。断熱目標は、木目を元に算定している。左頁：特注の機械学習ツールを用いたサンドブラスト加工は、節目部分の木目を検出し、露出させるために用いられる。本頁、上から、左から右へ：板材はニューヨーク市の建設現場から集められた／次に板材を撮影し、デジタル分析した／コンピュータ数値制御（CNC）のサンドブラスターは、節目の分析をもとに板材を成形するよう設定された／CNCサンドブラスターの方向に製作空間を見る／次に板材は木目や色合い、プロジェクト用の太陽光分析を元に分類され、切削される／サンドブラスト加工後の木目のディテール。

Original Board Image

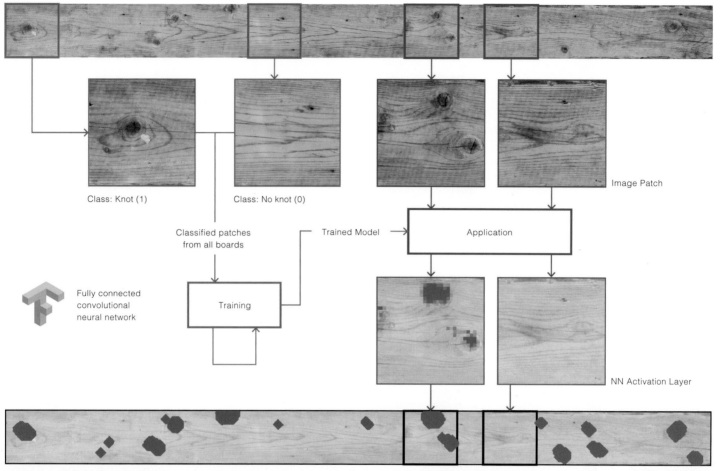

Class: Knot (1)

Class: No knot (0)

Image Patch

Fully connected convolutional neural network

Classified patches from all boards

Trained Model

Application

Training

NN Activation Layer

Board Image with knot detection after dilation

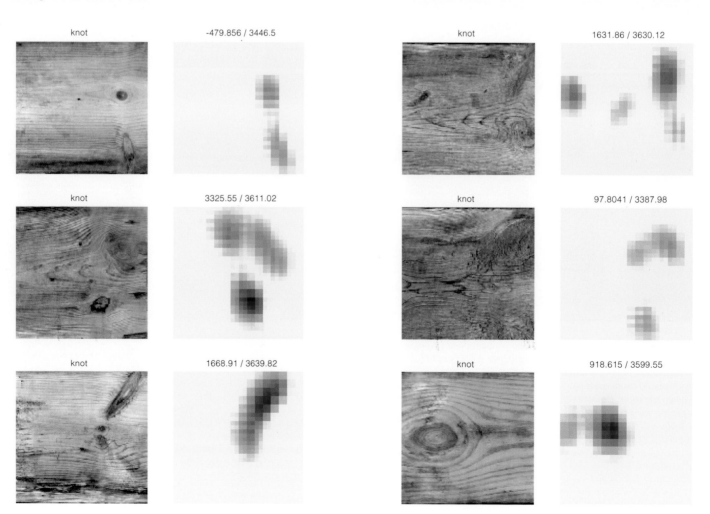

knot	-479.856 / 3446.5	knot	1631.86 / 3630.12
knot	3325.55 / 3611.02	knot	97.8041 / 3387.98
knot	1668.91 / 3639.82	knot	918.615 / 3599.55

Opposite, top: Diagram illustrating reclaimed board classifications, based on imaging and knots. Opposite, bottom: Knot imaging details. This page, top: A detail of the micro-contours after sand-blasting. This page, bottom: Photos of various boards before and after sand-blasting. All courtesy of The Living.

左頁、上：画像処理と節目をもとにした、再生板材の分類を示すダイアグラム。左頁、下：節目の画像処理ディテール。本頁、上：サンドブラスト加工後の木目ディテール。本頁、下：サンドブラスト加工前と後の様々な板材の写真。

BEFORE BEFORE BEFORE

AFTER AFTER AFTER

This is a facility for interdisciplinary research on robotics, sensors, and everywhere that computers meet the physical world and become "embodied computation." The building is both an experiment and a research instrument. Just as biologists use a microscope to study organisms, architects will use this structure to study buildings.

The project is also an "open source building," designed to evolve over time, with components and systems that can be swapped and upgraded. It proposes an alternative to architecture that is fixed, iconic, and driven by form or aesthetic signature.

The building features sustainable systems such as zero-energy radiant heating (via waste condensate from the neighboring building), and passive cooling with no air conditioning. Its structure is made of timber rather than steel. It uses repurposed scaffolding boards from New York City construction for its facade, giving new life to material that is otherwise discarded. It is the first building to use sand-blasted wood for its facade, and it led us to invent a CNC-sand blasting machine. And it is one of the first buildings to apply machine learning to the physical world, which we implemented through creating algorithms to detect knots in wood.

The resulting facade allows us to see materials in a new way, revealing natural variation rather than suppressing it with a lowest-common-denominator approach. It offers a new perspective on buildings as a temporary formation of materials, energy, and labor. Overall, the building suggests a new hybrid design approach that is high-tech and low-tech, familiar and new, functional and aesthetic, digital and biological.

これは、ロボット工学やセンサー、そしてコンピュータと物理的な世界の接点として「具現化された計算結果（エンボディド・コンピュテーション）」となるあらゆる場所に関する学際的研究のための施設である。この建物は実験であり、研究の道具でもある。生物学者が顕微鏡を使用して有機体を研究するように、建築家はこの構造体を使って建物を研究する。

このプロジェクトは、時の経過で進化するよう設計された「オープンソース・ビルディング」でもあり、コンポーネントやシステムを交換およびアップグレードすることができる。固定されたアイコン的存在として形態や審美的記号に依拠した従来の建築の代替となるものを提案している。

この建物は、ゼロ・エネルギー輻射暖房（近隣の建物から出る廃棄物凝縮処理物による）や、空調なしでの受動冷却など、持続可能なシステムを備えている。構造体は、スチールではなく木材でつくられている。ファサードにはニューヨーク市の建設現場で使われた足場板を再利用し、廃棄される運命にあった材料に新しい生命が与えられた。サンドブラスト加工した木材をファサードに使用した最初の建物であり、そのためCNCサンドブラスト機を発明することとなった。また、機械学習を物理的世界に適用した最初の建物の一つとして、木材の節を検出するアルゴリズムが創出され、実装された。

結果的に出来上がったファサードは、最小公倍数的アプローチで素材を抑制するのではなく、自然変異をそのままにみせ、素材への新たな見方を可能にする。このファサードは、素材、エネルギー、労働力を一時的に一つにまとめたもの、として建物をみる新たな視点を提供する。全体として、この建物は、ハイテクとローテク、見慣れたものと新しさ、機能性と美学、デジタルと生物学、これらをハイブリッドした真新しいデザインアプローチを提案する。

（松本晴子訳）

This page: The completed Embodied Computation Lab. Photo by Michael Moran. Opposite, top: The life cycle and processing of the reclaimed wood. Opposite, bottom: Diagram illustrating the arrangement of the reclaimed boards on the facade, with knot mapping. Enhancing shadows with micro-contours allows for greater thermal control. All courtesy of The Living.

本頁：完成したエンボディード・コンピュテーション・ラボ。右頁、上：再生木材のライフサイクルとその加工。右頁、下：節目のマッピングとともにファサードの再生板材の配置を示したダイアグラム。木目により陰影を強調することにより、より高い温度制御が可能になる。

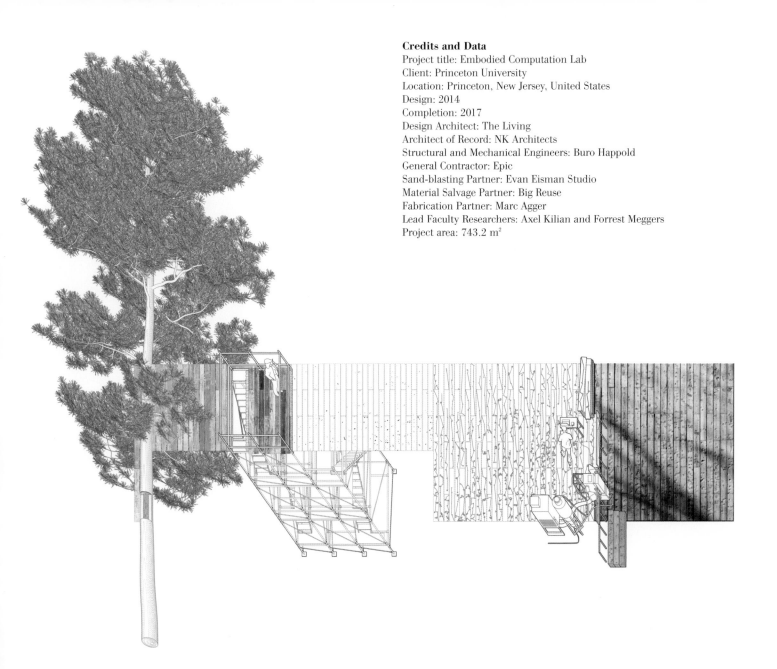

Credits and Data
Project title: Embodied Computation Lab
Client: Princeton University
Location: Princeton, New Jersey, United States
Design: 2014
Completion: 2017
Design Architect: The Living
Architect of Record: NK Architects
Structural and Mechanical Engineers: Buro Happold
General Contractor: Epic
Sand-blasting Partner: Evan Eisman Studio
Material Salvage Partner: Big Reuse
Fabrication Partner: Marc Agger
Lead Faculty Researchers: Axel Kilian and Forrest Meggers
Project area: 743.2 m²

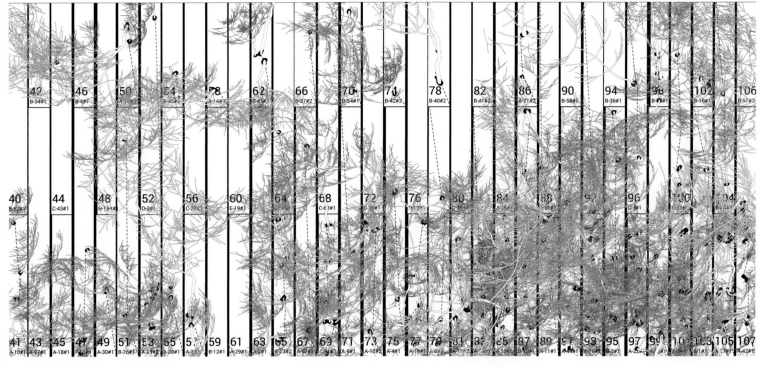

The Living
Hy-Fi
New York, U.S.A. 2014

ザ・リヴィング
Hy-Fi
米国、ニューヨーク　2014

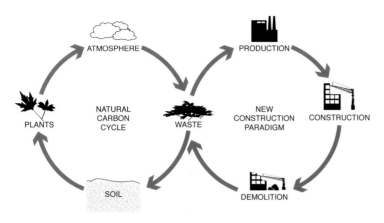

ATMOSPHERE

PRODUCTION

PLANTS

NATURAL
CARBON
CYCLE

WASTE

NEW
CONSTRUCTION
PARADIGM

CONSTRUCTION

SOIL

DEMOLITION

Sustainability diagram／サステイナビリティ・ダイアグラム

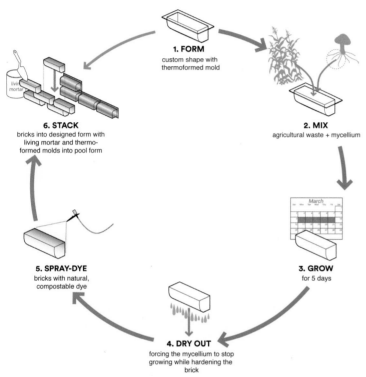

1. FORM
custom shape with
thermoformed mold

2. MIX
agricultural waste + mycellium

3. GROW
for 5 days

4. DRY OUT
forcing the mycellium to stop
growing while hardening the
brick

5. SPRAY-DYE
bricks with natural,
compostable dye

6. STACK
bricks into designed form with
living mortar and thermo-
formed molds into pool form

Brick manufacturing process／煉瓦生成プロセス

pp. 66–67: Photo looking toward Hy-Fi's apertures. Hy-Fi is a 13-meter-tall structure constituted by 10,000 biodegradable bricks. Photo by Iwan Baan, courtesy of The Living. Opposite: These bricks are grown from mycelium and agricultural waste, with almost no embodied energy or carbon emissions. Shown here are studies in mixing, brick growth, and casting. All photos courtesy of The Living.

66～67頁：Hy-Fiの開口部方向を見る。Hy-Fiは1万個の生分解性煉瓦で構成された高さ13mの構造物。右頁：これらの煉瓦は菌糸体と農業廃棄物から生成されたもので、内包エネルギーまたは二酸化炭素排出量はほぼゼロである。混合や煉瓦の生成、成形に関する研究の様子。

Hy-Fi, commissioned by the Museum of Modern Art and MoMA PS1, was developed for the Young Architects Program, an annual invited competition with a brief of creating a temporary, environmentally-friendly project for MoMA PS1's large courtyard.

We started by designing a new type of brick through an innovative combination of corn stalk waste and living mushrooms with root-like growth. The bricks are lightweight, low cost, and extremely sustainable. We then created the world's first large-scale outdoor construction out of this material. We used biological, physical, and computational technologies to test the material's durability, structure, and thermal performance, and to design a robust and viable temporary building.

This new construction material grows out of living materials and returns to the earth through composting at the end of the structure's lifecycle. The manufacturing process engages bio-technology, agriculture, and industrial manufacturing. The composting process engages the municipal solid waste stream. In contrast to typical short-sighted architecture, our project is designed to disappear as much as it is designed to appear.

Construction waste accounts for over 30% of landfill volume. Our project offers an alternative to this wasteful linear economy. We use low-value raw materials rather than high-value ones, we use almost no energy to create building blocks rather than using massive energy, and we return demolition material to the earth in 60 days rather than burying it in landfills for hundreds of years.

This project involves a multi-faceted engagement with people. It offers a direct relationship to regional agriculture and innovation culture, municipal artists and non-profits, and local community gardens. People working on the project included local artists, local trade school interns, international graduate students, construction professionals, engineering professionals, and non-profit organizations. All people involved were meaningfully engaged and fairly paid. The project also engaged a diverse public through its high-profile installation.

Hy-Fi offers a familiar-yet-completely-new building in the context of the glass towers and typical brick construction of New York City. The building creates mesmerizing light effects on its interior walls through reflected caustic patterns. The building frames the natural environment with a forward-looking perspective. The building plays with light, shadow, pattern, texture, and unique atmosphere. Both the architectural community and the general public have been enthusiastic about this pavilion and this new vision for design and manufacturing. This successful experiment offers many possibilities for future architecture and construction. Overall, the building is full of wonder and optimism.

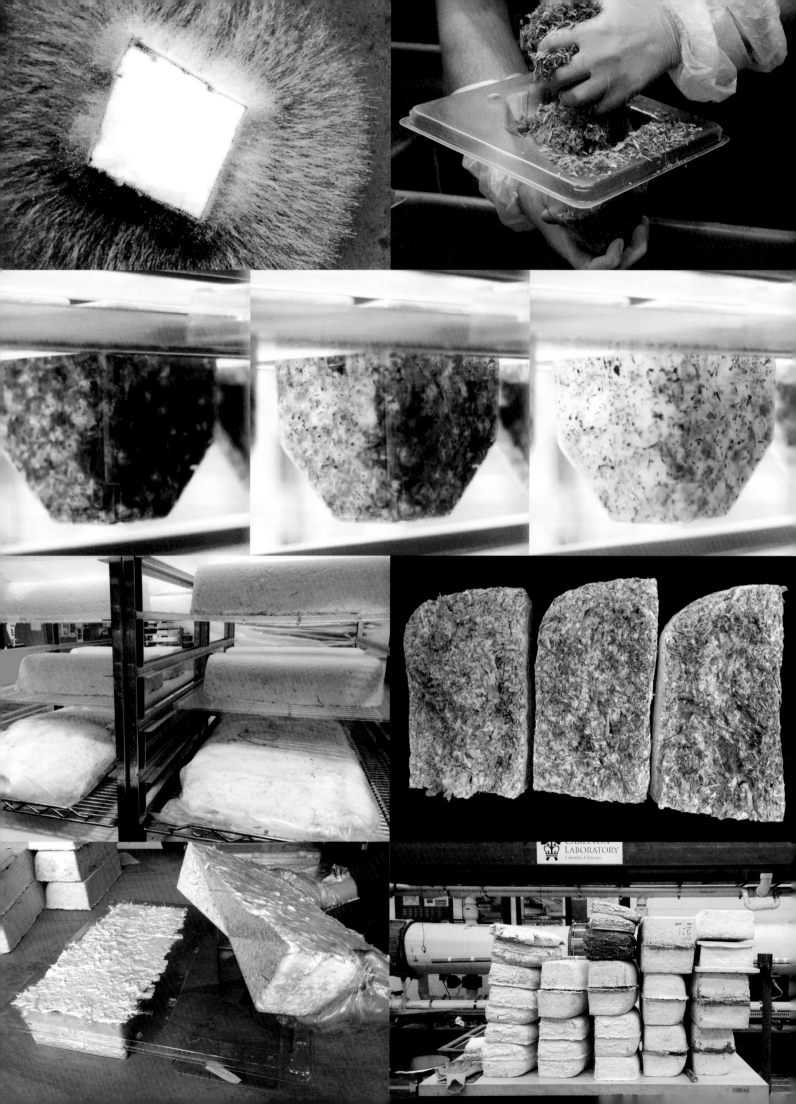

Hy-Fiは、ニューヨーク近代美術館（MoMA）とMoMA PS1から委託され、毎年開催の招待コンペであるヤング・アーキテクト・プログラムのためにつくられたものであり、その概要には、MoMA PS1の広々とした中庭に環境に優しい仮設のプロジェクトをつくりだす、と書かれていた。

私たちは、トウモロコシの茎の廃棄物と、根のように伸長する生きたキノコとの革新的な組み合わせによって新しいタイプの煉瓦をデザインすることからスタートした。この煉瓦は軽量かつ低コストであり、非常にサステイナブルである。私たちは次に、この素材を使用した世界初となる大規模な屋外向けの構造体を製作した。私たちは生物学的、物理的、およびコンピュテーショナル技術を使用して、材料の耐久性、構造、および熱性能をテストし、堅固で実現可能な仮設の建物をデザインした。

この新しい建設材料は、生きた材料から成長し、構造物のライフサイクルを終えると堆肥化され大地に戻る。製造過程は、バイオテクノロジー、農業、工業生産を用いている。堆肥化する過程は、自治体の固形廃棄物の流れに準じる。ありふれた近視眼的な建築とは対照的に、私たちのプロジェクトでは、出現と同様に消失もデザインされている。

建設廃棄物は、埋め立て処分量の30%以上を占める。私たちのプロジェクトは、この無駄の多い線形的経済（リニア・エコノミー）の代替となる。高価値の原料の代わりに低価値の原料を利用し、大量のエネルギーを使う代わりにほぼエネルギーを使うことなく建築用ブロックを製造し、埋め立て処分地に何百年も埋蔵する代わりに廃棄物を60日で大地に還す。

このプロジェクトには、人々との多面的な関与が含まれる。地域農業とイノヴェーション文化、市の芸術家と非営利団体、地域のコミュニティ・ガーデンとの直接的な関係を提供する。プロジェクトに携わる人々に

は、地元の芸術家、地元の職業訓練学校のインターン、世界各国からの大学院生、建設部門の専門家、エンジニアリングの専門家、非営利団体が含まれる。関係するすべての人々は有意義に関与し、公正な報酬を得ている。このプロジェクトはまた、その注目度の高いインスタレーションを通じて様々なパブリックも巻きこんでいる。

Hy-Fiは、ニューヨーク市のガラス張りのタワーと典型的な煉瓦造りを背景に、親しみがありながらまったく新しい建物をもたらす。建物は、内壁に魅惑的な光の効果をつくりだし、反射火線模様を描く。建物は、将来を見据えた視点で自然環境を構成する。建物は、光、影、模様、質感、独特の雰囲気で彩られる。建築コミュニティと一般市民の両方が、このパヴィリオンと、デザインや製造にたいする新たなヴィジョンに熱狂してきた。この成功した実験は、未来の建築と建設に多くの可能性をもたらす。この建物は全体として、驚きと楽観主義に満ちている。　　　　　（松本晴子訳）

This page: Variations of the bricks were tested for tensile and compressive strength using universal testing machines at Columbia University. Opposite: The project's fabrication and assembly involved engaging a variety of different people; shown are New York City brick masons and an international graduate student. All photos courtesy of The Living.

本頁：コロンビア大学の一般的な試験機器を用いた、様々な煉瓦の引張・圧縮強度にの試験。右頁：このプロジェクトの製作と組立てには、異なる分野の様々な人が携わった。ニューヨーク市の煉瓦職人達と、大学院の留学生を写す。

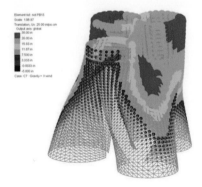

Full Model Iteration 01　　　　Full Model Iteration 07

Loading study／荷重スタディ

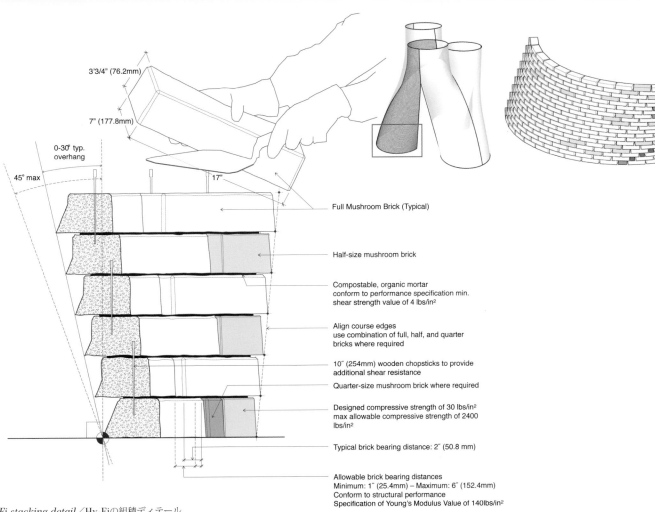

3'3/4" (76.2mm)

7" (177.8mm)

0-30° typ. overhang

45° max

17"

Full Mushroom Brick (Typical)

Half-size mushroom brick

Compostable, organic mortar
conform to performance specification min.
shear strength value of 4 lbs/in²

Align course edges
use combination of full, half, and quarter
bricks where required

10″ (254mm) wooden chopsticks to provide
additional shear resistance

Quarter-size mushroom brick where required

Designed compressive strength of 30 lbs/in²
max allowable compressive strength of 2400
lbs/in²

Typical brick bearing distance: 2″ (50.8 mm)

Allowable brick bearing distances
Minimum: 1″ (25.4mm) – Maximum: 6″ (152.4mm)
Conform to structural performance
Specification of Young's Modulus Value of 140lbs/in²

Hy-Fi stacking detail／Hy-Fiの組積ディテール

pp. 72–73: Hy-Fi on site at the MoMA PS1. Photo courtesy of The Living. This page: Hy-Fi hosted public cultural events for three months, after which it was disassembled, composted, and given, as a soil product, to local community gardens. Photo by Justin Lui, courtesy of The Living. Opposite: Reflective growing trays, used for brick casting, were reused as a finishing material on Hy-Fi's apertures to bring light into the interior. Copyright Amy Barkow, courtesy of The Living.

72〜73頁：MoMA PS1の敷地に設置されたHy-Fi。本頁：公共の文化イベントを3ヶ月にわたって開催、その後解体、コンポスト化され、地元のコミュニティ・ガーデンに土壌製品として提供された。右頁：煉瓦の成形のために使用された成育用反射トレーは、屋内に光をとり込むため、Hy-Fi開口部の仕上げ素材として再利用された。

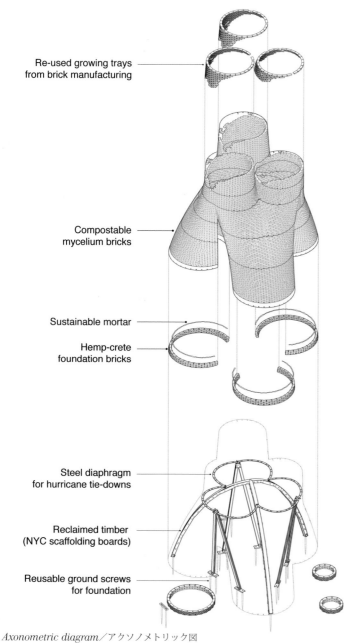

Re-used growing trays from brick manufacturing

Compostable mycelium bricks

Sustainable mortar

Hemp-crete foundation bricks

Steel diaphragm for hurricane tie-downs

Reclaimed timber (NYC scaffolding boards)

Reusable ground screws for foundation

Axonometric diagram／アクソノメトリック図

Credits and Data
Project title: Hy-Fi
Client: Museum of Modern Art and MoMA PS1
Location: MoMA PS1, Queens, New York, USA
Design: The Living
Construction and Completion: June 2014
Project area: 120.4 m²

Institute for Computational Design and Construction, University of Stuttgart

コメンタリー：
シュトゥットガルト大学、コンピュテーショナル・デザインおよび建設研究所（**ICD**）

a+u: *Generally speaking, how do you use computational design?*
ICD: We aim to tap the full potential of digital technologies in order to explore a novel computational material culture in architecture, which goes far beyond the mere digitalization of established design methods and the automation of existing building processes by seeking truly integrative computational design and construction. Forging new alliances between the fields of design, engineering and natural sciences, we conceive of digital technologies as catalysts for a new understanding of materiality in architecture, which is no longer seen to be a fixed property and passive receptor of preconceived form, but is transformed into an active generator of design and an adaptive agent of architectural performance.

a+u: *How are you expanding upon what you have done?*
ICD: At the center of our research lies the notion of co-design, which we define as the concurrent and feedback-based exploration and advancement of computational design methods, robotic fabrication processes and emerging material and building systems. In the first decade of our work we explored this approach primarily through research pavilions. In the next few years, we aim to expand this overarching co-design methodology significantly towards more common architectural typologies, as for example multi-story buildings, in order to contribute to addressing the severe ecological, economic and social challenges that architecture is facing.

a+u: *How would you describe the mess in your workplace?*
ICD: We strongly believe that scientific rigor can greatly contribute to design creativity. Both in design and in science the path towards a specific solution tends to be convoluted – even if the convolutions are typically of a different kind in both domains – but it is rarely messy. Accordingly, we embrace a workplace culture that reflects this situation: a place full of latent design possibilities to be uncovered and of genuine intellectual diversity, yet maintained with a high level of systematicity. At least, that's the idea – in reality, the occasional major cleanup is required!

a+u：コンピューテーショナル・デザインをどのように利用しているのか、概要を教えてください。

ICD：私たちは、デジタル技術の可能性を最大限に活用することを目指しており、建築における新しいコンピュテーショナル・マテリアル文化を探求するために、既存のデザイン手法の単なるデジタル化や、既存の建設プロセスの自動化など凌駕した、真に統合的なコンピュテーショナル・デザインと構築を追求している。デザイン、工学、自然科学の各分野間の新たな協力関係を構築し、建築における素材性を新たに理解するための触媒としてデジタル技術をとらえている。建築は、もはや固定資産や、先に考案された形態の受動的な受容体などではなく、活デザイン生成機、建築性能を適応させる仲介に変容した。

a+u：これまでの活動をいかに広げていきますか。

ICD：私たちの研究の中心にあるのは、コ・デザイン（共同設計）の思想である。これは、コンピュテーショナル・デザイン手法、ロボット製造プロセス、新素材、建設システムの同時的およびフィードバックベースの調査と進歩と定義されている。私たちは、最初の10年間の研究で、おもに研究棟を通じてこうしたアプローチを検討した。これから数年間のうちに、私たちはこの包括的なコ・デザイン手法を、高層ビルといったより一般的な建築のタイポロジーへと大幅に拡大することを目指している。建築が直面している生態学的、経済的、社会的難課題への対処に貢献していく。

a+u：仕事場の混沌とした状況をどのように表現しますか。

ICD：私たちが確信しているのは、科学的な厳密さがデザインの創造性に大きく貢献することである。デザインと科学の両方において、特定の解決方法への経路は包旋形になる傾向があり――こうした包旋形は、両領域で典型的に別種のものとなるにしても――雑然としたものにはめったにならない。したがって、私たちはこうした状況を反映した仕事場文化を受けいれる。そこは潜在的なデザインの可能性に満ち、真の知的多様性が明かされ、高度な体系によって維持された場所となる。少なくとも、理想的には。実際には、時々大がかりな掃除が必要だが！（松本晴子訳）

Photos by Wolfram Scheible, courtesy of ICD/ITKE University of Stuttgart.

Institute for Computational Design and Construction (ICD)

BUGA Fiber Pavilion 2019
Heilbronn, Germany 2019

コンピュテーショナル・デザインおよび建設研究所（**ICD**）
BUGAファイバー・パヴィリオン**2019**
ドイツ、ハイルブロン　**2019**

Novel Composite Building System Inspired By Nature

In biology most load-bearing structures are fiber composites. They are made from fibers, as for example cellulose, chitin or collagen, and a matrix material that supports them and maintains their relative position. The astounding performance and unrivalled resource efficiency of biological structures stems from these fibrous systems. Their organization, directionality and density is finely tuned and locally varied in order to ensure that material is only placed where it is needed. The BUGA Fiber Pavilion aims to transfer this biological principle of load-adapted and thus highly differentiated fiber composite systems into architecture. Man-made composites, such as the glass- or carbon fiber-reinforced plastics that were used for this building, are ideally suited for such an approach, because they share their fundamental characteristics with natural composites.

The project builds on many years of biomimetic research at the Institute for Computational Design and Construction (ICD) and the Institute for Building Structures and Structural Design (ITKE). It shows how an interdisciplinary exploration of biological principles together with the latest computational technologies can lead to a truly novel and genuinely digital fiber composite building system. Only a few years ago, this pavilion would have been impossible to design or build.

自然に学んだ新たな複合建設システム

自然の世界では生体構造のほとんどが、繊維（ファイバー）を元にした複合材でできている。セルロース、キチン質、コラーゲン、そしてそれらを支持し相互の間隔を保つマトリックス素材も繊維によるものである。生体構造の驚異的なパフォーマンスときわめて優れた物質的な効率性は、繊維によるシステムで生みだされている。繊維の構成、方向、密度は厳密に調整され、それぞれの場所に必要な素材のみが配されている。BUGAファイバー・パヴィリオンは、支えるべき荷重に対応する生体の仕組みを応用し、細かく調整された繊維の複合システムの建築への導入を目指している。パヴィリオンに使われているガラス繊維強化プラスティックや炭素繊維強化プラスティックなどの複合材は、基本的な特性が自然の合成物と共通していることから、このアプローチに最適なものであった。

プロジェクトは、コンピュテーショナル・デザインおよび建設研究所（ICD）と建築構造および構造デザイン研究所（ITKE）による、長年にわたるバイオミメティクス（生体模倣技術）の研究にもとづいている。ここでは、生体の仕組みについての分野横断的な研究を最新のコンピュータ技術と組み合わせることで実現された、繊維複合材による、まったく新しく完全にデジタルな建設システムが示されている。たった数年前でさえ、このパヴィリオンをデザインすることも、建てることも不可能だっただろう。

（中田雅章訳）

Winding Frames

Glass Fiber Lattice

**Carbon Fiber
Reinforcement**

**Carbon Fiber Corner
Reinforcement**

Integrative Computational Design and Robotic Fabrication

The pavilion is made from more than 150,000 meters of spatially arranged glass- and carbon fibers. They all need to be individually designed and placed, which is very hard to achieve with a typical linear workflow and established production technologies. Thus, it requires a novel co-design approach, where architectural design, structural engineering and robotic fabrication are developed in continuous computational feedback. In this way, the fiber arrangement, density and orientation of each building component can be individually calibrated, structurally tuned and architecturally articulated, while remaining directly producible.

The building components are produced by robotic, coreless filament winding, a novel additive manufacturing approach pioneered and developed at the University of Stuttgart. Fibrous filaments are freely placed between two rotating winding scaffolds by a robot. During this process, the predefined shape of the building component emerges only from the interaction of the filaments, eliminating the need for any mold or core. This allows for bespoke form and individual fiber layup for each component without any economic disadvantage. In addition, there is no production waste or material off-cuts. During manufacturing, a lattice of translucent glass fibers is generated, onto which the black carbon fibers are placed where they are structurally needed. This results in highly load-adapted components with a highly distinct architectural appearance.

Full production took place at the project's industrial partner, FibR GmbH. Each component takes between four to six hours to make, from around 1,000 meters of glass fiber and 1,600 meters of carbon fiber on average.

統合的なコンピューテーショナル・デザインとロボット製造

パヴィリオンは、15万mを超えるガラス繊維と炭素繊維を空間的に構成することでつくりだされている。それらはすべて個別にデザインされ、配置される必要があり、これまでの直線的な製造工程と定型化された生産技術では実現がきわめて難しいものである。ここで必要とされたのは、建築のデザイン、構造技術、ロボット製造がコンピュータによる継続的なフィードバックを通して進化していく、新たなコ・デザインのアプローチであった。これによって、それぞれのコンポーネントの繊維の配置、密度、方向を個別に調整し、構造に適合させ、建築として構築しながら、ダイレクトに生産していくことが可能になっている。

建物のコンポーネントは、シュトゥットガルト大学が世界に先駆けて試み開発した、新たな付加製造技術、ロボットによるコアをもたない繊維の巻きつけによってつくりだされている。2つの回転する巻きとり用の枠の間に、ロボットが自由に繊維を配していく。このプロセスによって、繊維の重なりのみで所定のコンポーネントがつくりだされる。そこでは、型枠やコアはまったく必要とされず、余計なコストをかけることなく、繊維を個別に積層し、あらかじめ指定された一つ一つのコンポーネントを生みだすことができる。加えてこの方式では、生産にともなう廃棄物や資材の無駄がまったく発生しない。その過程では透明なガラス繊維のラティスが形成され、構造上必要な場所に黒い炭素繊維が重ねられていく。これによって、きわめて特徴的な外観をもち、荷重に柔軟に対応するコンポーネントが生みだされている。

実際の生産は、プロジェクトの事業パートナーであるFibR社で行われた。それぞれのコンポーネントは平均1,000mのガラス繊維と1,600mの炭素繊維からなり、4〜6時間でつくりだされている。　　（中田雅章訳）

pp. 78–79: Membrane detail of the BUGA Fiber Pavilion. Opposite, top: Close-up of the composite structure. Opposite, middle: Coreless winding sequence. This page, from the top: Robotic winding unit; Fiber impregnation system; Testing setup ICD CCLab. All photos copyright ICD/ITKE University of Stuttgart.

78〜79頁：BUGAファイバー・パヴィリオン、膜のディテール。左頁、上：複合構造の近景。左頁、中：コアレスの巻きつけ手順。本頁、上から：ロボット巻きつけユニット／繊維含浸システム／ICD CCLabでの試験設置。

pp. 82–83: Close-up of the composite structure. Opposite, top: Crane lifting a composite building group. Opposite, bottom: BUGA Fiber Pavilion shortly before completion. Copyright BUGA Heilbronn 2019 GmbH. This page: Installation of the membrane. Copyright ICD/ITKE University of Stuttgart.

82〜83頁：複合構造の近景。左頁、上：複合構造グループの一つを吊り上げるクレーン。左頁、下：完成間近のBUGAファイバー・パヴィリオン。本頁：膜の設置。

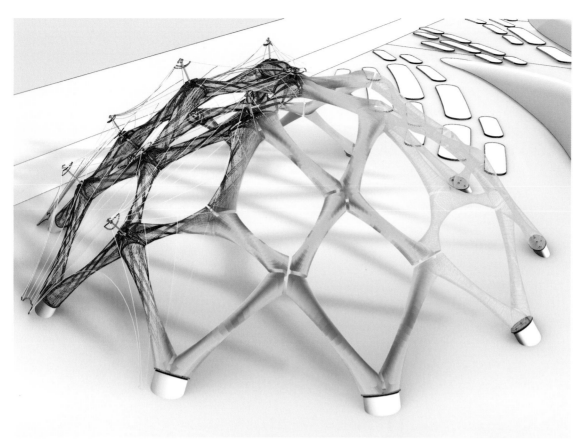

Unique Lightweight Structure and Expressive Architectural Space

The pavilion covers a floor area of around 400 square meters and achieves a free span of more than 23 meters. It is enclosed by a fully transparent, mechanically pre-stressed ETFE membrane. The primary load-bearing structure is made from 60 bespoke fiber composite components only. With 7.6 kilograms per square meter it is exceptionally lightweight, approximately five times lighter than a more conventional steel structure. Elaborate testing procedures required for full approval showed that a single fibrous component can take up to 250 kilo newton of compression force, which equals around 25 tons or the weight of more than 15 cars. The pavilion shows how a truly integrative approach to computational design and robotic fabrication enables the development of novel, truly digital fiber composite building systems that are fully compliant with the stringent German building regulations, exceptionally light, structurally efficient and architecturally expressive.

類のない軽量構造と表現的な建築空間

パヴィリオンは約400m²の空間を覆い、23mを超えるスパンを実現している。その空間は機械的にプレストレスを加えた透明なETFE膜（フッ素樹脂膜）に包まれている。基本的な構造は、計画された60個の繊維による複合部材のみで構成されている。1m²あたりの重量は7.6kgときわめて軽く、一般的なスティールの構造のおよそ5分の1である。最終的な認可のために実施された様々な試験の結果、繊維のコンポーネントは最大250kN（キロニュートン）の圧縮力（約25tあるいは自動車15台の重量に相当する）に耐えられることが示されている。コンピュータによるデザインとロボット製造の完全に一体的なアプローチによって、ドイツの非常に厳しい建築法規に全面的に適合し、きわめて軽く、構造的な効率性に優れ、建築的な表現力に富む、繊維によるこれまでにない完全にデジタルな複合的な建設システムが実現可能であることをパヴィリオンは示している。

（中田雅章訳）

Compression

0.0

Tension

C1　C2　C3　C4　C5　C6

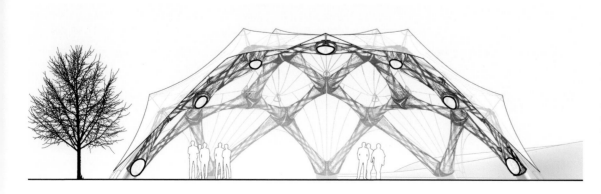

Section (scale: 1/250)／断面図（縮尺：1/250）

Opposite: View from underneath the membrane. The black carbon filament bundles, wrapping around the translucent glass fibre lattice, create a contrast in texture that is highlighted by the pavilion's transparent skin. Copyright Roland Halbe.

右頁：膜の下側からの眺め。黒い炭素繊維束が半透明のガラス繊維製の格子構造を包み込み、質感にコントラストを生みだす。そのコントラストを、パビリオンの半透明のスキンが強調する。

Embedded in the wave-like landscape of the Bundesgartenschau grounds, the pavilion translates the innovation on a technical level into a unique architectural experience. The black carbon filament bundles, wrapping around the translucent glass fiber lattice like flexed muscles, create a stark contrast in texture that is highlighted by the pavilion's fully transparent skin. This distinctive architectural articulation is further intensified by the gradient from sparser carbon filaments at the top towards their denser application on the slenderest components that meet the ground. While most visitors may not have seen anything like it before, the pavilion exposes its underlying design principles in an explicable yet expressive way. Its unfamiliar yet authentic architectural articulation evokes new ways of digital making, which no longer remain a futuristic proposition but already have become a tangible reality.

BUGA（連邦園芸博覧会）のゆるやかに起伏するランドスケープに置かれたパヴィリオンは、技術的な革新を独特な建築体験に転じている。透明なガラス繊維によるラティス様の折り曲げられた筋を包む黒い炭素繊維の束が表層に明確なコントラストを生みだし、その対比は完全に透明なパヴィリオンの皮膜によって強調されている。この特徴的な建築の構成は、頂部では疎らで、大地に接する最も細い部材では密度が高まる炭素繊維のグラデーションによって、さらに強められている。多くの来場者はこうした建物をはじめて体験することから、パヴィリオンはデザインに隠された原理を、その

表現の中にわかりやすく目に見えるものとしている。目新しく、しかし純粋に建築的な構成は、もはや夢物語ではなく手にすることができる現実となった、デジタルによるものづくりの新たな手法を実行に移している。

（中田雅章訳）

Credits and Data

Project title: BUGA Fiber Pavilion 2019

Location: Heilbronn, Germany

Completion: 2019

Design team: Prof. Achim Menges, Serban Bodea, Niccolo Dambrosio, Monika Göbel, Christoph Zechmeister (ICD – Institute for Computational Design and Construction, University of Stuttgart); Prof. Jan Knippers, Valentin Koslowski, Marta Gil Pérez, Bas Rongen (ITKE – Institute of Building Structures and Structural Design, University of Stuttgart); Moritz Dörstelmann, Ondrej Kyjanek, Philipp Essers, Philipp Gülke (FibR GmbH, Stuttgart); Hanspeter Faas, Oliver Toellner (Bundesgartenschau Heilbronn 2019 GmbH)

Project Building Permit Process: Dr. Stefan Brendler, Dipl.-Ing. Steffen Schneider (Landesstelle für Bautechnik); Dipl.-Ing. Achim Bechert, Dipl.-Ing. Florian Roos (Proof Engineer); Prof. Dr.-Ing. Götz T. Gresser, Pascal Mindermann (DITF German Institutes of Textile and Fiber Research)

Project area: 400 m²

Construction System: 60 load bearing robotically fabricated glass- and carbon fibre composite elements, out of 150,000 m glass- and carbon fibres; transparent, mechanically pre-stressed ETFE membrane

Project funding: Land Baden-Württemberg, Universität Stuttgart, Baden-Württemberg Stiftung, GETTYLAB, Forschungsinitiative Zukunft Bau, Pfeifer GmbH, Ewo GmbH, Fischer Group

Opposite: BUGA Fibre Pavilion in the morning light. Copyright ICD/ITKE University of Stuttgart. This page: View through the membrane and fibrous structure at night. Copyright Roland Halbe.

右頁：朝日の中の BUGA ファイバー・パヴィリオン。本頁：膜と繊維構造ごしの夜景。

Institute for Computational Design and Construction (ICD)
BUGA Wood Pavilion 2019
Heilbronn, Germany 2019

コンピュテーショナル・デザインおよび建設研究所（ICD）
BUGAウッド・パヴィリオン2019
ドイツ、ハイルブロン　2019

Robotic Prefabrication: Combining Automated Assembly with High-Precision Machining

Compared to a solid wood plate, as for example used in the team's LAGA Exhibition Hall, the hollow building segments significantly reduce weight and material, but they increase the number of building parts eightfold and lead to more complex manufacturing. Thus, striving for higher resource efficiency needs to go hand-in-hand with automated robotic manufacturing of the shell segments. For this, a novel, transportable, 14-axes robotic timber-manufacturing platform was developed by ICD University of Stuttgart and BEC GmbH, and located at the industrial partner MuellerBlaustein Holzbauwerke GmbH for production. The platform includes two high-payload industrial robots mounted on a 20-foot standard container base. The flexibility of industrial robots allows the integration of all pre-fabrication steps of the pavilion's segments within one compact manufacturing unit.

During production, each bespoke shell segment is robotically assembled. This entails the placement of preformatted timber plates and beams, their temporary fixation with beech nails, and the controlled application for the structural glue joint between plate and beam. In a second step, the intricate finger-joints and openings are machined into the segments with 300 μm accuracy. From the assembly of beams and plates, to multi-tool machining and sensorial process – and image-based quality control – everything happens in a fully automated workflow, controlled by 2 million custom lines of robotic code that were directly exported from the computational design framework. On average, the assembly time per segment is 8 minutes, with the high precision-milling taking another 20–40 minutes.

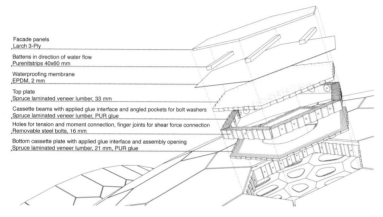

Facade panels
Larch 3-Ply

Battens in direction of water flow
Purenitstrips 40x60 mm

Waterproofing membrane
EPDM, 2 mm

Top plate
Spruce laminated veneer lumber, 33 mm

Cassette beams with applied glue interface and angled pockets for bolt washers
Spruce laminated veneer lumber, PUR glue

Holes for tension and moment connection, finger joints for shear force connection
Removable steel bolts, 16 mm

Bottom cassette plate with applied glue interface and assembly opening
Spruce laminated veneer lumber, 21 mm, PUR glue

Shell assembly detail／シェル組み立てディテール

ロボットによるプレファブリケーション：自動組み立てと高精度機械制御の連携

LAGAの展示ホールなどで使われたソリッドな木材のプレートに比べ、中空の部材は重量と資材量を大幅に減らしている。その反面、必要なパーツの数は8倍に増え、より複雑な生産工程が必要となった。したがって、優れた資材効率を目指す試みは、シェルのセグメントの自動化されたロボット製造と連動して進められる必要があった。このため、シュトゥットガルト大学のコンピューテーショナル・デザインおよび建設研究所（ICD）とBEC社によって運搬可能な14軸のロボットによる新たな製材プラットフォームが開発され、生産のために事業パートナーのミューラーブラウシュタイン・ホルツバウヴェルケ社に設置された。このプラットフォームは、20ft（約6.1m）の標準的なコンテナの台座上に設置された、重い部材にも対応可能な2台の産業用ロボットで構成されている。産業用ロボットのもち合わせる柔軟性によって、パヴィリオンの部材をプレファブリケートするためのすべての過程を、一つのコンパクトな生産ユニットに統合することが可能になっている。

生産工程では、計画されたシェルの一つ一つのセグメントが、ロボットによって組み立てられている。その工程は、あらかじめ成形された木材の板と梁材の配置、ブナの釘による仮止め、板と梁材を結着するため

の構造用接着材の適応を含んでいる。第二のステップでは、複雑なフィンガージョイントと開口部が、機械によって誤差300μmの正確さでセグメントに加工された。梁材と板の組み立てから、複数の装置による機械加工とセンサーによるプロセス、そして画像による品質管理に至るまで、すべてが完全に自動化されたワークフローの中で進められている。その工程は、コンピュテーショナル・デザインのフレームワークから直接書きだされた、200万行ものロボット専用のコードで制御されている。セグメントの組み立て時間は平均8分で、その他に高精度な製材のために20分から40分を要している。

（中田雅章訳）

pp. 90–91: Detail view of spine arch of the BUGA Wood Pavilion. Copyright ICD/ITKE University of Stuttgart. This page: Construction of Robotic Platform at BEC GmbH. Opposite, from the upper left, left-to-right: Multitool effector of robot 1: glue applicator, nailgun and spindle; Multitool effector of robot 2: parallel grippers for beams, vacuum grippers for plates, sensors for process control; Application of glue; Placement of beams; Fixation of beams with beech nails; Placement of top plate; Machining of cassette to form submillimeter precise detail features; Robotic fabrication overview with input modules and glue press docked to robotic platform. All photos copyright ICD/ITKE University of Stuttgart.

90〜91頁：BUGAウッド・パヴィリオンの背骨部分のアーチ構造のディテール。本頁：BEC社におけるロボット・プラットフォームの組立て。右頁、左上から時計回りに：ロボット1のマルチツール・エフェクター（接着剤のアプリケーター、釘打機、スピンドル）／ロボット2のマルチツール・エフェクター（梁用の平行グリッパ、板材用の真空グリッパ、プロセス制御用のセンサー）／接着剤塗布／梁の配置／ブナ材の釘による梁の固定／トップ・プレートの設置／サブミリ精度の詳細を形成するカセットの機械加工／ロボットプラットフォームに統合された入力モジュールと接着プレス機を備えるロボットファブリケーションの概観。

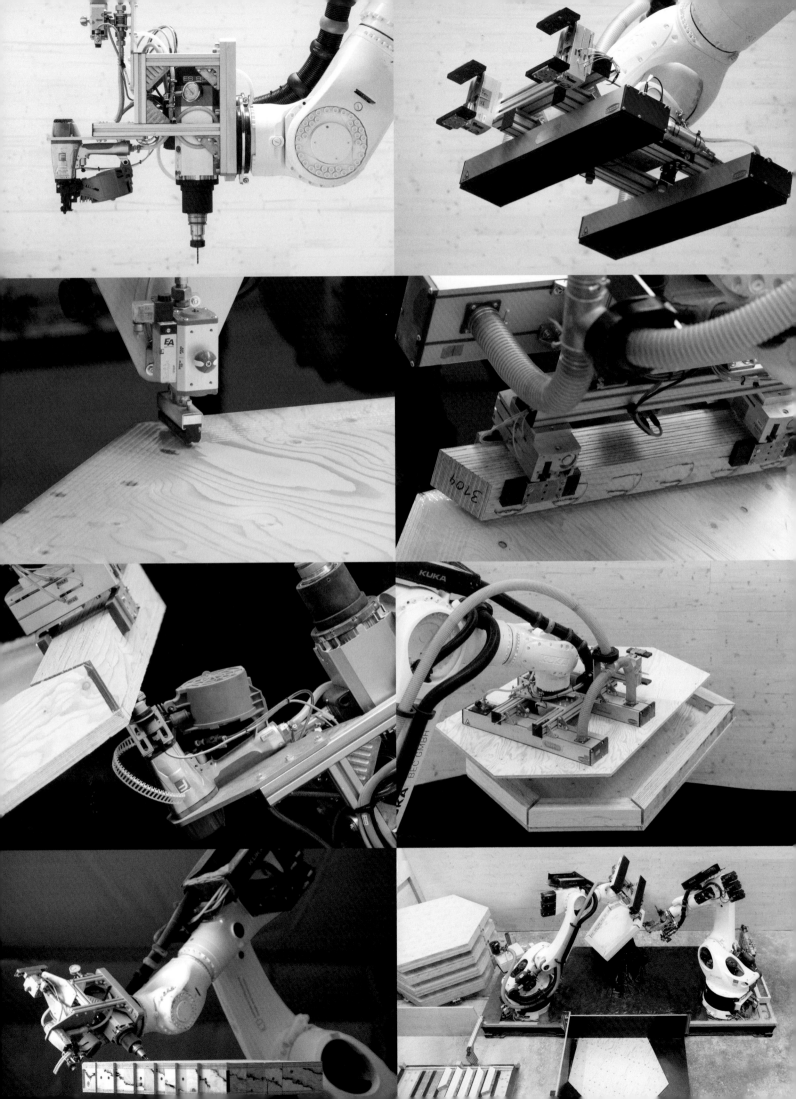

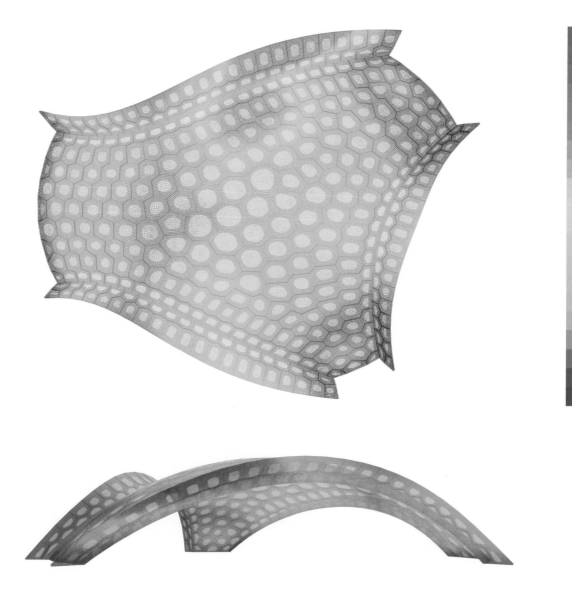

	mm
13.3	
12.77	
12.24	
11.7	
11.17	
10.64	
10.11	
9.58	
9.04	
8.51	
7.98	
7.45	
6.92	
6.38	
5.85	
5.32	
4.79	
4.26	
3.72	
3.19	
2.66	
2.13	
1.6	
1.06	
0.53	
0.0	

Integrative (Co)Design: Feedback-driven Design, Engineering and Fabrication Development

New ways of building require new ways of designing and manufacturing. The BUGA Wood Pavilion was conceived under the paradigm of Co-Design, where novel possibilities in design, engineering and fabrication are explored through continuous computational feedback within an interdisciplinary team. In this project, the co-design algorithms developed by the project team generate the shape of each element of the pavilion according to architectural design intent and structural requirements, while all robotic fabrication aspects are directly embedded and negotiated. The design of the pavilion happens concurrently and in feedback with the design of the robotic manufacturing set-up, which is a bespoke development for the project.

The highly integrative process enables the design and engineering of 376 unique plate segments with 17,000 different finger joints in response to multifaceted design criteria, from the scale of the overall structure down to sub-millimetre details. Without any loss of precision, this multi-scale approach allows addressing architectural and structural considerations concurrently. Despite the pioneering character of the project, and despite an incredible short development time of only 13 months from commission to the opening, the integrative computational process allows for the careful design of each building element in minute detail.

一体的な（コ・）デザイン：フィードバックにもとづくデザイン、エンジニアリング、ファブリケーションの進化

新たな建設方法は、これまでにないデザインと生産の進め方を必要としていた。BUGAウッド・パヴィリオンは、分野横断的なチーム内でのコンピュータによる継続的なフィードバックを通して、デザイン、エンジニアリング、ファブリケーションの新たな可能性を探求する、コ・デザインの考え方にもとづいて計画されている。このパヴィリオンでは、プロジェクト・チームによって開発されたコ・デザインのアルゴリズムが建築デザインの意図と構造上の必要性に応じて個々のエレメントの形状を生成する一方で、ロボットによる製造に必要なすべての要素が直接アルゴリズムに組み込まれ、調整されている。パヴィリオンのデザインは、プロジェクトに先行して開発されるロボット製造のための装置のセットアップのデザインと並行して、またセットアップされた製造装置からのフィードバックを通して生みだされている。

高度に一体化されたプロセスが、構造全体のスケールからミリ単位以下のディテールに至るまで、デザインの様々な条件に対応する17,000ものフィンガー・ジョイントをもつ、376枚のプレートによるセグメントのデザインと組み立てを可能にしている。このマルチ・スケールのアプローチは正確性を保ちながら、建築と構造の課題に同時に応えている。先駆的なプロジェクトであるにもかかわらず、そして発注から開幕までわずか13ヵ月という驚くほど短い開発期間であったにもかかわらず、コンピュータによる統合的なプロセスが、それぞれのエレメントを細部に至るまで注意深くデザインすることを可能にしている。

（中田雅章訳）

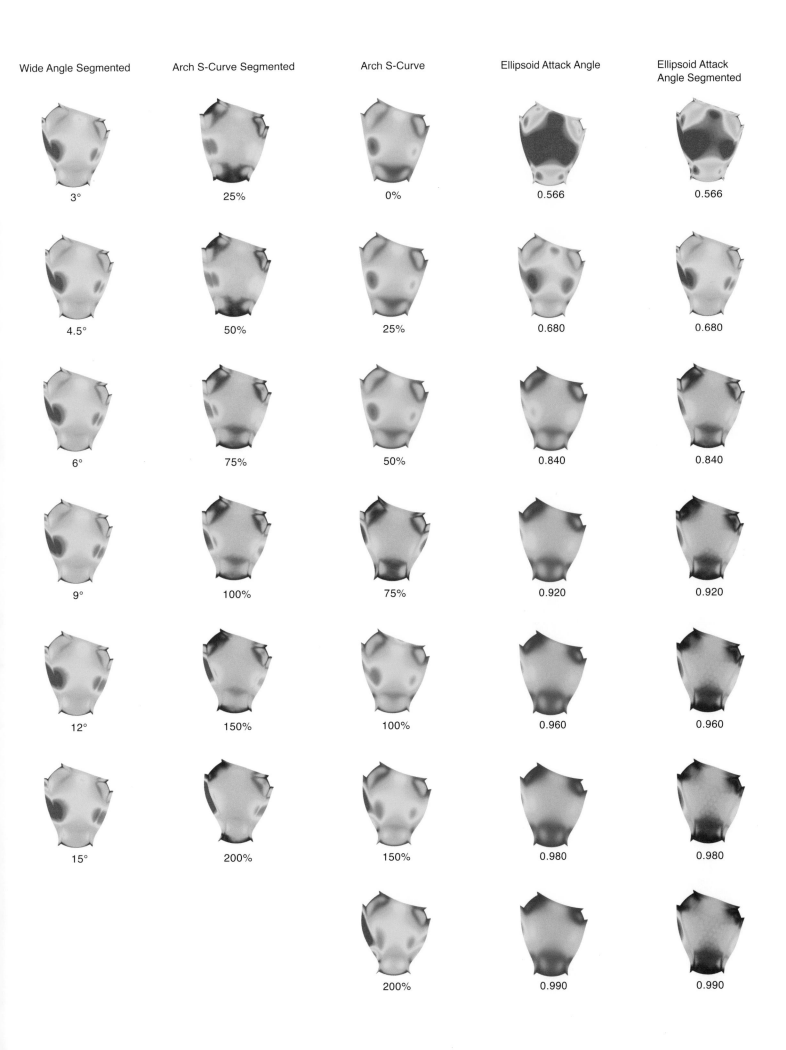

Wide Angle Segmented	Arch S-Curve Segmented	Arch S-Curve	Ellipsoid Attack Angle	Ellipsoid Attack Angle Segmented
3°	25%	0%	0.566	0.566
4.5°	50%	25%	0.680	0.680
6°	75%	50%	0.840	0.840
9°	100%	75%	0.920	0.920
12°	150%	100%	0.960	0.960
15°	200%	150%	0.980	0.980
		200%	0.990	0.990

The prefabricated shell segments were assembled in only 10 working days by a team of two craftsmen, without the usually required extensive scaffolding or formwork. After connecting all segments with removable bolts, a layer of EPDM foil was rolled over the pavilion in 8 strips to provide waterproofing. Untreated larch facade plates provide the external cladding of the pavilion. All building elements are designed for disassembly and reuse on a different site.

The pavilion's load-bearing wood shell achieves a column-free span of 30 meters, but weighs only 38 kg/m². This is less than the LAGA exhibition hall benchmark, despite a threefold increase in span and a fivefold increase in size. Drawing a line from traditional carpentry to high-tech robotic fabrication methods, the BUGA Wood Pavilion showcases the possibilities for efficient, economical, ecological and expressive wood architecture that arises at the intersection of master craft, digital innovation and scientific research.

プレファブリケートされたシェルのセグメントは、通常であれば必要になる足場や型枠を使うことなく、2人の職人のチームによって10日間で組み立てられた。とり外し可能なボルトですべてのセグメントを接合した後、防水性能を確保するために、8列のEPDM（エチレン・プロピレン・ジエンゴム）の膜材がパヴィリオンの上部全面に貼られている。パヴィリオンの外装は、仕上げを施していないカラマツのプレートである。すべてのエレメントは、解体し別の場所で再利用できるようデザインされている。

パヴィリオンの構造体となる木造シェルは

30mの無柱空間を実現しているが、1m²あたりの重量はわずか38kgである。スパンが3倍、規模が5倍になっているにもかかわらず、その重量はLAGAの展示ホールよりも軽い。BUGAウッド・パヴィリオンは伝統的な木造の施工技術とハイテクのロボット製造を1本の線で引き結び、職人の技、デジタルの進化、科学的な研究の交点に生まれる、効率的で経済的、そしてエコロジカルで表現的な木造建築の可能性を示している。

（中田雅章訳）

pp. 94, top: Structural model showing anticipated minimal deformations. pp. 95: Structural form-finding matrix. This page, from the top: The assembly of the shell on its site in Heilbronn, a "large three-dimensional puzzle"; Each shell segment was lifted in by crane and positioned in place by 2 carpenters; Bolts were tightened through the access hole on the bottom side of the segments; The shell was assembled without extensive formwork. Opposite, top: View of the half-assembled shell from across the Karlssee. Opposite, bottom: Build-up of the shell started at the three footpoints, and continued until the last cassette closed the shell. All photos copyright ICD/ITKE University of Stuttgart.

94頁、上：想定される最小変形を示す構造モデル。95頁：構造形状検討マトリクス。本頁、上から：ハイルブロン市にある敷地でのシェル構造「大型三次元パズル」の組立て／シェル構造の各セグメントはクレーンで吊り上げ、2人の大工によって所定の位置に配置される／ボルトは各セグメントの底面にある点検口から締めつける／このシェル構造は大規模な型枠工事無しで組立てられた。右頁、上：カールス湖を隔てて眺める施工途中のシェル構造。右頁、下：シェル構造の施工は3箇所の立上りから始まり、最後のカセットがシェル構造を閉じるまで続いた。

BUGA Wood Pavilion: A Novel Structure and Architectural Space

The BUGA Wood Pavilion is located at a central crossroad within the wavy landscape of the BUGA summer island. Three dynamic arches form inviting openings in the main directions and guide visitors into the pavilion's interior. Hosting concerts and public events, the shell creates a smoothly-curved space that provides very good acoustics and generates a unique architectural atmosphere. This is especially true at night, when thousands of LED lights embedded in the shells inner openings light up and bathe the pavilion's interior in subtle, warm and welcoming light.

BUGAウッド・パヴィリオン：新たな構造と建築空間

BUGAウッド・パヴィリオンは連邦園芸博覧会のサマー・アイランド会場の、ゆるやかに起伏するランドスケープの中央の交差点に面している。3つのダイナミックなアーチが人々を歓迎するかのように通路に向かって開き、来訪者をパヴィリオンへと招いている。コンサートやパブリック・イベントが開催されるシェルは、優れた音響と独特な雰囲気をもたらす柔らかな曲面の空間をつくりだしている。夜になり、シェルの内側の開口部に組み込まれた数千のLEDライトが光を放ち、パヴィリオンの内部が繊細で暖かく包み込むような光に満たされると、その特徴はさらに際立ったものとなる。 （中田雅章訳）

pp. 98–99: South-east view of the wood pavilion on the BUGA Summer Island. Copyright ICD/ITKE University of Stuttgart. Opposite: Dynamic arches create openings within the self-supporting shell. Copyright Roland Halbe. This page: Aerial view of the wood pavilion. Copyright Nikolai Benner.

98〜99頁：BUGAサマー・アイランドにあるウッド・パヴィリオンの南東側の眺め。左頁：ダイナミックなアーチ構造が、自立シェル構造内に開口部をつくりだしている。本頁：ウッド・パヴィリオンの鳥瞰写真。

Credits and Data

Project title: BUGA Wood Pavilion
Location: Heilbronn, Germany
Completion: 2019
Project Partners:
    ICD – Institute for Computational Design and Construction, University of Stuttgart: Prof. Achim Menges, Martin Alvarez, Monika Göbel, Abel Groenewolt, Oliver David Krieg, Ondrej Kyjanek, Hans Jakob Wagner.
    ITKE – Institute of Building Structures and Structural Design, University of Stuttgart: Prof. Jan Knippers, Lotte Aldinger, Simon Bechert, Daniel Sonntag Müllerblaustein Bauwerke GmbH, Blaustein: Reinhold Müller, Daniel Müller, Bernd Schmid
    BEC GmbH, Reutlingen: Matthias Buck, Zied Bhiri
    Bundesgartenschau Heilbronn 2019 GmbH: Hanspeter Faas, Oliver Toellner
Project Building Permit Process:
    Landesstelle für Bautechnik: Dr. Stefan Brendler und Dipl.-Ing. Willy Weidner
    Proof Engineer: Prof. Dr.-Ing. Hugo Rieger
    MPA Stuttgart: Dr. Simon Aicher
Project Support: State of Baden-Wuerttemberg, University of Stuttgart, EFRE European Union, GETTYLAB, DFG German Research Foundation, Carlisle Construction Materials GmbH, Puren GmbH, Hera Gmbh co.KG, Beck Fastener Group, J. Schmalz GmbH, Niemes Dosiertechnik GmbH & Co. KG, Jowat Adhesives SE, Raithle Werkzeugtechnik, Leuze electronic GmbH & Co. KG, Metsä Wood Deutschland GmbH
Project Data:
    Dimensions: 32 x 25 x 7 m (LxWxH), Covered Area: 500 m², Shell Area: 600 m², Weight of load-bearing wood structure: 36.8 kg/m²
Construction System:
    Structural Shell: robotically fabricated hollow, polygonal wood case segments of spruce laminated veneer lumber with UV-protection coating
    Cladding: EPDM-water proofing, 3-Axis CNC-cut natural larch 3-ply wood plates

Institute for Computational Design and Construction (ICD)
ICD/ITKE Research Pavilion 2016–17
Stuttgart, Germany 2016–2017

コンピュテーショナル・デザインおよび建設研究所（ICD）
ICD/ITKEリサーチ・パヴィリオン2016〜17
ドイツ、シュトゥットガルト　2016〜2017

Lightweight, Long-Span Fibrous Construction

Fiber composite materials have tremendous potential in architectural applications. Due to performative material characteristics, they are readily used in highly-engineered applications, such as in the automotive and aerospace industries. The potentials within architecture, however, remain still largely unexplored. Within architectural scale production, where material self-weight is of high concern for larger span structures, lightweight fiber composites provide unparalleled performance. However, we currently lack adequate fiber composite fabrication processes to produce at this scale without compromising the design freedom and system adaptability required for the architecture and design industries. Traditional methods of fabrication require full-scale surface molds and often restrict the process to serialized production of identical parts. Previous research at the ICD and ITKE has explored fiber composite construction without the need for surface molds or costly formwork. These novel manufacturing processes have been utilized to create highly-differentiated multi-layered structures, functionally integrated building systems and large element assemblies. They have freed the relatively formable material from the limitations of traditional fiber composite fabrication processes. However, the scale of these early investigations has been limited by the working space of the industrial robotic arms that were utilized. The goal of the ICD/ITKE Research Pavilion 2016–17 is to envision a scalable fabrication process and to test alternative scenarios for architectural application by developing a manufacturing process for long-span continuous fiber structures.

繊維による軽量、長スパンの建築

繊維複合材は建築への応用という面で、非常に大きな可能性を秘めている。それらは素材の機能的な特性から、自動車や航空機などの高度な工業製品に広く用いられている。しかし建築での可能性については、いまだほとんど研究されていない。軽量の繊維複合材が建築のスケールで用いられる場合、資材の自重が問題になる長スパンの構造物で圧倒的な強みを発揮する。しかし現時点では、建築やデザインに求められる設計上の自由やシステムの応用面で妥協することなく、繊維複合材で大スケールの構造物をつくりだしていくことができる有効な製作方法が存在しない。一般的な製作方法では仕上げ面と同じ大きさの型が必要になり、その工程は同じ部品の大量生産の制約を受けることが多い。ICDとITKEはこれまでの研究で、仕上げ面の型、あるいはコストがかかる型枠を必要としない、繊維複合材による建築物を探求してきた。これらの新たな工程は、これまでのものとはまったく異なる積層による構築物、機能を組み合わせた建設システム、そして大きなエレメントの組み立てを実現するものである。それらは比較的自由に造形可能な素材を、一般的な繊維複合材の製作工程の制約から解放している。しかし初期の実験の規模は、使用された産業用ロボット・アームの稼働範囲の制約を受けていた。ICD/ITKEリサーチ・パヴィリオン2016〜17の目的は、連続する繊維による長スパンの構造物を構築する技術を開発することで、様々な規模に対応可能な製作工程をつくりだし、建築への新たな応用のシナリオを検証することである。

（中田雅章訳）

Process Biomimetic Investigation

The focus of the project is a parallel bottom-up design strategy for the biomimetic investigation of natural construction processes of long-span fiber composite structures and the development of novel robotic fabrication methods for fiber reinforced polymer structures. The aim was to develop a fiber winding technique over a longer span, which reduces the required formwork to a minimum whilst taking advantage of the structural performance of continuous filament. Therefore, functional principles and construction logics of natural lightweight structures were analysed and abstracted in cooperation with the Institute of Evolution and Ecology and the Department for Paleobiology of the University of Tübingen. Two species of leaf miner moths, the *Lyonetia clerkella* and the *Leucoptera erythrinella*, whose larvae spin silk "hammocks" stretching between connection points on a bent leaf, were identified as particularly promising for the transfer of morphological and procedural principles for long-span fibrous construction. Several concepts were abstracted from the biological role models and transferred into fabrication and structural concepts, including: the combination of a bending-active substructure and coreless wound fiber reinforcement to create an integrated composite winding frame, fiber orientation and hierarchy over a long-span structure and multi-stage volumetric fiber laying processes for the generation of complex three-dimensional geometries.

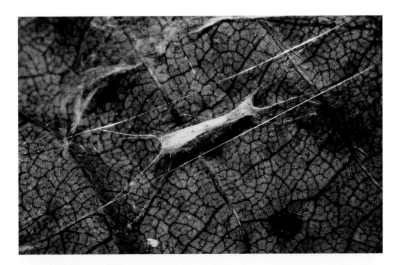

バイオミメティクスによる工程の探求

このプロジェクトの焦点は、自然の世界での繊維による長スパンの構築物の生成過程に関するバイオミメティクス（生体模倣技術）にもとづく研究と、繊維強化ポリマーによる構築物のロボットによる新たなファブリケーションを開発するための、同時並行のボトムアップのデザイン・ストラテジーである。その目的は、必要な型枠を限界まで減らす一方で、連続する繊維の構造的な有効性を活かし、より長いスパンを架け渡す繊維の巻きつけ技術を開発することであった。そのため、自然の世界での軽量な構築物の機能的な原理とその構築手順が、テュービンゲン大学の進化および生態学研究所と古生物学部の共同で分析され、まとめられた。その結果、形態と工程の原理を繊維による長スパンの建築に応用するうえでは、幼虫が木の葉の曲面に糸を張り、繭の「ハンモック」をつくる2種類のハモグリガ、モモハモグリガとエリスリナハモクリガが特に有望なものとされた。生物学的な手本からいくつかのコンセプトが導かれ、ファブリケーションと構造のコンセプトに転換された。そのコンセプトには、複合材を巻きつけるフレームとなる折り曲げ可能なサブストラクチュアと巻きつけられたコアをもたない繊維による強化の融合、長ス

パンの構築物全体での繊維の方向づけと層化、そして複雑な3次元の形状を生成するための多段階の立体的な繊維の積層プロセスが含まれている。　　　（中田雅章訳）

p. 103: View from within the long-span fiber composite structure. Opposite: Detail of the fiber composite structure. Photos by Burggraf / Reichert, copyright ICD/ITKE. This page, from the top: Lyonetia prunifoliell, "Apple Leaf Miner" cocoon; Leucoptera erythrinella, Leaf miner cocoon; Microscopic image of "Apple Leaf Miner" cocoon, illustrating volumetric structure; Microscopic image of "Apple Leaf Miner" cocoon, illustrating fiber hierarchy and directionality. All courtesy of ICD/ITKE.

103頁：長スパン繊維製複合構造物の内部からの眺め。左頁：繊維複合構造のディテール。本頁、上から：リンゴ・ハモクリガ（Lyonetia prunifoliell）の繭／エリスリハモクリガ（Leucoptera erythrinella）の繭／リンゴ・ハモクリガの繭の顕微鏡写真。容積構造を示す／リンゴ・ハモクリガの繭の顕微鏡写真。繊維の階層構造と方向性を示す。

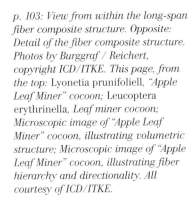

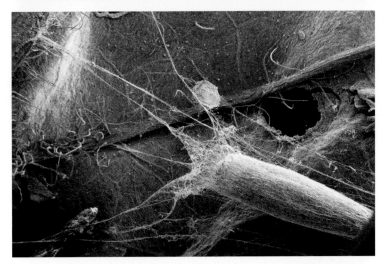

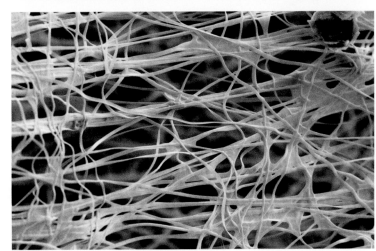

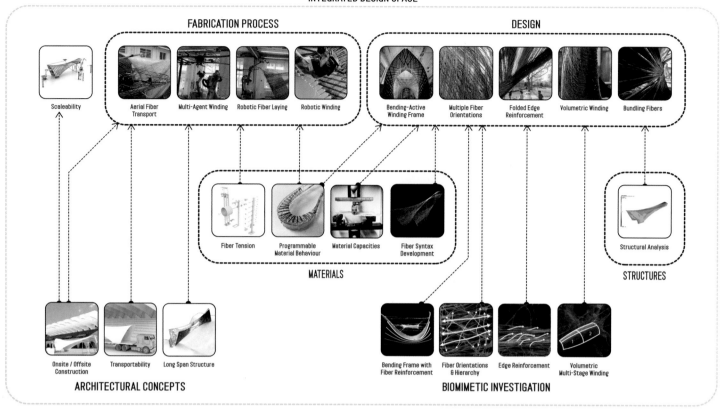

INTEGRATED DESIGN SPACE

FABRICATION PROCESS

Scaleability

Aerial Fiber Transport · Multi-Agent Winding · Robotic Fiber Laying · Robotic Winding

DESIGN

Bending-Active Winding Frame · Multiple Fiber Orientations · Folded Edge Reinforcement · Volumetric Winding · Bundling Fibers

MATERIALS

Fiber Tension · Programmable Material Behaviour · Material Capacities · Fiber Syntax Development

STRUCTURES

Structural Analysis

ARCHITECTURAL CONCEPTS

Onsite / Offsite Construction · Transportability · Long Span Structure

BIOMIMETIC INVESTIGATION

Bending Frame with Fiber Reinforcement · Fiber Orientations & Hierarchy · Edge Reinforcement · Volumetric Multi-Stage Winding

Diagram of integrated design space／一体型デザイン・スペース・ダイアグラム

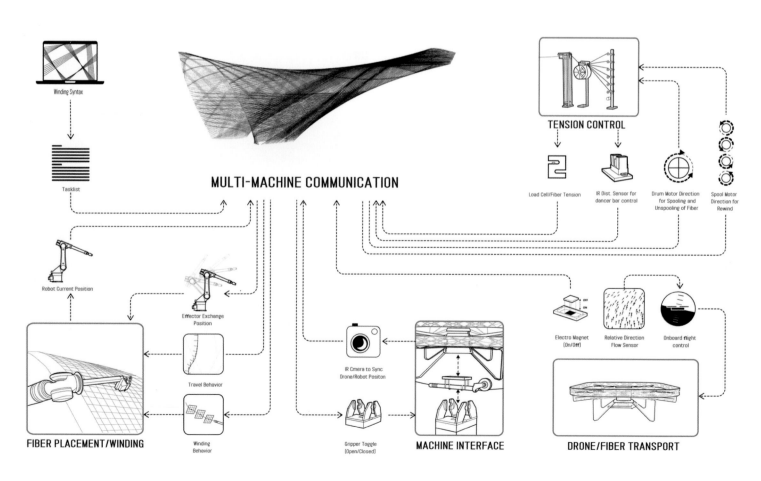

Winding Syntax

Tasklist

MULTI-MACHINE COMMUNICATION

TENSION CONTROL

Load Cell/Fiber Tension · IR Dist. Sensor for dancer bar control · Drum Motor Direction for Spooling and Unspooling of Fiber · Spool Motor Direction for Rewind

Robot Current Position

Effector Exchange Position

Travel Behavior

Winding Behavior

IR Cmera to Sync Drone/Robot Positon

Gripper Toggle (Open/Closed)

Electro Magnet (On/Off) · Relative Direction Flow Sensor · Onboard flight control

FIBER PLACEMENT/WINDING

MACHINE INTERFACE

DRONE/FIBER TRANSPORT

Diagram of multi-machine communication for fiber winding process／ファイバー巻きつけプロセスの機械間コミュニケーション図

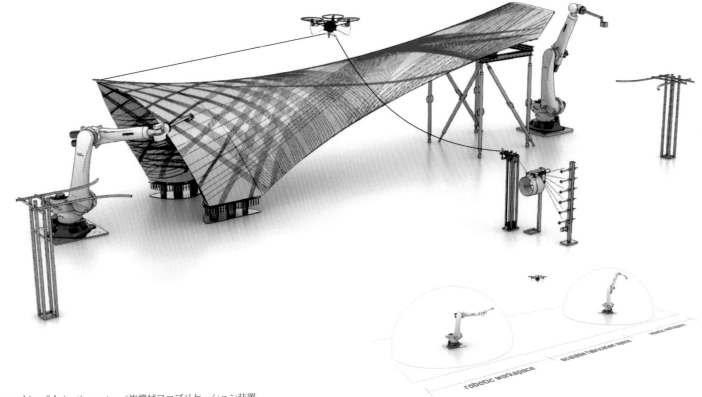

Multi-machine fabrication setup／複機械ファブリケーション装置

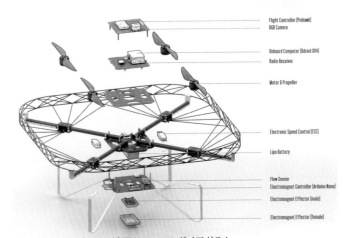

Flight Controller (Pixhawk)
RGB Camera

Onboard Computer (Odroid XU4)
Radio Receiver

Motor & Propeller

Electronic Speed Control (ESC)

Lipo Battery

Flow Sensor
Electromagnet Controller (Arduino Nano)
Electromagnet Effector (male)
Electromagnet Effector (female)

Diagram of custom drone／専用ドローン・ダイアグラム

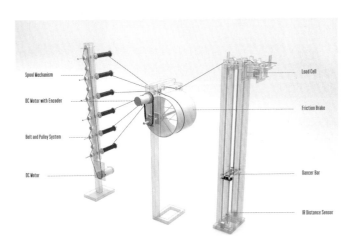

Spool Mechanism

DC Motor with Encoder

Belt and Pulley System

DC Motor

Load Cell

Friction Brake

Dancer Bar

IR Distance Sensor

Diagram of tension control mechanism／張力コントロール機構ダイアグラム

Multi-Machine Cyber-Physical Fabrication

Creating a long-span structure, beyond the working space of standard industrial fabrication equipment, required a collaborative setup where multiple robotic systems could interface and communicate to create a seamless fiber laying process. A fiber could be passed between multiple machines to ensure a continuous material structure. The concept of the fabrication process is based on the collaboration between strong and precise, yet stationary, machines with limited reach and mobile, long-range machines with limited precision. In the specific experimental setup, two stationary industrial robotic arms with the strength and precision necessary for fiber winding work are placed at the extremities of the structure, while an autonomous, long-range but less precise fiber transportation system is utilized to pass the fiber from one side to the other, in this case a custom-built UAV. Combining the untethered freedom and adaptability of the UAV with the robots, opened up the possibilities for laying fibers on, around, or through a structure, creating the potential for material arrangements and structural performance not feasible with the robot or UAV alone.

マルチ・マシンによるサイバー＝フィジカル・ファブリケーション

標準的な産業用製造装置の稼働範囲を超えて長スパンの架構をつくりだすためには、シームレスな繊維の積層工程を実現するため、複数のロボット・システムが協調して動作する連携の仕組みが必要であった。製作工程のコンセプトは、強力で正確ではあるものの稼働範囲と移動性が限られた据え置き型の機械と、正確さには限界があるものの移動範囲が広い装置の協調にもとづくものである。実験用に構成された装置のセットアップでは、繊維の巻きつけ作業に必要な強度と正確さを備えた2台の据え置き型の産業用ロボットが架構の端部に置かれ、繊維を一方から他方へと受け渡すために、正確さは劣るものの長い移動距離をもつ自律した運搬システムが使われている。プロジェクトの運搬システムには、専用のUAV（無人航空機）が導入された。ロボットにUAVの自由さと柔軟性を組み合わせることで、構築物の上部や周囲、そして内部に繊維を積層することが可能になり、それらが単体では実現できなかった素材の配置と構造の可能性がもたらされている。　　（中田雅章訳）

An adaptive control and communication system was developed to allow multiple industrial robots and a UAV to interact throughout the winding and fiber laying processes. An integrated sensor interface enabled the robots and UAV to adapt their behaviors, in real time, to the changing conditions during fabrication. The UAV could fly and land autonomously without the need of human pilots, the tension of the fiber was actively and adaptively controlled in response to both the UAV and robot behaviors. A localization system was utilized to create a digital and physical "handshake" between the robot and the UAV in order to pass the fiber back and forth throughout the winding process. The series of adaptive behaviors and integrated sensors lay the foundation for developing novel multi-machine, cyber-physical fabrication processes for large-scale fiber composite production.

Opposite, top: Multi-machine cyber-physical fabrication system. Opposite, bottom: Autonomous flight of custom drone carrying a fiber between robots. This page, top: Fabrication setup of fiber winding robotic arms and autonomous drone carrying a fiber. This page, bottom: Transport of long-span fiber composite structure to site. All photos copyright ICD/ITKE.

左頁、上：複数機によるサイバー・フィジカルファブリケーション・システム。左頁、下：ロボット間で繊維を運ぶ特注ドローンの自律飛行。本頁、上：繊維巻きつけ用のロボットアームと繊維を運ぶ自律ドローンの製作セットアップ。本頁、下：長スパン繊維製複合構造物の現場への輸送。

巻きつけと繊維の積層工程で複数の産業用ロボットとUAVの連携を可能にするため、応答性をもつ制御・通信システムが開発された。統合されたセンサーのインターフェースが、製造工程での状況の変化に、ロボットとUAVがリアルタイムに応答することを可能にしている。自律的に飛行・着陸するUAVは操作の必要がなく、繊維のテンションはUAVとロボットの動きによって能動的かつ応答的に制御されている。繊維を受け渡していくうえで欠かせないロボットとUAVのデジタルと物理的な「ハンドシェイク」のために、位置測定システムが用いられた。一連の応答的な動作と統合されたセンサーが、繊維複合材を大きなスケールで構築するための、複数の装置による新たなサイバー＝フィジカル・ファブリケーション・プロセスを開発する基盤となっている。

（中田雅章訳）

Integrative Demonstrator

The ICD/ITKE Research Pavilion 2016–17 was created by laying a combined total of 184 km of resin-impregnated glass and carbon fiber. The lightweight material system was employed to create and test a single long-spanning cantilever with an overall length of 12 m as an extreme structural scenario. The surface covers an area of about 40 m² and weighs roughly 1,000 kg. The realized structure was manufactured off-site and thus the size was constrained to fit within an allowable transport volume. However, variations of the setup were found suitable for on-site or in-situ fabrication, which could be utilized for much longer span and larger fiber composite structures.

The pavilion's overall geometry demonstrates the possibilities for fabricating structural morphologies through multi-stage volumetric fiber winding, reducing unnecessary formwork through an integrated bending-active composite frame, and increasing the possible scale and span of construction through integrating robotic and autonomous lightweight UAV fabrication processes. It explores how future construction scenarios may evolve to include distributed, collaborative and adaptive systems. This research showcases the potential of computational design and construction through the incorporation of structural capacities, material behavior, fabrication logics, biological principles and architectural design constraints into integrative computational design and construction. The prototypical pavilion is a proof-of-concept for a scalable fabrication process of long-span, fiber composite structural elements, suitable for architectural applications.

統合の実証

ICD/ITKEリサーチ・パヴィリオン2016〜17は、全長184kmの樹脂含浸ガラス繊維と炭素繊維を積層することでつくりだされている。極端な構造のシナリオとして、長さ12mの長スパンのキャンチレヴーを構築し、検証するために、軽量の素材によるシステムが用いられた。キャンチレヴーはおよそ40m²の空間をカバーし、重量は1,000kgほどである。実際の架構は別の場所でつくられたため、大きさは運搬可能なヴォリュームに制限された。しかしその製作工程は、装置の組み合わせを変えることで現場での作業に応用でき、繊維複合材によるより長く、より大きな架構を構築できることが明らかになっている。

パヴィリオンの全体的な形状は、多段階の立体的な繊維の巻きつけで構造的な形状をつくりだし、折り曲げ可能な複合材のフレームの組み合わせによって不要な型枠を減らし、ロボットと自律的な軽量のUAVを連携した製作工程によって実現可能な架構の規模とスパンを拡張できることを示している。それは建設の未来が、いかにして包括的、分散的、協働的、そして応答的なシステムに進化しうるかの探求である。この研究は、統合的なコンピュータを用いたデザインと建設に、構造の強度、材料の振る舞い、製作手順、生物学的な原理、そして建築デザインの制約を織り込むことによって、コンピュータによるデザインと建設の連携がもたらす新たな可能性を示している。プロトタイプとしてのパヴィリオンは、建築への応用に適した繊維複合材による長スパンの構造的なエレメントをつくりだす、様々な規模に対応可能な製造工程の概念実証である。

(中田雅章訳)

Opposite: The structure was fabricated off-site, though variations of its set-up could be utilized for on-site fabrication. Photo by Burggraf / Reichert, copyright ICD/ITKE. This page: The structure being interacted with. Copyright ICD/ITKE/Laurian Ghinitoiu.

左頁：この構造物は現場外で製作されたが、このセットアップのヴァリエーションは、現場での製作にも使用可能である。本頁：人々が構造物を利用する様子をとらえた写真。

Credits and Data

Project title: ICD/ITKE Research Pavilion 2016–17
Location: Stuttgart, Germany
Start: 2016
Completion: 2017
Project team: Prof. Achim Menges (ICD Institute for Computational Design and Construction); Prof. Jan Knippers (ITKE Institute of Building Structures and Structural Design); Benjamin Felbrich, Nikolas Früh, Marshall Prado, Daniel Reist, Sam Saffarian, James Solly, Lauren Vasey (Scientific Development); Miguel Aflalo, Bahar Al Bahar, Lotte Aldinger, Chris Arias, Léonard Balas, Jingcheng Chen, Federico Forestiero, Dominga Garufi, Pedro Giachini, Kyriaki Goti, Sachin Gupta, Olga Kalina, Shir Katz, Bruno Knychalla, Shamil Lallani, Patricio Lara, Ayoub Lharchi, Dongyuan Liu, Yencheng Lu, Georgia Margariti, Alexandre Mballa, Behrooz Tahanzadeh, Hans Jakob Wagner, Benedikt Wannemacher, Nikolaos Xenos, Andre Zolnerkevic, Paula Baptista, Kevin Croneigh, Tatsunori Shibuya, Nicoló Temperi, Manon Uhlen, Li Wenhan. With the support of Artyom Maxim and Michael Preisack. (System Development, Fabrication and Construction)
Collaborators: Prof. Dr.-Ing. P. Middendorf, Markus Blandl, Florian Gnädinger (Institute of Aircraft Design (IFB)); Prof. Dr.-Ing. habil. Volker Schwieger, Otto Lerke (Institute of Engineering Geodesy (IIGS)); Prof. Oliver Betz (Department of Evolutionary Biology of Invertebrates, University of Tuebingen); Prof. James Nebelsick (Department of Palaeontology of Invertebrates, University of Tuebingen)
Supported by: Volkswagen Stiftung; GETTYLAB Kuka Roboter GmbH Peri GmbH; SGL Technologies GmbH; Hexion Stuttgart GmbH; Ed. Züblin AG Lange Ritter GmbH; Stahlbau Wendeler GmbH; Leica Geosystems GmbH; KOFI GmbH
Project area: 26.5 m²

Essay:
Towards a Computational Material Culture in Architecture
Achim Menges, Director of Institute for Computational Design and Construction at University of Stuttgart

エッセイ：
建築におけるコンピュテーショナルな物質文化をめざして
アヒム・メンゲス（シュトゥットガルト大学コンピュテーショナル・デザイン・建設研究所）
土居純訳

Architecture forms the material space in which most of our everyday life takes place. It unfolds its cultural and social significance, as well as its ecological and economic relevance, through the creation of the built environment. How this built environment is conceived and shaped is directly related to the intellectual and material becoming of architecture, that is the processes of designing and construction. Digital technologies question the established relation in which these processes of generating and materializing form and space have hitherto been conceived. In our work, we aim to explore digital technologies' impact on architecture as a material practice, and how computation gives rise to a novel, computational material culture.

Digital technologies and their relation to design and construction have been researched for more than half a century. What is remarkable about this is not only the long period of time, but also the fact that concepts such as parametric modelling and rule-based design were developed and investigated at a very early stage. Initially, however, this required extensive computer facilities, which were only available at selected academic institutions and a few companies. Only with the invention of the microprocessor and the personal computer were the hardware requirements for a broader application in practice available from the beginning of the 1980s onwards. In the context of the advance and spread of Computer-Aided Design (CAD) applications, however, the digitization of the technical draftsman's work was the main focus of related developments. The change from analogue to digital techniques therefore had no major impact on the prevailing concept of design.

This also did not change when the creation of complex geometry became more accessible in the early 1990s. Technologies such as NURBS and mesh modelling were transferred from highly-specialized CAD applications, which until then had mostly been the preserve of expert domains, as for example in the automotive industry, to more general computer graphics applications. This was taken up by architects in order to supplement two-dimensional drawing with three-dimensional modelling and to considerably expand the possible canon of architectural shapes from basic geometric elements to free-form surfaces. The resulting, sometimes shockingly new forms of architecture, which, depending on one's point of view, were either enthusiastically received or deeply despised, continue to shape the general idea of so-called "digital architecture" to this day, with all the associated reservations. However, they should not hide the fact that the seemingly radical designs originated from a methodically conventional process of designing, and that behind the digitally generated, double-curved facade there usually is a conventional, pre-digital construction system.

Thinking Digitally: From Computerization to Computation

An essential aspect of our research is the investigation of digital technologies, not as a continuation of existing methods and processes, but as a point of departure and a vehicle for rethinking design and construction. This is not about the unconventional as an end in itself, but rather about exploring alternative approaches that do justice to the possibilities of the means of our time, that take up epochal changes as an architectural opportunity and that shape their disruptive potential critically but positively. In order to do so, the very notion of "digitization" must already be questioned, as it suggests that the use of digital technologies is essentially aimed at merely digitizing or computerizing previously analogue methods, processes and systems. Computerization here essentially refers to the automation, mechanization and conversion of entities or processes that are already given and precisely defined in non-digital form[1]. Actually, this applies to a large extent to the use of digital technologies in architecture: With the introduction of conventional CAD applications, the ink pen and drawing board was digitized by means of mouse and screen. Then analogue modelling and sculpting in three-dimensional space was computerized through NURBS and mesh modelling. BIM now digitizes design using standard construction elements, products and details and transfers them into a database-based modeling. From a conceptual point of view, computerization is thus merely an evolutionary step in existing approaches.

Computation, on the other hand, represents a genuinely digital approach. In contrast to computerization, the focus here is on the development of undetermined, vague or insufficiently defined spaces of possibilities and solutions, for which the computer can be employed generatively and exploratively, using algorithmic and logical methods. In architecture, computation, or its application in computational design and computational construction, allows rethinking conventional approaches, established processes and traditional typologies. In this way, computation forms the basis for our research of genuinely digital design and construction methods whose specific characteristics and logics cannot be derived linearly from pre-digital concepts. This is especially true of the above-mentioned interrelation between the design and materialization of form, structure and space in architecture, which is a focus of our research. The connecting element between design and

我々は日常の大半を、建築によってつくられる物的空間で過ごしている。建築の文化的・社会的価値ならびに環境や経済への影響は、ビルト・エンヴァイロメントの創出とともに表面化する。このビルト・エンヴァイロメントがどのように構想され形成されるかは、ひとえに知性と物質の産物たる建築に、すなわち設計と施工のプロセスにかかっている。ところがデジタル技術が出現すると、こうした既成の構図のままに形態と空間を生成し物質化するという従来のプロセスにたいし、疑念が生じる。はたしてデジタル技術は建築という物的営為をどれほど変えるだろうか、またコンピュテーションはどんな新種の物質文化をもたらすのだろうか。これが私たちのテーマである。

デジタル技術とその設計・施工への応用については、すでに半世紀あまり前から研究が進んでいる。これほどの歴史があるというのも意外だが、それにもまして、そのごく初期段階でパラメトリック・モデリングやルールベース・デザインといった概念が考えられ検討されたという事実に驚かされる。とはいえ、こうした研究にはまだ大掛かりなコンピュータ設備を必要とする時代であったから、当時それができるのはおのずとごく一部の学術機関と企業に限られた。このハードウェア面での実用化にあたっては、マイクロプロセッサとパーソナル・コンピュータの開発を待たねばならず、これが実現したのはようやく1980年代に入ってからのことだ。その後、コンピュータ支援設計（CAD）ソフトが進化し普及するが、ただしその開発目的は、せいぜい製図工の行なう作業のデジタル化でしかなかった。アナログ技術からデジタル技術へ移行したとはいえ、結局、一般的な設計概念を覆すほどのインパクトはなかった。

1990年代初頭には誰でも手軽に複雑なジオメトリーを描けるようになるが、やはり設計概念を塗り替えるには至らなかった。NURBS（非一様有理Bスプライン）やメッシュ・モデルといった技術は、それまでは自動車産業などの特殊な分野に特化したCADソフトにしか搭載されなかったが、ここに来てようやく一般的なCGソフトにも応用された。これに目をつけた建築家は、二次元の図面を三次元モデルに膨らませ、またそれまで基礎幾何学図形を組み合わせるしかなかった建築に自由曲面を用いることで、従来の規範を緩めようとした。その結果が往々にしてひどく斬新な建築形態となったため、世間では好悪が激しく分かれたものの、さしあたりこれらがいわゆる「デジタル・アーキテクチュア」の典型となり、様々な留保はつくものの今に至る。ただし正直に打ち明けると、いくら見るからにラディカルなデザインであっても、方法論的には従来の設計プロセスと何ら変わるところがなく、またCGで描かれた複曲面ファサードにしても、えてしてデジタル時代以前と同じ工法でつくられている。

デジタルに考える：コンピュータライゼーションからコンピュテーションへ
もとより私たちは、デジタル技術を既存の手法やプロセスの延長線上には位置づけておらず、むしろ設計と施工のあり方を見直す契機にして手段というふうにと

らえている。といって、決して慣例に逆らうつもりはなく、むしろ我々が今日せっかく手にした手段を存分に使いこなしたいというのが本意である。うまくいけば、この時代の変化が建築にとって追い風となるかもしれないし、良い意味で既存の価値観を打ち砕くことにもなるかもしれない。そのためには、さしあたり「デジタル化」という概念をこそ疑ってかかることだ。なぜなら、これではまるで、従来のアナログ的な手法・プロセス・仕組みを単にデジタル化しコンピュータ化することが、デジタル技術の使いみちのように受けとられてしまうからだ。ここでいうコンピュータライゼーションとは、正確に定義された所与の非デジタル形式の事物なりプロセスなりを、自動化、機械化、変換することを指す[1]。現に、建築に用いられるデジタル技術についても同じことがいえる。たとえば、一般的なCADソフトは、ペンと製図板をマウスとスクリーンにデジタル化した。つぎに、NURBSとメッシュ・モデルが、模型や粘土でこしらえた三次元の空間をコンピュータ化した。現在はBIMが、規格の部材・製品・ディテールをとり合せた設計図をデジタル化し、データベースと連動したモデルを制作する。こうして見ると、コンピュータライゼーションとは、あくまで現行アプローチの発展型にすぎない。

他方のコンピュテーションは、正真正銘デジタルなアプローチである。コンピュータライゼーションとは反対に、こちらの目的は、不確定、曖昧、定義不十分な解空間や可能空間を発現させることにある。もしそうした空間がみつかれば、コンピュータ上のアルゴリズムやロジックを介して生成・精査が可能になる。建築の場合、コンピュテーションの導入もしくはその応用であるコンピュテーショナル・デザインやコンピュテーショナル・コンストラクションの導入が、従来のアプローチや既成のプロセスや伝統的なタイポロジーを見直すきっかけになる。逆にいうと、私たちのリサーチはコンピュテーション抜きには成り立たない。なぜなら、私たちの目指す真にデジタルな設計手法・工法は、その特性上、また理屈からしてもデジタル時代以前の発想から一直線には引きだせないからだ。まして、建築の形態・構造・空間の設計と物質化とを連動させるつもりなら、なおのことだ。設計と施工を橋渡しするのが建築図面である。近代建築図面の発祥は13世紀から15世紀の間とされる。ルネサンスに透視図法と平行射影が考案されると状況は一転し、中世における職人の親方に代わって近代建築家が登場し、設計業務は建設工事とは切り離される。ここに来て画法幾何学という表記形式が決定的な役割を演ずる。図面には建築家の意図が込められ、なおかつ施工者への指示も記載される。こうして図面が主役となった以上、その表記法次第で建築という一芸術形式のありようも変わってくる。ところが、まさにこの物質的性質を失った幾何学図面という表記法こそに、建築思考は長年縛られ、それこそ幾何学と物質化との間に上下関係を定着させるのである。かくて、設計者の間では、幾何学形態を優先させ物質をそれに従わせるのが常識となる。むろん、大半の建築家は、自分は素材に合わせて設計をする、と反論するだろう。だが、これこれの素材であれば類型的に建物のこの部分に、この構造に、この空間に用いるものだといった先入観が往々にしてあるからには、やはり先述の上下関係に縛られているのだ。

construction is the architectural plan. The modern building plan was created between the thirteenth and fifteenth centuries. With the development of perspective and parallel projection in the Renaissance, the conditions were created on the basis of which the transformation from medieval master builder to modern architect took place, whose design activity is no longer directly integrated into the building process. The notational form of the descriptive geometry plays a decisive role in this. It generates the architectural intent and at the same time provides the instructions for its implementation. Due to its central role, architecture is considered one of the art forms that is dependent on a system of notation. However, it is precisely in this dematerialized system of notation of the geometric drawing or plan that an essential convention of architectural thinking is laid down, namely the primacy of geometry and its hierarchical relationship to materialization. Accordingly, common design thinking prioritizes the geometric form and understands the material as its passive recipient. Of course, most architects claim to design in a way that is appropriate for the material. However, the specific materiality is mostly assigned to preconceived, constructive, structural and spatial typologies that remain locked in the aforementioned hierarchy.

In contrast, our research explores a highly integrative approach to generation of form, structure and space, and its materialization. This requires an understanding of the processes of materializing architecture – that is: fabrication and construction – not as a merely facilitative step from plan to building, but as generative agency in design. The change from process-specific CNC machines, which in most cases represent a computerized or automated variant of conventional manufacturing processes, to generic manufacturing units such as industrial robots, offers the possibility of designing the manufacturing process itself. In our project BUGA Wood Pavilion, we explored how this opens up the possibility for a design-integrated feedback between the materialization process and the form to be materialized.

Designing Form in Feedback with Designing Fabrication: BUGA Wood Pavilion

The BUGA Wood pavilion serves as an event space at the central island of the Bundesgartenschau 2019 in Heilbronn. Located at the crossroad of two major axes in the BUGA grounds, it provides an architectural attraction that celebrates a new approach to digital timber construction. The pavilion embraces the genuinely digital design principle of using "less material" by having "more form", both on the level of the overall shell and its individual segments. In order to minimize material consumption

and weight, each wood segment is built up from two thin plates that plank a ring of edge-beams on top and bottom, forming large-scale hollow wooden cases with polygonal forms. The bottom plate includes a large opening, which constitutes a distinctive architectural feature and provides excellent acoustics. The hollow building segments significantly reduce weight and material, but they increase the number of building parts eightfold and lead to more complex manufacturing. Thus, striving for higher resource efficiency needs to go hand-in-hand with automated robotic manufacturing of the shell segments. For this, a novel, transportable, 14-axes robotic timber-manufacturing platform was designed and developed as part of the project.

In this way, the BUGA Wood pavilion is emblematic for a new paradigm of Co-Design, where novel possibilities in design, engineering and fabrication are explored through continuous computational feedback within an interdisciplinary team. In this project, the Co-Design algorithms developed by the project team generate the shape of each element of the pavilion according to architectural design intent and structural requirements, while all robotic fabrication aspects are directly embedded and negotiated. The design of the pavilion happens concurrently and in feedback with the design of the robotic manufacturing setup, which is a bespoke development for the project. The highly integrative process enables the design and engineering of 376 unique plate segments with 17,000 different finger joints in response to multifaceted design criteria, from the scale of the overall structure down to sub-millimetre details. Without any loss of precision, this multi-scale approach allows addressing architectural and structural considerations concurrently. Despite the pioneering character of the project, and despite an incredible short development time of only 13 months from commission to the opening, the integrative computational process allows for the careful design of each building element in minute detail. The pavilion's stunning wooden roof spans 30 meters over one of BUGA's main event and concert venues, using a minimum amount of material while also generating a unique architectural space.[2]

Genuinely Computational Design and Construction: BUGA Fiber Pavilion

Embedded in the wave-like landscape of the Bundesgartenschau grounds, there is a second project that offers visitors a profoundly different architectural experience, and a glimpse of genuinely digital design and construction methods. In contrast to the BUGA Wood Pavilion, which explores novel facets of building with one of the oldest construction materials we have,

これにたいして私たちは、形態・構造・空間の生成、ならびに空間の物質化までをも網羅するような、すぐれて統合的なアプローチを探っている。そのためには、建築の物質化——すなわち製作と施工——プロセスがどのようなものであるかを認識し、つまりプロセスを単に図面から建物へと一足飛びに移行させる手段ととらえるのではなく、むしろそれ自体がデザインを生成する因子であるというふうにとらえる必要がある。たとえばCNC加工は、個別の工程に用いられるものだから、所詮は従来の製作工程の単なるコンピュータ化か自動化でしかないが、代わりに産業用ロボットなどの汎用製造装置を用いれば、製作工程そのものを設計できるようになるだろう。そこで「BUGAウッド・パヴィリオン」では、建物の物質化と形態の物質化との間のフィードバックループを設計プロセスに組み込み、両者を並行して進めることにした。

工程設計を形態設計にフィードバックさせる：BUGAウッド・パヴィリオン

「BUGAウッド・パヴィリオン」は、2019年にハイルブロン市で開かれたブンデスガルテンシャウ（連邦園芸博覧会）（BUGA）会場の中洲につくられたイヴェント・スペースである。BUGA会場を貫く2本の主軸が交差する位置にあるこのパヴィリオンは、木造デジタル・コンストラクションの新機軸を全面に打ちだした建築アトラクションでもある。ここではデジタル・デザインの大原則に則り、全体を覆うシェルであれ個別のセグメント（弧）であれ、「形態を増やす」ことで「材料を減らし」ている。材料の使用量と重量を極力減らすべく、エッジビーム（縁梁）のセグメントには、穴の空いた厚板の上下を薄板で覆って大ぶりの多角形の木箱に仕立てている。木箱の底板には大きな穴が空いており、これが建築の個性になると同時に優れた音響効果を発揮する。この中空セグメントのおかげで全体の重量と材料使用量が大幅に軽減されるが、あいにく部材の種類は8倍に増え、そのぶん製作に手間がかかる。となると、資源効率を高めるために、シェルのセグメントをロボットで自動製作する必要がある。そこで、14軸ロボットの木材加工用可搬プラットフォームを、これまたプロジェクトの一環として新規に設計・開発した。

「BUGAウッド・パヴィリオン」はしたがって、これからの「コ・デザイン」のあり方を象徴する事例といえる。つまりここでは、多分野共同チーム内で継続的にコンピュテーショナル・フィードバックを行ないながら、意匠・技術・製作の3分野において未知の可能性を探っている。具体的には、まずプロジェクト・チームがコ・デザイン用のアルゴリズムを開発し、つぎにそのアルゴリズムが建築の設計意図と構造条件に応じてパヴィリオンの各要素の形状を生成するのだが、この時点でロボットによる製作を前提として各種調整も済ませる。パヴィリオンの設計とロボット工程の設定・設計とは互いにフィードバックを繰り返しながら同時進行するため、ロボット工程はおのずから本プロジェクト用にカスタマイズされる。このようにプロセスを完全に統合すると、全体の構造からミリ未満のディテールに至るまでの各尺度に一度に応えるかたちで、計376枚のセグメントとこれに付随する全17,000種類のフィンガージョイントを誤差ミリ未満の精度で設計・工

This page, from the top: BUGA Fiber Pavilion 2019, BUGA Wood Pavilion 2019. Photos courtesy of ICD.

本頁、上から：BUGAファイバー・パヴィリオン。BUGAウッド・パヴィリオン。

115

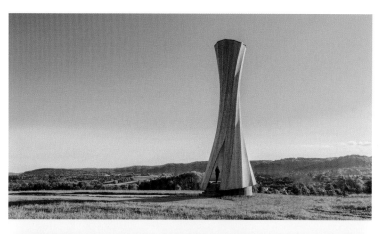

the BUGA Fiber Pavilion explores a similar integrative approach to design and fabrication, but employs radically different materials. The pavilion's load-bearing structure is robotically produced from advanced fiber composites only, that is more than 150,000 meters of spatially arranged glass and carbon fibers. They all need to be individually designed and placed, which is very hard to achieve with a typical linear workflow and established production technologies. Thus, it requires a novel Co-Design approach, where architectural design, structural engineering and robotic fabrication are developed in continuous computational feedback. In this way, the fiber arrangement, density and orientation of each building component can be individually calibrated, structurally tuned and architecturally articulated, while remaining directly producible.

The building components are produced by robotic, coreless filament winding, a novel additive manufacturing approach pioneered and developed at the University of Stuttgart. Fibrous filaments are freely placed between two rotating winding scaffolds by a robot. During this process, the predefined shape of the building component emerges only from the interaction of the filaments, eliminating the need for any mold or core. This allows for bespoke form and individual fiber layup for each component without any economic disadvantage. In addition, there is no production waste or material off-cuts. During manufacturing, a lattice of translucent glass fibers is generated, onto which the black carbon fibers are placed where they are structurally needed. This results in highly load-adapted components with a distinctive architectural appearance. The pavilion achieves a free span of more than 23 meters. With 7.6 kilograms per square meter, it is exceptionally lightweight, approximately five times lighter than a more conventional steel structure, and it also provides a distinctive yet authentic architectural expression and an extraordinary spatial experience.[3]

Material Programming: Urbach Tower

Computation makes accessible aspects of the material world that were previously far beyond the designer's intuition and beyond the grasp of conventional forms of notation. The computer thus represents a direct interface between the virtual and physical world, allowing material behavior to be activated in the design process. Moreover, our understanding of computation is not limited to purely digital processes. Rather, it involves material computation, that is the possibility that material itself can create specific forms or even be programmed, as shown in our Urbach Tower project.

The Urbach Tower is one of 16 stations designed by some of the

作できる。このマルチスケール方式ならば、精度を少しも落とさずに建築設計と構造計算を同時に処理できるということだ。これほど先駆的なプロジェクトであろうと、おまけに受注から開館まで実質わずか13ヶ月という納期しか与えられなかろうと、いっさいをコンピューテーショナル・プロセスに統合すれば、各建物要素の設計を周到に詰めてゆける。BUGAイヴェント会場兼コンサート会場をスパン30mですっぽりと覆うこの大胆な木造屋根は、最小限の材料しか消費せず、それでいて独特な建築空間を出現させる[2]。

純然たるコンピューテーショナルな設計と施工：BUGAファイバー・パヴィリオン

BUGA会場の波打つ地形に埋め込まれた二作目は、来場者に前作とはまるで異なった建築体験を与え、と同時にその設計・施工におけるデジタル技術の真骨頂を垣間見せる。さきのBUGAウッド・パヴィリオンが、人類最古の建材から多彩な面を引きだしたとすれば、このファイバー・パヴィリオンでは、似たような統合的アプローチを設計・製作段階でとるものの、使用する素材はがらりと変わる。躯体には、高強度繊維複合材のみ（ガラス繊維と炭素繊維を総長15万m以上）を用い、これをロボットで立体的に組み立てている。ただし、この複合材を一本一本設計し配置するには、通常の直線的なワークフローや既存の生産技術では至難であろう。となると、建築設計と構造設計とロボット工程とを継続的なコンピューテーショナル・フィードバックで連携させた新式のコ・デザインにおのずと行き着く。これなら各部材の繊維の配列や密度や方向を、構造や建築表現に応じて個別に調整できるうえに自作も可能である。

ここでは建物の部材を、ロボット工程のフィラメント・ワインディングによって中空円筒形に仕上げている。シュトゥットガルト大学の開発したこの新手の積層成形法では、ロボットが2台の回転式ヘッドの間にフィラメント（繊維束）を自在に架け渡して撚ってゆく。この工程ではフィラメントどうしが絡み合って所定の形状を生じさせるので、金型や芯棒が不要となる。こうして部材ごとに逐一形態をカスタマイズし、繊維を積層させるのだが、そのわりには不経済な点が一つもない。しかもゴミも端材もない。この製作工程では、ガラス繊維を編んで半透明メッシュに仕立てたところへ、補強が必要な部分にのみ黒い炭素繊維を纏わす。建築らしからぬ見かけの部材になるが、これなら荷重をうまく逃せる。パヴィリオンのフリー・スパンは23mを超える。重量は平米あたりわずか7.6kg、つまり従来の鉄骨造のおよそ五分の一の軽さで済むうえに、建築表現としては個性的なのに嘘がなく、来場者にはまたとない空間体験を提供する[3]。

素材のプログラミング：ウルバッハ・タワー

コンピューテーションのおかげで、設計者の直観だけではいわずもがな、従来の表記形式でさえとらえきれなかった物質界に少しは手が届くようになる。コンピュータはこのように仮想世界と物理世界とを直結するインターフェースであるからして、設計者がコンピュータ越しに材料の挙動を増幅させることも可能である。た

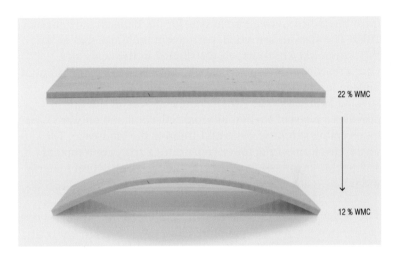

22 % WMC

12 % WMC

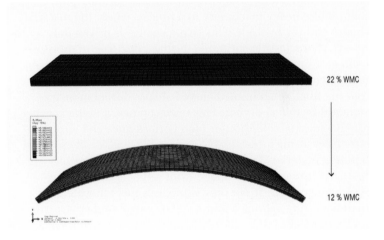

22 % WMC

12 % WMC

Opposite: Urbach Tower. This page, from top: Material Programming: Self-shaping wood and computational model. Photos courtesy of ICD.

左頁：ウルバッハ・タワー。本頁：素材のプログラミング。上から：自己形成プロセス。コンピューテーショナル・モデル。

most renowned German architects for the Remstal Gartenschau 2019. The stations are small, permanent buildings that evoke the traditional white chapels distributed in the fields and vineyards along the scenic Rems Valley. Located on a prominent hillside in the center of the valley, the 14m tall tower is a striking landmark that visually connects several stations. It provides a place of shelter, internal reflection and outward view by revealing stunning vistas and framing the landscape. The distinctive form of the tower constitutes a truly contemporary architectural expression of the traditional construction material wood.

The design of the tower emerges from a new self-shaping process of the curved wood components. This pioneering development constitutes a paradigm shift in timber manufacturing from elaborate and energy-intensive mechanical forming processes that require heavy machinery to a process where the material shapes entirely by itself. This shape change is driven only by the wood's characteristic shrinking during a decrease of moisture content. Components for the 14m tall tower are designed and manufactured in a flat state and transform autonomously into the final, programmed curved shapes during industry-standard technical drying. This opens up new and unexpected architectural possibilities for high performance and elegant structures, using a sustainable, renewable, and locally sourced building material. The Urbach Tower constitutes the very first structure worldwide made from self-shaped, building-scale components. It not only showcases this innovative manufacturing approach and resultant novel timber structure; it also intensifies the visitors' spatial involvement and landscape experience by providing a striking landmark building for the City of Urbach's contribution to the Remstal Gartenschau 2019.[4]

Computational Material Culture
Through our larger body of research, we have begun to explore the profound integration of design and construction enabled by digital technologies and to investigate how genuinely digital building systems, construction methods, structures and thus architecture can unfold from this. The selected projects presented above begin to suggest how material performance and architectural performativity can be synthesized in ways that go far beyond the mere digitization of established design methods, the simple automation of essentially pre-digital construction processes, and the related fixed and conventional structural and spatial typologies. This computational convergence of the processes of form generation and materialization enables new modes of architectural speculation and experimentation, which will contribute to the definition of a truly contemporary,

computational material culture, rather than an architectural style.[5] A humble indication of this may be given by the project examples presented above, which all stem from one coherent body of design research, but display a considerable variety in formal, spatial and structural articulation.

Notes:
1. Kostas Terzidis, *Algoritmic Architecture*, Elsevier Architectural Press, Oxford, 2006, S.XI.
2. For more details and full project credits view: www.icd.uni-stuttgart.de/projects/buga-wood-pavilion-2019/
3. For more details and full project credits view: www.icd.uni-stuttgart.de/projects/buga-fiber-pavilion/
4. For more details and full project credits view: www.icd.uni-stuttgart.de/projects/remstal-gartenschau-2019-urbach-turm/
5. Achim Menges, "Computational Material Culture", *Architectural Design*, Vol. 86 No. 2, Wiley, London, 2016, pp. 76-83.

だし、デジタル処理ばかりがコンピュテーションではない。たとえば、素材をコンピュテーションにかけると、素材自体が固有の形態を生み、もしくは素材自体がプログラミングされる。その具体例が「ウルバッハ・タワー」である。

「ウルバッハ・タワー」は、レムシュタール・ガルテンシャウ（園芸博覧会）2019の全16基地のうちの一つであり、ほかの基地についてはドイツ国内の有名建築家が設計を担当している。こうした小ぶりな常設基地の佇まいが、風光明媚なレムス渓谷沿いの野原やブドウ畑にかつて点在したであろう白い礼拝堂を彷彿させる。レムス渓谷のほぼ中間地点にあたる丘陵地の斜面に建てられたこの高さ14mのタワーは、堂々たるランドマークであり、それだけに周辺の基地を視覚的に統率する存在でもある。ここは隠れ場にして内省の場であり、あるいは外に目をやれば切りとられた風景があり、一歩外へ出れば絶景が開ける。タワーの特異な形態はさしずめ、伝統的な建材たる木材に当世風の建築表現を施したものである。

このタワーのデザインは、曲板材の自己成形プロセスから生まれる。まさに製材におけるパラダイム・シフトともいうべき展開である。というのも、従来の機械式の成形加工には手間とエネルギーがかかるうえに重機も必要だったが、いまや素材がひとりでに形を変えるからだ。しかも、単に水分が抜けると収縮するという木の性質が、この変形をうながしてくれる。高さ14mのタワーに用いられる部材は、設計・製作の時点では平らな板だが、標準的な乾燥装置にかけるとプログラムどおりにおのずから湾曲する。わずかこれだけのことで、建築には持続可能で再生可能な地産材を用いた高性能かつエレガントな構造がそなわる。「ウルバッハ・タワー」は、世界ではじめて自己成形素材を建材に用いた構造物である。このタワーの売りは、製作工程における革新的なアプローチと、その産物たる世にも珍しい木構造にとどまらない。レムシュタール・ガルテンシャウ2019の参加都市ウルバッハ市にひときわ高くそびえるランドマークは、来場者をその空間と風景に引き込む力をもつ[4]。

コンピュテーショナルな物質文化

私たちはこれまでの膨大な研究蓄積を通じて、デジタル技術による設計と施工の完全なる統合を目指し、そのうえで真にデジタルな構法・工法・構造を、ひいてはデジタルな建築を実現する方法を探ってきた。本稿に紹介したプロジェクトにもいくらかその兆しがうかがえるように、材料の性能がそのまま建築の機能遂行性※に直結するようになれば、既存の設計手法の単なるデジタル化でもなければ、デジタル時代以前の工程の自動化でもなく、はたまた既定の構造・空間タイポロジーでもない、まったく次元の異なるものが生まれる。形態の生成と物質化の両プロセスをこのようにコンピュテーションで集約すると、従来にないかたちで建築を考察し実験できるようになり、そしていずれは、建築様式を単にまた一つ増やすのではなく、コンピュテーショナルな物質文化のもつ真に今日的な意義を解明できるだろう[5]。上述した事例には、そのささやかな徴候がみられるかもしれな

い。いずれも、同一のデザイン・リサーチから引きだされた事例ではあるが、形態・空間・構造の表現という点ではじつに多種多彩である。

訳註：
※ "performativity" とは本来は社会言語学で用語であり、「行為遂行性」と訳されるが、この場合は建築が主体であるため、「機能」が「行為」に相当すると解釈した。

原註：
1. 邦訳：コスタス・テルシディス『アルゴリズミック・アーキテクチュア』田中浩也・荒岡紀子・重村珠穂・松川昌平訳、彰国社、2010。
2.〜5. 英文参照。

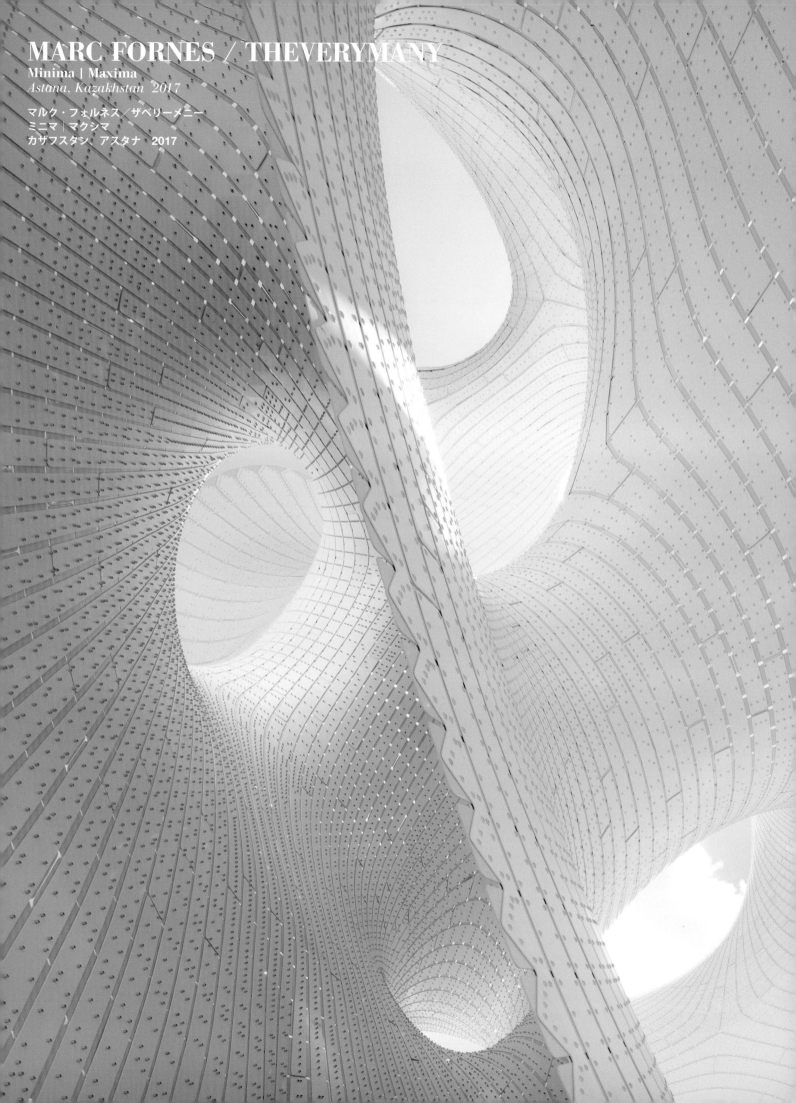

MARC FORNES / THEVERYMANY
Minima | Maxima
Astana, Kazakhstan 2017

マルク・フォルネス／ザベリーメニー
ミニマ｜マクシマ
カザフスタン、アスタナ　2017

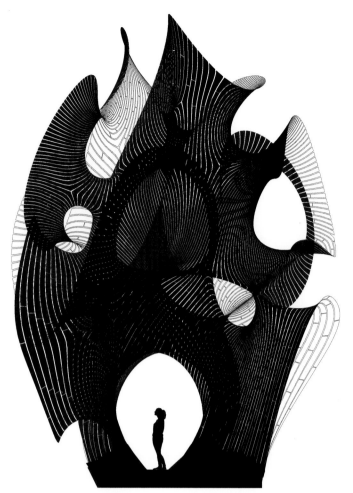

Section (scale: 1/200)／断面図（縮尺：1/200）

p. 120–121: Detail of Minima | Maxima's 6 mm aluminum stripes bent into self-supporting, double-curved surfaces. This page, bottom: The project is a multi-ply composite of three layers. These layers were constructed in tandem, supporting one another as they assumed curvature and gained height. The resulting composite system is mechanically bonded, allowing for recomposition and corrections during construction. All photos copyright NAARO, courtesy of MARC FORNES / THEVERYMANY. Opposite: Diagrams showing the assembly of stripes, and the forces acting upon them.

120〜121頁：ミニマ｜マクシマのディテール。幅6mmのアルミニウム製の帯が曲がって自立式の複曲面をつくりだす。本頁、下：このプロジェクトは3層の複合構造である。これらのレイヤーは、曲率と有効高を想定した上で互いに支持し合うよう、同時に施工された。その結果生みだされた複合システムは機械的に結合されているため、施工中に組み替え・修正することが可能である。右頁：帯の組立てと、これらの帯にかかる力を示すダイアグラム。

Minima | Maxima stands at a crossroad of extremes: an ultra-thin shell of just 6 mm rises to a height of 43 feet (13 m) by way of its sprawling, double-curved surfaces. In this whimsical yet durable universe created by MARC FORNES / THEVERYMANY, curves win out over angles. Branches, splits, and recombinations make columns and beams irrelevant. A "networked'" surface rolls in, on and around itself, transforming into a space that upends preconceived notions of enclosure, threshold, and limit, while also providing its own support. Towards the base of the Minima | Maxima, its rolling surfaces begin to softly corrugate, its zig-zag angles gently tuck into a full pleat as they meet the ground platform. The visual transition – from pleated base to smooth and doubly-curved, continuous surface – is subtle, yet its structural effect is significant, allowing it to rise to impressive heights. It bends in all directions but still manages to stand upright on its own.

This project is the tallest-thinnest freestanding work by MARC FORNES / THEVERYMANY, and extends the studio's research and development efforts to achieve structural integrity through ultra-thin, self-supporting assemblies that find strength in the double curvature of their form. The studio's innovative "structural stripes" accumulate in different directions to compose and strengthen these complex surfaces.

Three layers of flat, aluminum stripes – white and white sandwiching pink – are cross-laminated, supporting one another as they assume curvature and gain height. One layer never exists independently, but contributes to and benefits from the unified whole. The innovation lies in this multiplication, where aluminum, an isotropic or non-directional structural material takes on anisotropic (directional) structural properties in its patterned, composite form. The system warrants comparison to fiber technology – such as carbon or glass fiber – yet is unique in that unlike fibers, each individual component does not need to be in tension. The assembly requires no mold or temporary scaffolding, and because it is mechanically bonded, the system allows for recomposition and correction during construction.

Minima | Maxima was commissioned for World Expo 2017, an event with a history of architectural and engineering innovations. It is situated prominently on the grounds in Astana, Kazakhstan, where it will continue to live as a permanent structure. There it remains a destination of interest for visitors to the rapidly developing city, an environment that incites curiosity from afar and opportunities for play, discovery and quiet contemplation inside.

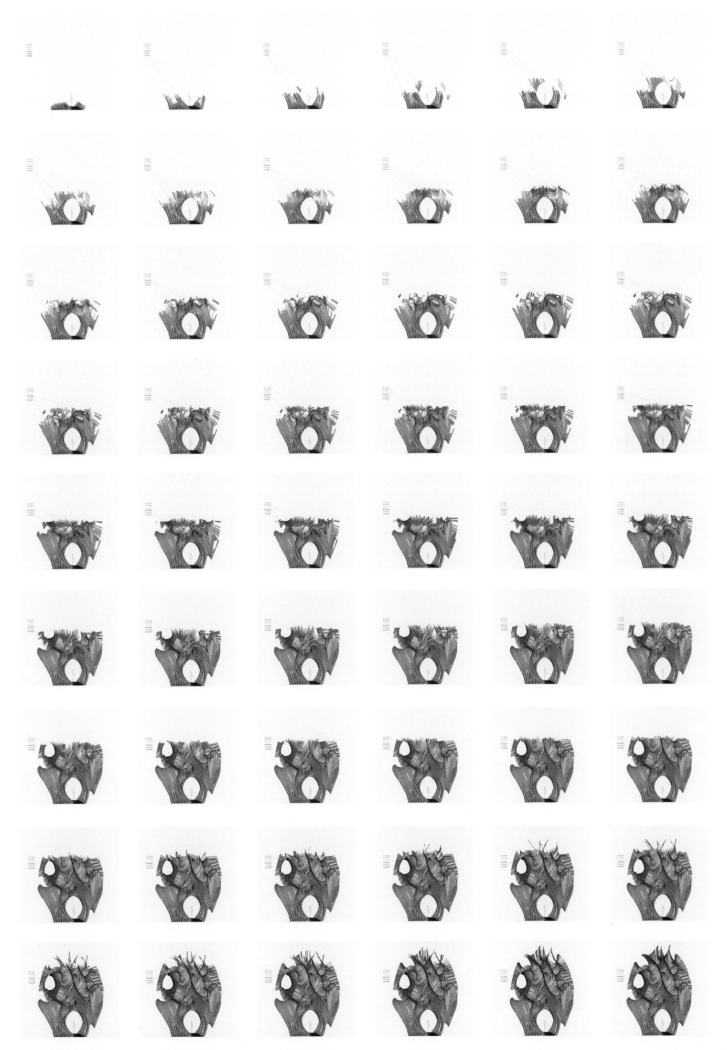

123

ミニマ｜マクシマは極端の十字路に立つ。厚さわずか6mmの超薄型シェルは、ゆったりと広がる複曲面により、高さ43フィート（約13m）まで立ちあがる。マーク・フォルネス／ザベリーメニーが創造したこの気まぐれだが頑丈な宇宙において、曲面は角に勝っている。分岐、分裂、再結合により柱と梁は無関係となる。「ネットワーク化された」面は、自らの支えとなりながらも、自身の内部、上部、周囲にすべりこみ、囲いや敷居、境界といった先入観を覆す空間に変化していく。緩やかに起伏する面は、ミニマ｜マクシマの基礎に向かうにつれ、緩やかに折りたたまれはじめ、ジグザグの角度は地面のプラットフォームに触れる部分では襞の間に完全に吸収される。襞状の基礎から、なめらかで連続した複曲面へと展開する視覚的変化は微細であるが、その効果は構造的には重要で、この印象的な高さを実現している。あらゆる方向に折れ曲がってはいるが、構造体そのものでは直立している。

このプロジェクトは、マーク・フォルネス／ザベリーメニーが手がけた自立作品の中では、最も背が高く、最も薄い作品であり、複曲形態によって必要強度を獲得する超薄型・独立型の集合体の完全構造をつくりだすという目的をもった当スタジオの研究開発を一歩進める作品である。こうした複雑な面を構成、強化するため、スタジオの革新的な「ストラクチャル・ストライプ」は様々な方向に積層されている。

3層の平らなアルミニウム製ストライプ（白いレイヤーどうしでピンクのレイヤーを挟む）が交差積層されており、曲率を受けいれ高さを増しながら相互に支えあう。レイヤーは決して一層では存在せず、それぞれが統合された全体に貢献し、そこから恩恵を受けている。こうした「乗」法にこそ革新があ

り、等方性もしくは非方向性の構造材料であるアルミニウムが、パターン化された複合形態をとることで異方性（方向性）の構造特性を帯びている。このシステムはたしかに繊維技術──炭素繊維やガラス繊維──と類似してはいるが、繊維とは異なり個々の構成要素に張力をかける必要がない点で独自である。組立て時には金型や仮設の足場は不要であり、機械的に接合されているため、このシステムを用いれば建設途中での構成の変更修正が可能となる。

ミニマ｜マクシマは、建築やエンジニアリングの革新の歴史となるイベント、2017年アスタナ国際博覧会に出展された。この傑出した構築物は、カザフスタンの首都アスタナの土地に設置され、恒久的な建造物として使われ続ける。この場所は、急速な発展に関心を抱いた人々が訪れる都市となり、遠方の人々の好奇心を刺激し、遊び、発見、静かな熟考の機会を提供する環境となっている。

（松本晴子訳）

Opposite: The aluminum stripes move perpendicularly from one another, creating an anisotropic composite material from an isotropic material. This page: At the base of the structure, the continuous surface begins to corrugate. All photos copyright NAARO, courtesy of MARC FORNES / THEVERYMANY.

左頁：アルミニウム製の帯は互いに垂直方向に伸びており、一つの等方性素材から、異方性の複合素材を生みだしている。本頁：構造物の底部では、連続した表面が波形になっていく。

Credits and Data
Project title: Minima | Maxima
Client: Epazote Sa. Vladislav Sludskiy for World Expo 2017
Location: Astana, Kazakhstan
Design: 2017
Completion: 2017
Design Team: MARC FORNES / THEVERYMANY

Commentary:
Jenny Sabin Studio & Sabin Lab

コメンタリー：
ジェニー・セイビン・スタジオ、セイビン・ラボ

Drawing on historian Detlef Mertins's term bioconstructivisms, we continue to emphasize and expand the analogic negotiation of morphological behavior as a dynamic template that is then filtered through material organizations, employing digital handcraft in the co-production of materiality and seeking a biosynthesis of the natural model with material manifestation. In contrast to biomimicry, biosynthesis fosters process-based research where design solutions and applications emerge in a shared collaborative space through bottom-up, materially directed, ecological and systemic thinking in design. Our methodology and design process, both in studio projects (Jenny Sabin Studio) and through fundamental research in the lab (Sabin Lab), may be organized into three distinct phases: (1) New Tools and Forms – The production of catalogs of visualization and simulation tools that are then used to discover new behaviors in geometry and matter; (2) Architectural Prototyping – An exploration of the material and ecological potentials of these tools through the production and digital fabrication of experimental structures and material systems, and (3) Building Ecology – Generation of scientifically-based, design-oriented applications in contemporary architecture practice for adaptive building systems, protocols, and material assemblies. The scope of our work probes the visualization and simulation of complex spatial datasets alongside issues of craft, fabrication and production in a diverse array of material systems (woven, knitted, and braided textiles, Rapid Prototype and 3D printed ceramics, bio-plastics and hydrogels, water-jet cut metals). This interest probes the productive tinkering with digital fabrication machines, informed by scientific principles and issues of digital craft and making, to produce bio-inspired material systems and software design tools that have the capacity to facilitate embedded expressions in our built environment. The 'mess' in both the lab and the studio is about process, productive failures, rigorous and playful experimentation, and the production of new knowledge.

To summarize some of my key projects and their innovative biosynthetic approaches, networks, datasets, emerging technologies such as artificial intelligence and adaptive material systems inform one of the featured projects: Ada for Microsoft Research's Artist in Residence program 2018–2019. In parallel, the PolyBrick series brings together biological principles with advancements in additive manufacturing and 3D printing. In both projects, by investigating loops that filter datasets through material organizations, the work forms a bridge between the human body and technology as an active overlay that influences and contributes to an alternative material practice in architecture, which frequently touches upon pressing global issues such as material performance and building energy. One of the most important deliverables of the studio and lab concerns fostering new habits of thought and material intuition where non-standard tectonic elements emerge through the rigorous investigation of the behaviors of natural models and their corresponding translation into novel material systems. These transformative models may in parallel provide potent contributions towards issues of construction, digital fabrication and material ecologies in architecture. Critical to this approach are design processes rooted in experimentation across disciplinary boundaries without predetermination of form.

私たちは、歴史家デトレフ・メルティンズの用語「生物構成主義」に依拠し、材料組織を通じてフィルタリングされるダイナミックなテンプレートとしての、形態学的行動の類推的交渉の強調・拡大を行ってきた。デジタル・ハンドクラフトを使用して素材性の共同生産を行い、物質の顕在をともなう自然モデルの生合成を追求する。生物模倣とは対照的に、生合成はプロセス・ベースの研究を促進する。ここではボトムアップ、素材主導、生態学的、体系的なデザイン思考を通じ、デザインによる解決策とアプリケーションは共用のコラボレーション空間に現れている。スタジオ（ジェニー・セイビン・スタジオ）でのプロジェクトと、研究室（セイビン・ラボ）での基礎研究の両方で、私たちの方法論とデザイン・プロセスは、以下3段階で構成されている。（1）新しい道具と形態——視覚化のためのカタログ作成とシミュレーション用ツールは、幾何学と物質の新しい動作を発見するために使用される。（2）建築プロトタイピング——実験的構造と材料システムの生産とデジタル製作により、これらのツールの材料面、生態学面の可能性を探求。（3）建築生態学——現代建築の実践における応用建設システム、プロトコル、および材料アセンブリのための科学にもとづいたデザイン指向のアプリケーション生成。私たちは、複雑な空間データセットの視覚化・シミュレーションを対象とし、多種多様な素材のシステム（織物、編物、編み上げ織物、ラピッドプロトタイピングされ3Dプリントされたセラミック、バイオプラスチック、ハイドロゲル、ウォータージェット切断された金属など）の手工や製造、生産とともに探求を行なっている。この活動は、化学原理とデジタルのものづくりにもとづいたデジタル製造において、意味のある機械いじりをすることを目指している。また、結果としてバイオインスパイアード素材の構造とソフトウェア・デザインの道具を生みだし、構築環境に組み込まれた表現をつくりだすことを目的としている。ラボとスタジオの両方の「混沌」は、プロセス、意味のある失敗、厳格でありながらも遊び心のある実験、新しい知識の生成なのである。

主要プロジェクトと、それを可能にした新興テクノロジー（革新的な生合成アプローチ、ネットワーク、データセット、また人工知能や適応材料システムなど）を要約するものとして、「エイダ」マイクロソフト・リサーチによる2018〜19年アーティスト・イン・レジデンス・プログラムが挙げられる。またこれに並行し、ポリブリック・シリーズは、付加製造・3Dプリント技術の進歩と生物学的原理を結びつける。これらプロジェクトに共通して、材料組織を通じてデータセットをフィルタリングするループを研究することで、作品は人体とテクノロジーを繋いでいる。活きたオーバーレイとして建築の代替素材関係に影響を与え、貢献し、素材性能や建物エネルギーといった世界的に差し迫った問題に言及している。スタジオとラボの最も重要な成果物の一つは、新しい思考習慣と材料的直観の育成に関するものである。自然モデルの振る舞いと、それに対応する新しい材料システムへの変換に関する厳密な研究を通じて、非標準的な構造要素が出現する。これらの変形モデルには、それと並行して、建築、建設、デジタル製造、および材料生態学の問題に向けた強力な貢献を提供する可能性がある。このアプローチで重要なのは、事前に形態を決定せずに、専門領域の境界を越えた実験に根ざしたデザイン・プロセスである。

（松本晴子訳）

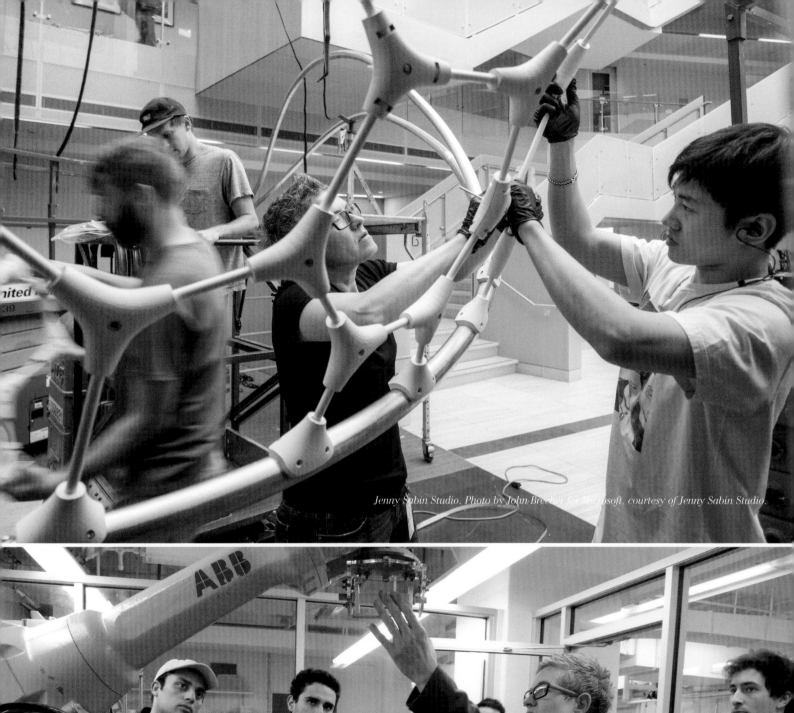

Jenny Sabin Studio and Microsoft Research

Ada
Seattle, U.S.A. 2018–2019

ジェニー・セイビン・スタジオ、マイクロソフト・リサーチ
エイダ
米国、シアトル　2018〜2019

Named after the polymath, mathematician, first computer programmer, and early innovator of the computer age, Ada Lovelace, this collaborative project with Microsoft Research embodies performance, material innovation, human-centered adaptive architecture and emerging technologies, including artificial intelligence. Ada builds upon 13 years of collaborative work and innovation across architecture and science, where projects embrace and are informed by technology, non-standard and bio-steered concepts, and the hidden spatial structures within data; projects that have the capacity to facilitate and reveal hidden expressions and emotion in the built environment. The first architectural pavilion project to incorporate AI, Ada is also knitted light, immersing visitors in a responsive and interactive glow of photo-luminescence. Importantly, Ada is human-driven; Ada is a cyber-physical architecture that is adaptive, personal, data-driven and informed by individual and collective participation. It is a project that celebrates AI, an architecture that is 'happy to see you' and 'smiles back at you'.

A lightweight knitted pavilion structure of responsive and data-driven tubular and cellular components employs textiles and photo-luminescent fibers that absorb, collect, and emit light. An external rigid, experimental shell structure assembled from a compressive network of 895 unique, 3D-printed nodes and fiberglass rods holds Ada's form in continuous tension. Working with researchers and engineers at Microsoft Research, Ada is driven by individual and collective sentiment data collected and housed within the Microsoft Research Building 99. A network of sensors and cameras located throughout the building offers multiple opportunities for visitors and participants to engage, interact with, and drive the project. The data includes facial patterns, voice tones, and sounds that are processed by AI algorithms and correlated with a sentiment. Three scales of responsive and gradated lighting including a network of addressable LEDs, a custom fiber optic central tensegrity cone, and five external PAR lights respond in real-time to continuous streams of data. Specific sentiment data are correlated with colors, spatial zones within the project, and responsive materials.

Suspended from three points and hovering above the ground floor of the atrium, Ada is a socially and environmentally responsive structure that is interactive and transformative. This environment offers spaces for curiosity and wonder, individual and collective exchange, and rigorous research experimentation as the pavilion filters light, casts dynamic shadows, and changes in response to your input. It is an open responsive system featuring digitally-knitted lightweight, high-performing, form-fitting, and adaptive materials.

このマイクロソフト・リサーチとの共同プロジェクトは、博識な数学者かつ、最初のコンピュータ・プログラマー、そしてコンピュータ時代の先駆であったエイダ・ラブレスに因んで名づけられ、パフォーマンス、新素材イノヴェーション、人間中心の適応型建築（アダプティブ・アーキテクチュア）、そして人工知能などを含む新しいテクノロジーを具現化する。エイダは建築と科学を横断する13年にわたる共同作業と革新にもとづき構築され、プロジェクトは、テクノロジーや非標準的かつ生物学に刺激を受けたコンセプト、データ内の隠れた空間構造を包含し、これら要素から情報を与えられている。そして構築環境に隠された表情や感情を促進し表出させる力をもつ。エイダは、人工知能を組みこんだ初の展示館計画でもあり、光の編み物として、応答型かつ対話型のフォトルミネセンスの輝きに訪問者を浸しこむ。エイダが人間主導であることは特筆に値し、サイバー＝フィジカル・アーキテクチュアとして適応型、個別的、データ駆動、そして個人および集団の参加により情報を取得する、という特徴をもち合わせている。人工知能を称えるプロジェクトであり、「人との邂逅を喜び」「微笑みかえしてくれる」建築である。

応答型でデータ駆動型の管／多孔性組成でできた軽量ニット構造の展示館は、織物と光を吸収、収集、放出するフォトルミネセンス・ファイバーを使用している。外側の堅固な実験的シェル構造は、3Dプリントされた全895種の結節点とファイバーグラス製ロッドによる圧縮ネットワークで構成され、連続的な張力でエイダの形状を保持している。マイクロソフト・リサーチの研究者、エンジニアらとの協働から、エイダはマイクロソフト・リサーチ・ビルディング99内で採取、保存された個人、集団的な感情データにより駆動している。建物中にとりつけられたセンサーとカメラのネットワークは、訪問者・参加者にたいしてプロジェクトとかかわり、交流し、それを駆動させる様々

な機会を提供する。これらデータは、表情パターン、音声トーン、および音を含み、人工知能アルゴリズムで処理され、感情と結びつけられる。3段階の応答型で段階的な照明は、アドレス指定可能なLEDのネットワーク、カスタムによる光ファイバーのセントラル・テンセグリティ構造のコーン、および5つの外づけPAR（放物線アルミ反射鏡）ライトを含み、データの連続的な流れにリアルタイムで応答する。特定の感情データは、色、プロジェクト内の空間ゾーン、応答型素材と相互に関連づけられる。

エイダは、3点で吊り下げられ、アトリウムの地上階上方をホバリングし、社会および環境に反応する構造体であり、対話型で変形可能である。パヴィリオンは光のフィルターとなり、ダイナミックな影を生みだし、様々なインプットに応じて変化する。そしてつくりだされた環境は、好奇心と驚き、個人・集団間のやりとり、そして厳密な研究実験のための空間をもたらしている。この構造は開放系の応答システムであり、デジタルで編まれた軽量性、高性能で形態に合わせた適応型素材を特徴とする。

（松本晴子訳）

Opposite: Detail of the textiles and photo-luminescent fibers that absorb, collect, and emit light in response to Ada's data collection. Photo by Jake Knapp, courtesy of Jenny Sabin Studio.

右頁：エイダの集積データに反応して光を吸収、収集、放出するテキスタイルと蛍光繊維のディテール。

values		
● Angry	0.12	
● Serious	0.03	
● Frowning	0.01	
● Enthusiastic	0.34	
● Grinning	0.00	
● Normal	0.03	
● Upset	0.94	
● Surprised	0.27	

CONTINUOUSLY UPDATING
VALUES

PYTHON APP

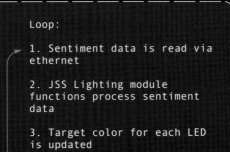

1. Sentiment data is read every three seconds from MS cameras
2. Sentiment values are processed and stored
3. JSS DMX Lighting module functions define relationships between sentiment data and global lighting behaviors

Loop:

1. Sentiment data is read via ethernet

2. JSS Lighting module functions process sentiment data

3. Target color for each LED is updated

4. Current LED colors are smoothly transitioned to target colors with interpolation behaviors defined in JSS module

5. 3 second delay

RASPBERRY PI + LED

1. Data continuously translated to DMX signals

2. Signals transmitted to PAR lights via Serial and Arduino

ARDUINO DMX INTERFACE

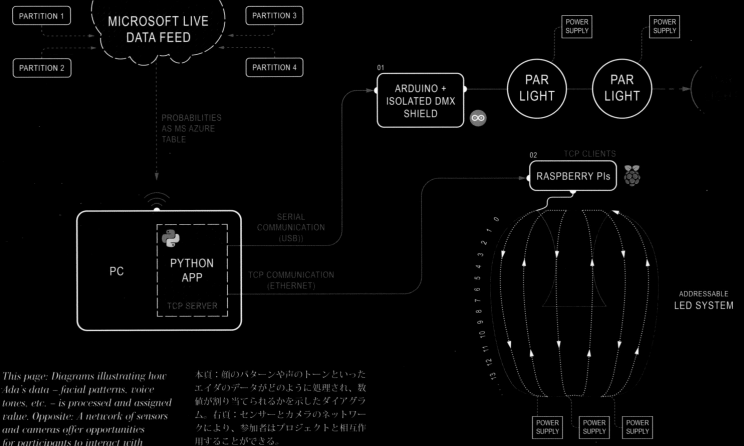

PARTITION 1
PARTITION 2
PARTITION 3
PARTITION 4

MICROSOFT LIVE DATA FEED

PROBABILITIES AS MS AZURE TABLE

PC
PYTHON APP
TCP SERVER

SERIAL COMMUNICATION (USB))

TCP COMMUNICATION (ETHERNET)

01
ARDUINO + ISOLATED DMX SHIELD

PAR LIGHT

PAR LIGHT

POWER SUPPLY

POWER SUPPLY

02
TCP CLIENTS
RASPBERRY PIs

ADDRESSABLE LED SYSTEM

POWER SUPPLY
POWER SUPPLY
POWER SUPPLY

This page: Diagrams illustrating how Ada's data – facial patterns, voice tones, etc. – is processed and assigned value. Opposite: A network of sensors and cameras offer opportunities for participants to interact with the project. Photos by Jake Knapp, courtesy of Jenny Sabin Studio.

本頁：顔のパターンや声のトーンといったエイダのデータがどのように処理され、数値が割り当てられるかを示したダイアグラム。右頁：センサーとカメラのネットワークにより、参加者はプロジェクトと相互作用することができる。

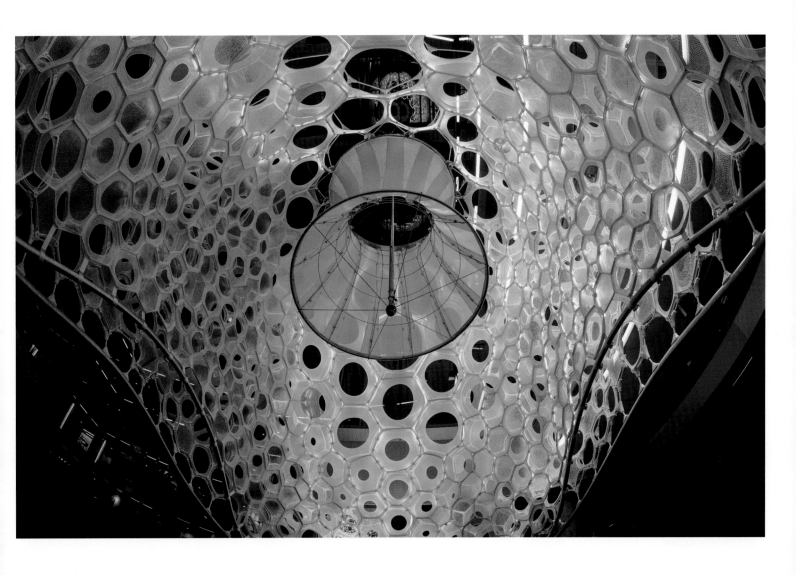

Credits and Data

Project title: Ada
Client: Microsoft Research
Location: Seattle, Washington, USA
Design: 2018
Completion: 2019
Design Team:
   Jenny Sabin Studio Team: Jenny E. Sabin (Architectural Designer and Artist); Dillon Pranger (Project Manager); John Hilla, Jeremy Bilotti, William Qian (Design, Production, Installation); Clayton Binkley and Judy Guo (Arup – Design Engineer)
   Microsoft Research Ada Core: Eric Horvitz (Technical Fellow and Director);Shabnam Erfani (Director of PM and Special Projects); Asta Roseway (Principal Research Designer/Fusionist); Wende Copfer (Principal Design Director); Jonathan Lester (Principal Electrical Engineer); Daniel McDuff (Principal Researcher); Mira Lane (Partner Director/Ethics)
Consultants: GoProto, Dazian, Avatar Knit, Fabric Images, Accufab (Fabrication and Manufacturing)
Project area: 23'-2" (length) x 15'-10" (width) x 24'-6" (height)
Special Thanks to Allison Linn, Kiesha Clayton, John Roach, John Brecher, Henry Honig, Evelina Barhudarian, Christopher O'Dowd, Abhishek Udupa, Gregory Lee, Kathleen Walker, Stef Letman, Vaishnavi Ranganathan, Lex Story, Todd Jurgenson, Teresa LaScala, Tracy Tran, Trey Bagley, Jin Kim, Nicolas Villar, Chris Lovett, Cornell AAP, and the Blank Family

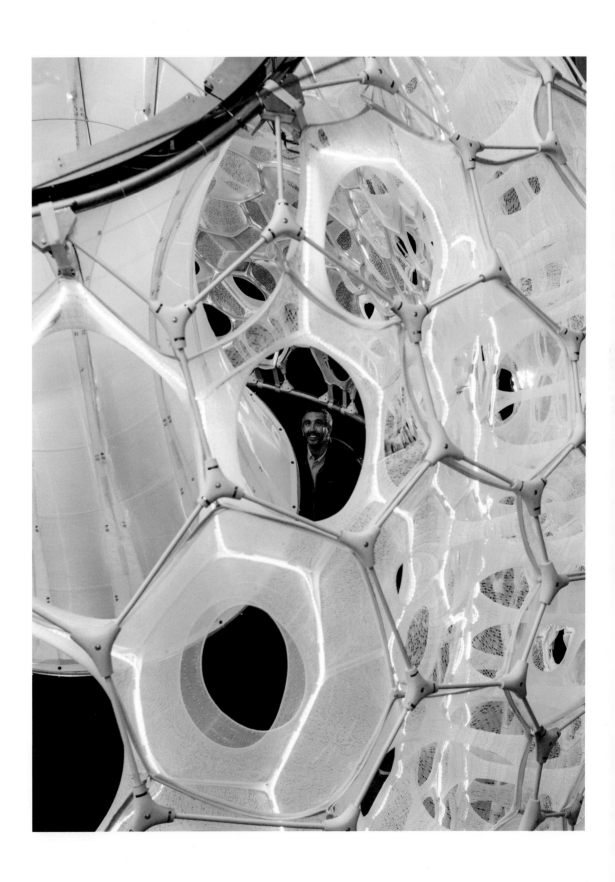

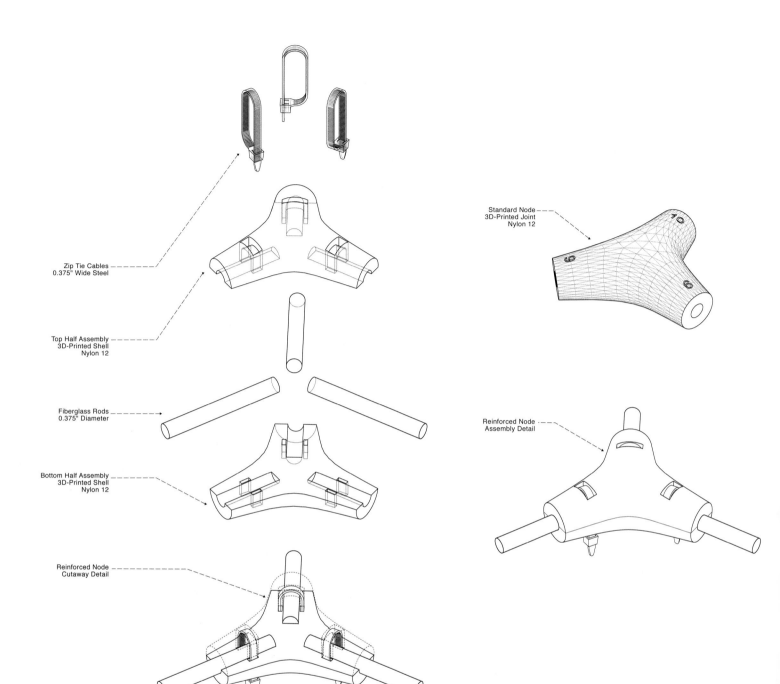

Zip Tie Cables
0.375" Wide Steel

Top Half Assembly
3D-Printed Shell
Nylon 12

Fiberglass Rods
0.375" Diameter

Bottom Half Assembly
3D-Printed Shell
Nylon 12

Reinforced Node
Cutaway Detail

Standard Node
3D-Printed Joint
Nylon 12

Reinforced Node
Assembly Detail

Exoskeleton node details／外骨格結節ダイアグラム

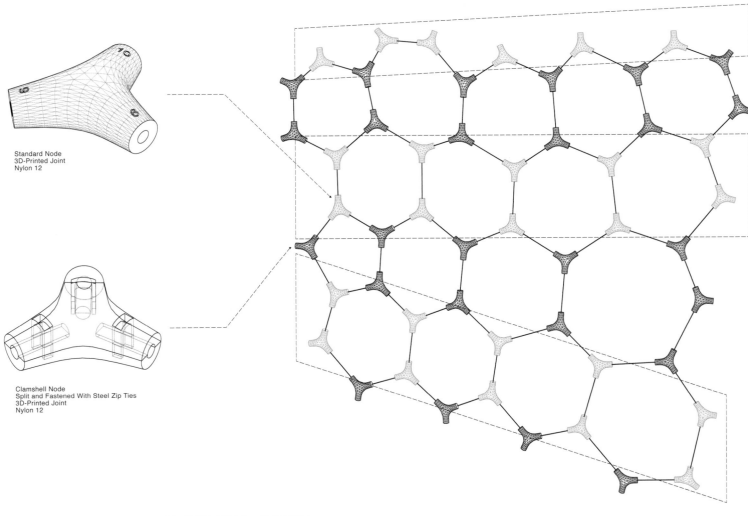

Standard Node
3D-Printed Joint
Nylon 12

Clamshell Node
Split and Fastened With Steel Zip Ties
3D-Printed Joint
Nylon 12

Exoskeleton node assembly system／外骨格結節点組み立てダイアグラム

pp. 132–133: Photos depicting user experiences and Ada's responses. Photos by Jake Knapp, courtesy of Jenny Sabin Studio. Opposite, left to right: Jing Wei Qian, a designer at Jenny Sabin Studio, sorts through 895 custom 3D-printed nodes that help form Ada's exoskeleton; John Hilla, a designer at Jenny Sabin Studio, inserts fiberglass rods into the nodes. This page, left to right: Jing Wei Qian,

John Hilla, and Jenny Sabin assemble the exoskeleton; The team works to suspend the exoskeleton. Photos by John Brecher for Microsoft, courtesy of Jenny Sabin Studio.

132〜133頁：ユーザー体験とエイダの反応を表した写真。 左頁、左から：ジェニー・セイビン・スタジオ のデザイナー、ジン・ウェイ・キアンは、3Dプリント成形された895個の特注結節点を分類する。この結

節点はエイダの外骨格の成形を助ける／ジェニー・セイビン・スタジオ のデザイナー、ジョン・ハイラは、この結節点にガラス繊維製の棒を挿入する。本頁、左から：ジン・ウェイ・キアン、ジョン・ハイラ、ジェニー・セイビンが外骨格を組み立てる／外骨格を吊り下げる作業の様子。

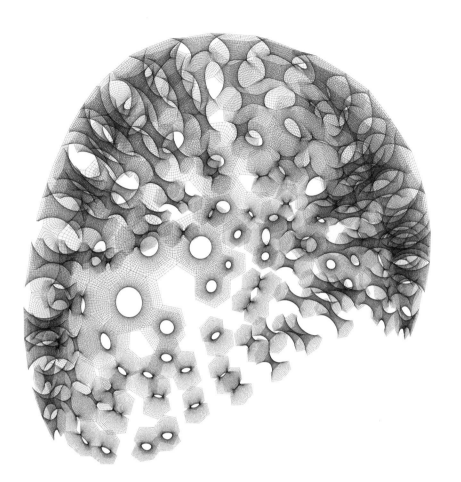

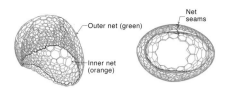

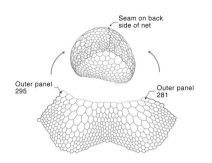

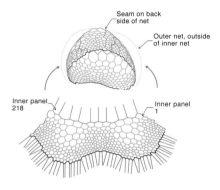

Knit geometry ／編みの幾何学図

Assembly ／組み立て

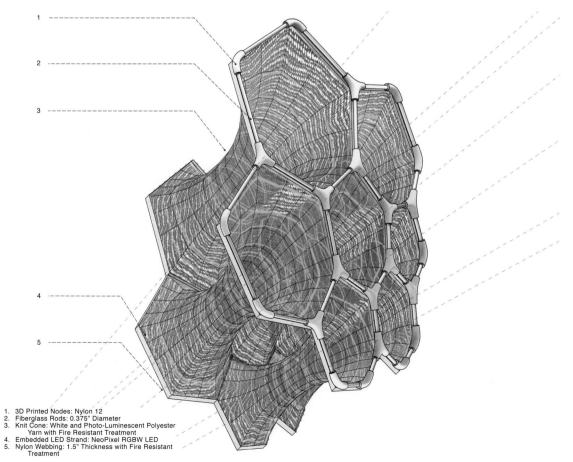

1. 3D Printed Nodes: Nylon 12
2. Fiberglass Rods: 0.375" Diameter
3. Knit Cone: White and Photo-Luminescent Polyester Yarn with Fire Resistant Treatment
4. Embedded LED Strand: NeoPixel RGBW LED
5. Nylon Webbing: 1.5" Thickness with Fire Resistant Treatment

Opposite: Ada suspended in site.
Photos by Jake Knapp, courtesy of
Jenny Sabin Studio.

Cluster of cones ／円錐形の集まり

右頁：現場で吊り下げられたエイダ。

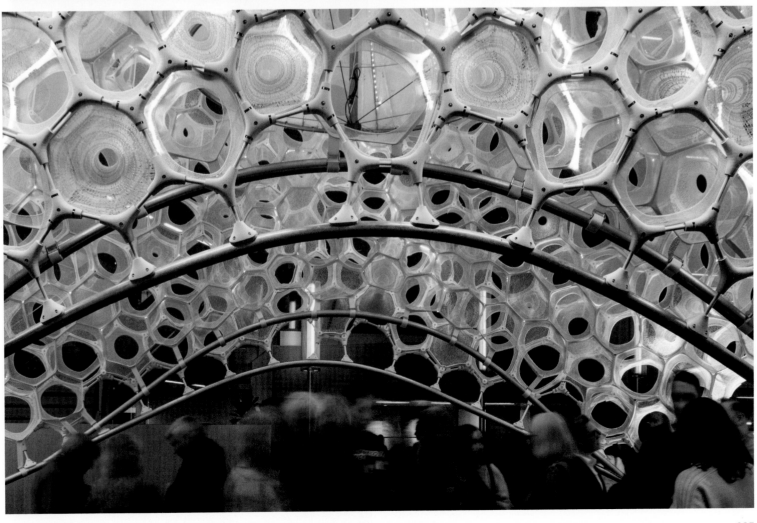

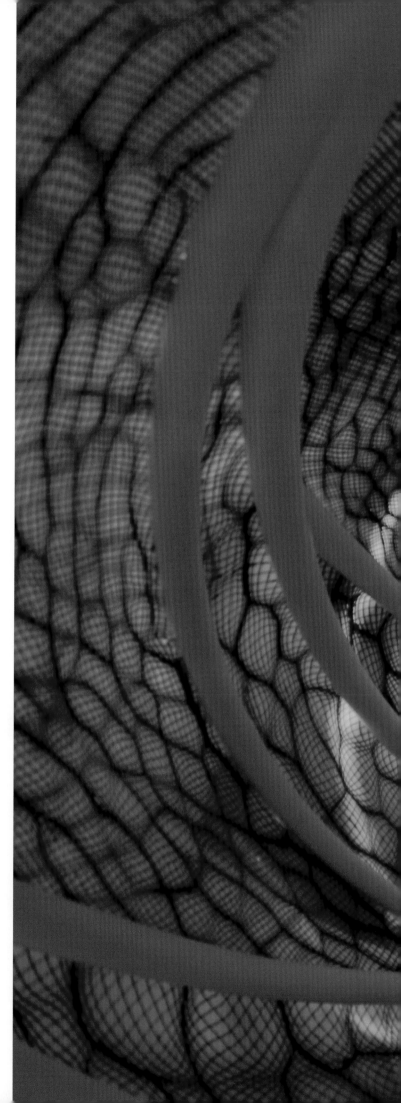

Commentary:
Neri Oxman and The Mediated Matter Group, Massachusetts Institute of Technology

コメンタリー：
ネリ・オックスマン、メディエイティド・マター・グループ（**MIT**）

The Mediated Matter group focuses on Nature-inspired design and design-inspired nature. We conduct research at the intersection of computational design, digital fabrication, materials science, and synthetic biology, and apply that knowledge to design across scales – from the microscale to the building scale. We create biologically inspired and engineered design fabrication tools and technologies and structures aiming to enhance the relation between natural and man-made environments. Our research area, entitled Material Ecology, integrates computational form-finding strategies with biologically inspired fabrication. This design approach enables the mediation between objects and the environment; between humans and objects; and between humans and the environment. Our goal is to enhance the relation between natural and man-made environments by achieving high degrees of design customization and versatility, environmental performance integration, and material efficiency. We seek to establish new forms of design and novel processes of material practice at the intersection of computer science, material engineering, and design and ecology, with broad applications across multiple scales.

メディエイティド・マター・グループは、自然から着想を得たデザインと、デザインから着想を得た自然に焦点をあてる。私たちはコンピューテーショナル・デザイン、デジタル・ファブリケーション、材料科学、合成生物学の交わる点で研究を行い、ミクロのスケールから建築のスケールまで多様なスケールのデザインに知識を応用する。私たちは、生物学に着想を得て考案されたデザイン・ファブリケーション・ツール、テクノロジー、およびストラクチャーを創出し、自然環境と人工環境の関係の強化を目ざす。マテリアル・エコロジーと名づけられた私たちの研究領域は、コンピュータによる形状決定の戦略と、生物学から着想を得た製造を統合する。こうしたデザイン・アプローチにより、物体と環境、人間と物質、人間と環境間が調停可能となる。私たちの目標は、デザインのカスタマイズと汎用化、環境性能の統合、材料効率の高度化を達成することにより、自然環境と人工環境の関係を強化することである。私たちは、コンピュータ科学、材料工学、デザインとエコロジーの交差点で、新たなデザイン形態と材料実践の新しいプロセスを確立しようとしている。

（松本晴子訳）

Nexi Oxman and The Mediated Matter Group

Silk Pavilion
Cambridge, U.S.A. 2013

ネリ・オックスマン、メディエイティド・マター・グループ
シルク・パヴィリオン
米国、ケンブリッジ 2013

The Silk Pavilion explores the relationship between digital and biological fabrication on product and architectural scales. The primary structure was created of 26 polygonal panels made of silk threads laid down by a CNC (Computer Numerical Control) machine. Inspired by the silkworm's ability to generate a 3D cocoon out of a single multi-property silk thread (1km in length), the overall geometry of the pavilion was created using an algorithm that assigns a single continuous thread across patches providing various degrees of density.

Overall density variation was informed by the silkworm itself deployed as a biological "printer" in the creation of a secondary structure. A swarm of 6,500 silkworms was positioned at the bottom rim of the scaffold spinning flat nonwoven silk patches as they locally reinforced the gaps across CNC-deposited silk fibers. Following their pupation stage the silkworms were removed. Resulting moths can produce 1.5 million eggs with the potential of constructing up to 250 additional pavilions.

Affected by spatial and environmental conditions including geometrical density as well as variation in natural light and heat, the silkworms were found to migrate to darker and denser areas. Desired light effects informed variations in material organization across the surface area of the structure. A season-specific sun path diagram mapping solar trajectories in space dictated the location, size and density of apertures within the structure in order to lock-in rays of natural light entering the pavilion from South and East elevations. The central oculus is located against the East elevation and may be used as a sun-clock.

Parallel basic research explored the use of silkworms as entities that can "compute" material organization based on external performance criteria. Specifically, we explored the formation of non-woven fiber structures generated by the silkworms as a computational schema for determining shape and material optimization of fiber-based surface structures.

シルク・パヴィリオンは、工業製品と建築のスケールでの、デジタルと生物学的なファブリケーションの関係を探究している。基本的な構造はCNC（コンピュータ数値制御）によって絹糸を置き重ねた、26枚の多角形のパネルで構成されている。様々な特性をもつ1本の絹の繊維（長さ1km）から3次元の繭をつくりだす蚕の能力に着想を得て、パヴィリオンの全体的な形状は、連続した1本の糸をパネル全体に配し、様々な密度をもたらすアルゴリズムによってつくりだされている。

全体的な密度の違いは、副次的な構造をつくりだす過程で生物学的な「プリンター」として配された、蚕そのものから情報がもたらされている。蚕がCNCによって配された絹の繊維に点在する隙間を場所ごとに補強するよう、絹糸を置き重ねた平らなパネルを吊り下げる牽引材の下端に、6,500匹の蚕の群れが置かれた。蛹化を迎えると、蚕はとり去られる。やがて成虫になった蛾は150万個の卵を産み、最大で250の追加的なパヴィリオンをつくりだす可能性をもっている。

幾何学的な密度や光、温度など、空間や環境が変化すると、蚕はより暗く、より密度が高い場所に移動していくことが明らかになった。必要に応じて光を調整することで、構造の表層全体の素材構成を変動させる情報が与えられている。季節ごとの太陽の軌道を空間の中にマッピングしたダイアグラムが、南と東の面からパヴィリオンに自然光をとり入れるために、架構内部の開口部の位置、大きさ、数を定めている。中央の「オクルス（眼）」は東の立面に置かれ、日時計と

しても使うことができる。
関連の基礎研究では、外的な性能評価基準にもとづいて素材の構成を「計算」するために、蚕を利用することが研究された。特に我々は、繊維による面構造の最適な形状と素材を決定するコンピュータの理論的な枠組みとして、蚕が生成する置き重ねられた繊維による構造物の成り立ちを詳細に研究している。

（中田雅章訳）

This page: View through the Silk Pavilion's apertures as the silkworms skin the structure. Courtesy of The Mediated Matter Group.

本頁：蚕が構造物に膜を張っているときの
シルク・パヴィリオンの開口部からの眺め。

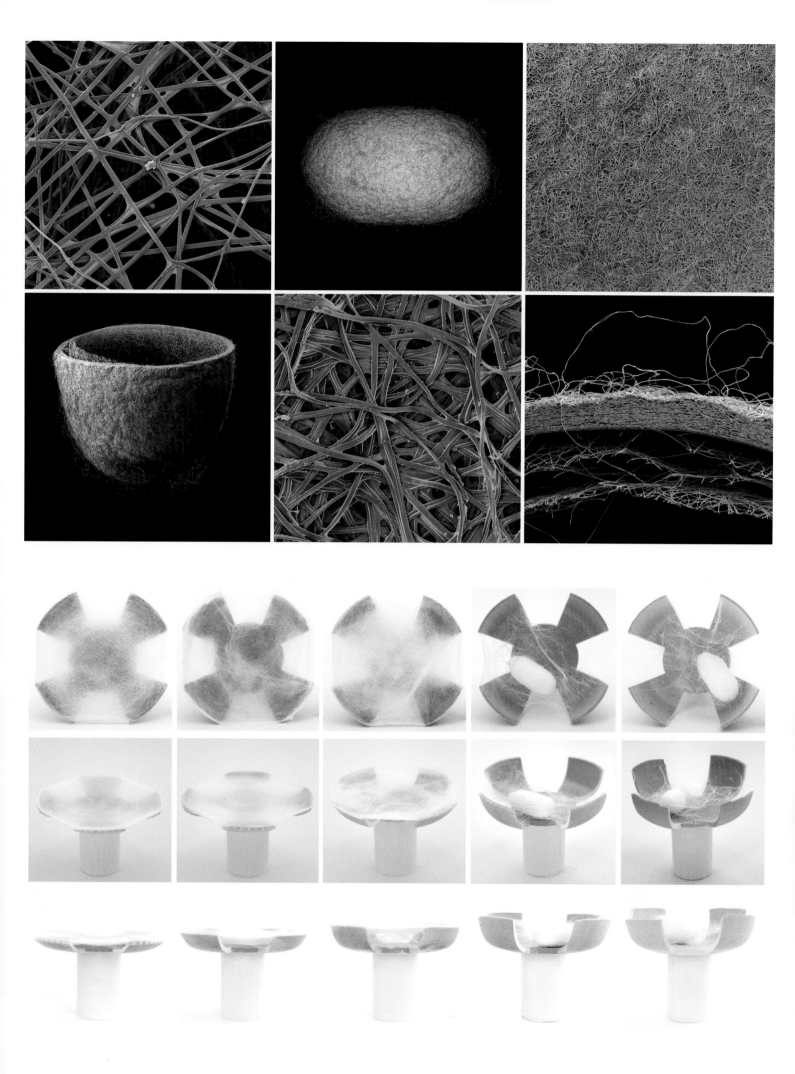

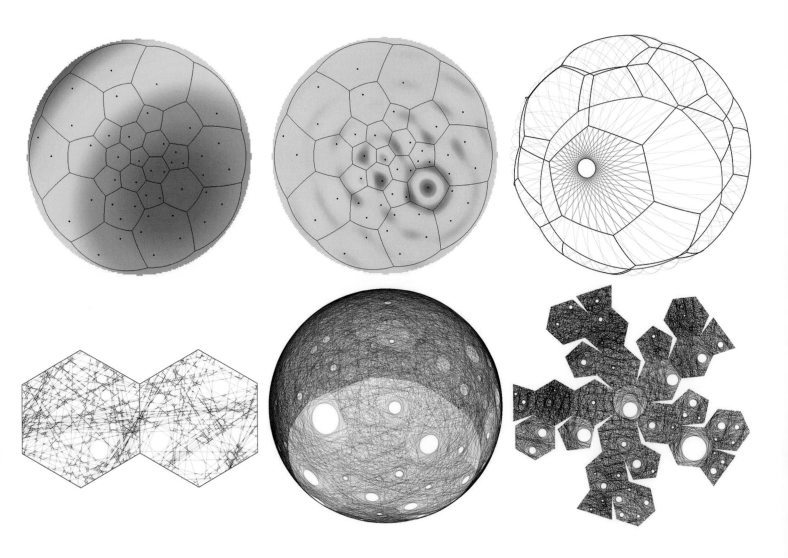

Credits and Data

Project title: Silk Pavilion

Location: Cambridge, MA, USA

Completion: 2013

Project team (Mediated Matter Group): Neri Oxman (Director), Markus Kayser (Research Assistant), Jared Laucks (Research Assistant), Carlos David Gonzalez Uribe (Research Assistant), Jorge Duro-Royo (Research Assistant), Neerja Aggarwal (UROP), Zachary Tribbett (UROP), Trevor Walker (UROP), Sarah Ryan (Administrative Assistant)

Collaborators: James Weaver (WYSS Institute, Harvard University), Prof. Fiorenzo Omenetto (TUFTS University)

Research: Leslie Brunetta (Co-Author of "Spider Silk" and silk expert), Catherine L Craig (Co-Author of "Spider Silk" and silk expert), Nereus Patel (Researcher, TUFTS University), Prof. Markus Buehler (Dept. of Civil Engineering, MIT)

Sponsors: National Science Foundation, Bentley Systems, MIT Media Lab

Finance: Christina Williams (Director of Finance and Development)

Facilities: Greg Tucker (Director of Facilities, MIT Media Lab), Kevin Davis (Facilities Manager (MIT Media Lab), Cornelle N. King (Office Assistant, MIT Media Lab), Katie Blass (Assistant Officer, MIT Health & Environment)

Fabrication Facilities: Center for Bits & Atoms (MIT Media Lab), Tom Lutz (Administrative Assistant, MIT Media Lab), Martin Seymour (Technical Advisor, MIT Media Lab)

Communications: Ellen N. Hoffman (Director of Communications, MIT Media Lab), Alexandra Kahn (Senior Press Liaison, MIT Media Lab)

Video & Photography: Steven Keating (Research Assistant, Mediated Matter, MIT Media Lab); Andy Ryan (Photographer); Michail Bletsas (Director of Network and Computing Systems, MIT Media Lab); Harlan Reiniger (Operations Manager, MIT Video Productions (AMPS))

Silkworms Storage Space: Prof. Hugh Herr (Director of the Biomechatronics Group, MIT Media Lab); Prof. Ed Boyden (Director of the Synthetic Neurobiology Group, MIT Media Lab)

Special Gratitude: Joi Ito (MIT Media Lab); Ryan Walsh (Administrative Assistant, The MIT Media Lab Community)

Opposite, top, left to right: 2300x magnification, polychromatic micrograph of the silk support scaffold of a Bombyx mori [silkworm] cocoon; 25x magnification, overview micrograph of a Bombyx mori cocoon; 300x magnification, polychromatic micrograph of the external surface of a Bombyx mori cocoon color coded to reflect surface typography; 40x magnification, isometric view micrograph of an equatorially bisected Bombyx mori cocoon; 2500x magnification, polychromatic micrograph of the external surface of a Bombyx mori cocoon; 230x magnification, plan view micrograph of an equatorially bisected Bombyx mori cocoon. Scanning electron micrographs in collaboration with James Weaver, Wyss Institute, Harvard University. Opposite, bottom, left to right: Top and elevation views of the Maltese Cross study series where surface morphologies vary in sectional height from 0 (flat) to 25mm. Flat patches are spun onto morphological patches less than 20mm in sectional height beyond which the full 3D silkworm cocoon appears. Variations in designed surface morphology yield corresponding variations in fiber density, property and overall organization. This page, from left to right: Digital form-finding process and computational tools – solar mapping, aperture distribution mapping, aperture generation logic, spinning range calculation, overall distribution, unfolded panels for fabrication. All courtesy of The Mediated Matter Group.

左頁、上、左から：蚕（Bombyx mori）の繭を支える、シルクの足場。2300倍率の多染性顕微鏡写真／繭の全体像を示す 25 倍率の顕微鏡写真／外部表面のタイポグラフィを反映するよう色分けされた、繭の外部表面の300倍率の多染性顕微鏡写真／赤道上で2等分された繭の40倍率の等角図顕微鏡写真／繭外部表面の 2500 倍率の多染性顕微鏡写真／赤道上で2等分された蚕繭の 230 倍率の平面図顕微鏡写真。走査電子顕微鏡写真はハーヴァード大学ヴィース研究所のジェームズ・ウィーバーとの共同により得られた。左頁下、左から：一連のマルタ十字スタディの上面図と立面図。断面高0（平坦）から25mmまで表面の形態が変化している。平坦なパッチが紡がれ、形態学的なパッチとなり、その断面高が20mmを超えると完全な3次元繭が現れる。表面形態のデザイン・ヴァリエーションに対応して、繊維の密度、特性、および全体構成のヴァリエーションが生みだされる。本頁、左から：形態決定のデジタル・プロセスとコンピュテーショナル・ツール。太陽光分布／開口部分布／開口部生成方法／回転範囲の計算／全体分布／パネル組み立て時の展開図。

Opposite, top: Top view of the Silk Pavilion as approximately 1,500 silkworms construct the fibrous composite. Bottom: Bombyx mori silkworms deposits silk fiber on a digitally-fabricated scaffolding structure. This page: Perspective view of the completed Silk Pavilion and the basic research exhibit focusing on fiber density distribution studies (far right). All courtesy of The Mediated Matter Group.

左頁、上：約1,500匹の蚕によってつくりだされた繊維複合構造によるシルク・パヴィリオンを上から見る。左頁、下：デジタル製作された足場構造上に、蚕がシルク繊維を付着させる。本頁：完成したシルク・パヴィリオンの外観と、繊維密度の分布スタディに焦点を当てた基礎研究の展示（右端）。

Nexi Oxman and The Mediated Matter Group

Aguahoja
Cambridge, MA, USA 2019

ネリ・オックスマン、メディエイティド・マター・グループ
アグアオハ
米国、ケンブリッジ　2019

The Aguahoja project – comprised of completed works (Aguahoja I) and works-in-progress (Aguahoja II) – aims to subvert the industrial vicious cycle of material extraction and obsolescence through the creation of biopolymer composites that exhibit tunable mechanical and optical properties, and respond to their environments in ways that are impossible to achieve with their synthetic counterparts.

Aguahoja I

Works included in this project are digitally designed and robotically manufactured out of the most abundant materials on our planet – the very materials found in trees, insect exoskeletons, apples and bones. Cellulose, chitosan, pectin and calcium carbonate are combined and compounded with high spatial resolution over material tunability producing biodegradable composites with mechanical, chemical and optical functional properties across length scales ranging from millimeters to meters. These water shaped skin-like structures ('hojas') are designed and manufactured as if they were grown: no assembly is required.

Standing five meters tall, the Aguahoja I pavilion is composed of biocomposites constructed with varying degrees of stiffness, flexibility and opacity acting as facade or 'structural skin' manufactured without components the surface area of which is limited only by the robotic gantry – a continuous construction modeled after human skin – with regions that serve as structure, window, and environmental filter. At the end of its life cycle, when no longer useful, the structure can be programmed to degrade in water (e.g. the rain!), thereby restoring its constituent building blocks to their natural ecosystem, augmenting the natural resource cycles that enabled its creation. This level of 'environmental programming' can in the future enable the construction of structures that modify their properties relative to the season: even small alterations to the molecular composition of biocomposites can have a dramatic impact on their design and their decay.

The Aguahoja I artifacts represent 6 years of exploration into computationally 'grown' and robotically manufactured biocompatible material composites that together make up a 'library' of functional biopolymers. The artifacts in this collection are diverse in their appearance and structural make up and environmental behavior; yet they are all composed from the same components: chitosan, cellulose, pectin, and water.

The wide array of forms and behaviors embodies in both pavilion and artifacts reflects the manner in which they are expressed in Nature, where a material such as chitin can compose both the exoskeletons of crustaceans and the cell walls of fungi. In contrast to steel and concrete, the composites formed by these materials are in constant dialogue with their environment. Some artifacts exhibit dramatic changes in conformation in response to humidity and heat, while others darken or lighten as the seasons change. Some are brittle and transparent with a glassy texture while others remain flexible and tough like leather. Despite their emergent diversity, these artifacts share a common quality – in life their properties are mediated by humidity; in death they dissociate in water and return to the ecosystem.

The Aguahoja I platform is comprised of a robotic gantry for 3D printing biomaterials where shape and material composition are directly informed by physical properties (e.g., stiffness and opacity), environmental conditions (e.g., load, temperature, and relative humidity), fabrication constraints (e.g., degrees-of-freedom, arm speed, and nozzle pressure), etc. Entitled Water-based Digital Fabrication the platform fosters tight integration between form, function and fabrication at scales that approach and often match the biological world.

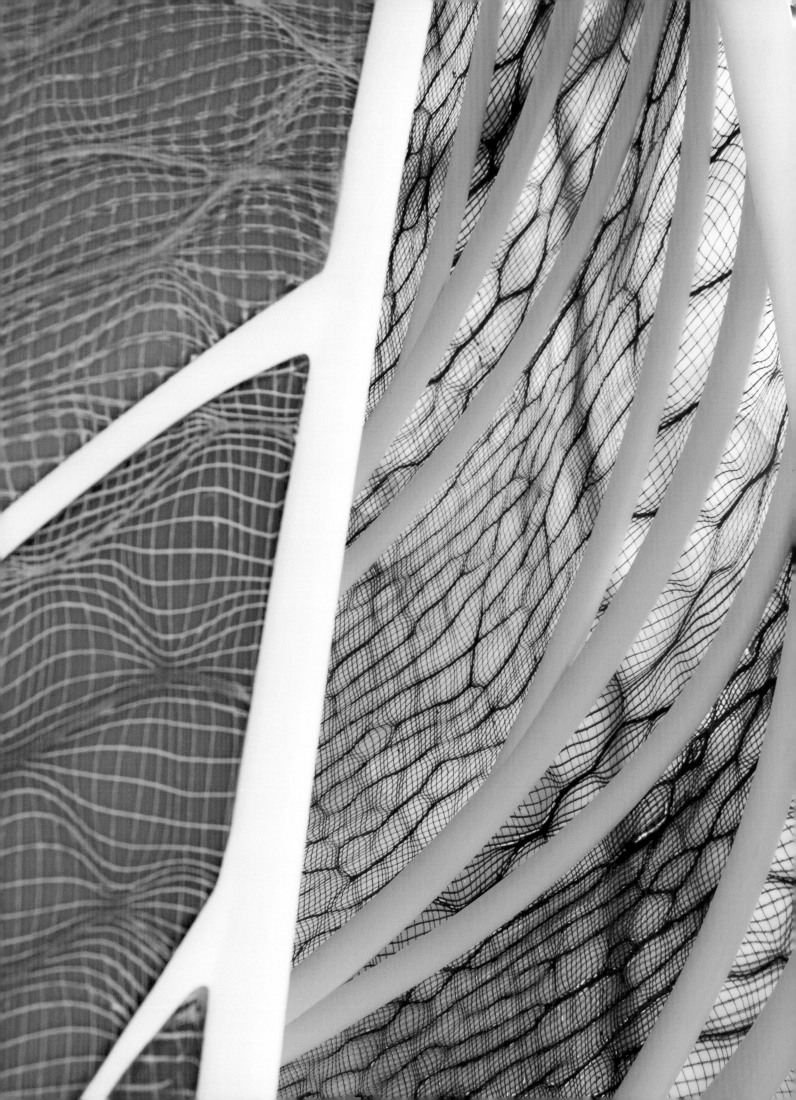

p. 147: Close view of a backlit section of the Aguahoja Pavilion, showing a slight bulging of the panels due to absorption of water from ambient humidity. This page, from the top: An ABB IRB6700 robot was outfitted with a custom pneumatic extrusion system for water-based bio-composites; Large-scale chitosan structure printed using the first generation of the Water-Based Digital Fabrication Platform. The extension of this research allowed for the creation of the Aguahoja series. All courtesy of The Mediated Matter Group.

147頁：背面から照明を当てたアグアオハ・パヴィリオンの近景。周辺環境の湿気を吸収するため、パネルにわずかな膨らみが見られる。本頁、上から：ABB IRB6700ロボットは、水性バイオコンポジット用の特注圧縮空気押出システムを搭載／第一世代水性デジタル・ファブリケーション・プラットフォームを用いて3Dプリントされた大型のキトサン構造。この研究の延長で、アグアオハ・シリーズの製作が可能になった。

Credits and Data
Project title: Aguahoja
Location: Cambridge, USA
Completion: 2019
Project team (Mediated Matter Group): Jorge Duro-Royo, Joshua Van Zak, Yen-Ju (Tim) Tai, Andrea Ling, Nic Hogan, Barrak Darweesh, Laia Mogas-Soldevilla, Daniel Lizardo, Christoph Bader, João Costa, Sunanda Sharma, James Weaver, Prof. Neri Oxman
Research Collaborators: Joseph Faraguna, Matthew Bradford, Loewen Cavill, Emily Ryeom, Aury Hay, Yi Gong, Brian Huang, Tzu-Chieh Tang, Shaymus Hudson, Prof. Pam Silver, Prof. Tim Lu
Substructure Production: Stratasys, Ltd., Stratasys Direct Manufacturing
Acknowledgements: MIT Media Lab, NOE. LLC, Stratasys Ltd, MIT Research Laboratory of Electronics, Wyss Institute at Harvard, Department of Systems Biology at Harvard, GETTYLAB, Robert Wood Johnson Foundation, Autodesk BUILD Space, TBA-21 Academy, Thyssen-Bornemisza Art Contemporary, Stratasys Direct Manufacturing, National Academy of Sciences, San Francisco Museum of Modern Art, Esquel Group

完成した「アグアオハ」と進行中の「アグアオハII」からなるアグアオハ・プロジェクトは、バイオポリマー・コンポジットをつくりだすことで、素材を濫用し廃棄物を生みだす産業の悪循環を断ち切ることを目指している。バイオポリマー・コンポジットは機構と視覚の両面で調整可能な特性を有し、それに相当する人工物では実現不可能な方法で周囲の環境に応答している。

アグアオハI

このプロジェクトの作品は、私たちの惑星に最も豊かに存在する素材──樹木、昆虫の殻（外骨格）、リンゴ、骨にも存在する普遍的な素材を使い、デジタルでデザインされ、ロボットで製作されている。セルロース、キトサン、ペクチン、炭酸カルシウムを組み合わせ、調整可能な素材の特性を利用して微細な空間的解像度で合成し、機械的、化学的、視覚的な機能特性を備えたミリメートルからメートル単位の大きさの生分解性コンポジットをつくりだした。水でかたちづくられた皮膚のようなこれらの構造体「オハス」は、あたかも成長するかのようにデザインされ、製作されている。そこでは、組み立て作業は必要とされていない。

高さ5mのアグアオハIのパヴィリオンは、様々な硬度、フレキシビリティ、不透明度をもつバイオコンポジットで構成され、表層あるいは「構造的な皮膚」として機能している。構造、窓、環境フィルターとして機能する部分を有するその表層は人体の皮膚をモデルにした連続的な構築物で、コンポーネントを使うことなくつくりだされ、ロボットのガントリーのみが構築上の制約になっている。その構造物は、使われなくなりライフ・サイクルの終わりを迎えると水（たとえば雨！）で分解するようにプログラムすることができ、それによってパヴィリオンを構成するビルディング・ブロックは、自然のエコシステムに戻り、その創造の源となった自然物の循環を豊かにする。このレヴェルの「環境的なプログラミング」は将来、季節によってその特性を変化させる構造物の建設を可能にしていく。バイオコンポジットの分子構成をわずかに変えるだけでも、そのデザインや分解に大きなインパクトをもたらすことができる。

アグアオハIの制作物は、コンピュータによって「成長し」ロボットで製作されたバイオコンパチブルな素材の組み合わせに関する、6年にわたる研究の成果を示すもので、その全体が機能的なバイオポリマーの「ライブラリー」になっている。このコレクションの制作物は、外観と構造の組み立て、環境的な振る舞いがそれぞれ異なっているが、すべて同じ要素、キトサン、セルロース、ペクチン、そして水で合成されている。

パヴィリオンと制作物の双方が具現化している形態と振る舞いの多様性は、自然の中でそれらがかたちづくられていく姿を反映している。そこではキチン質などの素材が、甲殻類の殻（外骨格）も、菌類の細胞壁も構成することができる。スティールやコンクリートとは対照的に、これらの素材によって生成された合成物は、周囲の環境と恒常的に対話している。制作物のあるものが湿度と温度に反応して形態を大きく変える一方で、別のものは季節の変化に応じて暗く、あるいは明るくなる。外観の多様性にもかかわらず、これらの制作物は同じ性質を共有している。それは、命ある状態ではそれぞれの特性が湿度によって調整され、命を終えた段階では水で分解され、エコシステムに戻っていくことである。

アグアオハIのプラットフォームは、形態と素材の構成に関する情報が物理的な特性（たとえば硬度や不透明度）、環境条件（たとえば荷重、温度、湿度）、製作上の制約（たとえば自由度、アームの速度、ノズル圧）などから直接的にもたらされる、バイオマテリアルのための3Dプリンターを中心としたロボットのガントリーで構成されている。ウォーターベイスト・デジタル・ファブリケーションと呼ばれるこのプラットフォームは、生物の世界に近づき、時にはそれに迫るスケールで、形態、機能、ファブリケーションの緊密な統合を生みだしている。

（中田雅章訳）

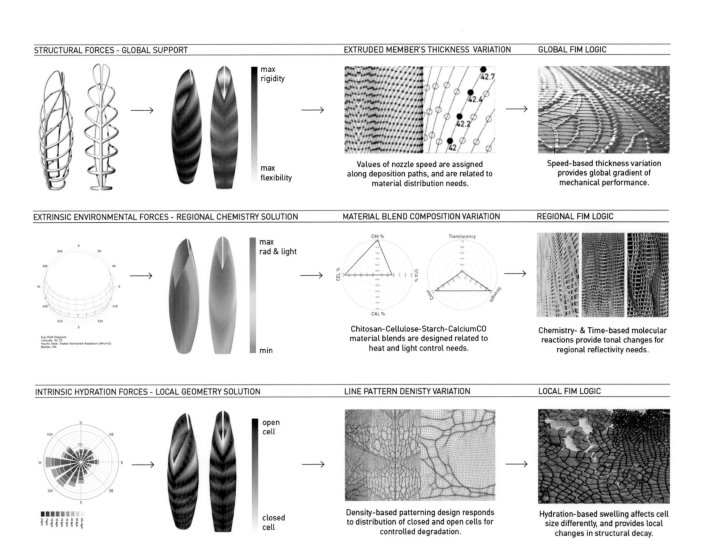

STRUCTURAL FORCES - GLOBAL SUPPORT

max rigidity

max flexibility

EXTRUDED MEMBER'S THICKNESS VARIATION

Values of nozzle speed are assigned along deposition paths, and are related to material distribution needs.

GLOBAL FIM LOGIC

Speed-based thickness variation provides global gradient of mechanical performance.

EXTRINSIC ENVIRONMENTAL FORCES - REGIONAL CHEMISTRY SOLUTION

Sun-Path Diagram
Latitude: 42.37
Hourly Data: Global Horizontal Radiation (Wh/m2)
Boston, MA

max rad & light

min

MATERIAL BLEND COMPOSITION VARIATION

CHI %

CEL %

CAL %

Translucency

Chitosan-Cellulose-Starch-CalciumCO material blends are designed related to heat and light control needs.

REGIONAL FIM LOGIC

Chemistry- & Time-based molecular reactions provide tonal changes for regional reflectivity needs.

INTRINSIC HYDRATION FORCES - LOCAL GEOMETRY SOLUTION

open cell

closed cell

LINE PATTERN DENISTY VARIATION

Density-based patterning design responds to distribution of closed and open cells for controlled degradation.

LOCAL FIM LOGIC

Hydration-based swelling affects cell size differently, and provides local changes in structural decay.

MULTISCALE INTERPLAY OF STRUCTURAL BEHAVIOR STRATEGIES

COMPUTATIONAL MAPPING DIAGRAM

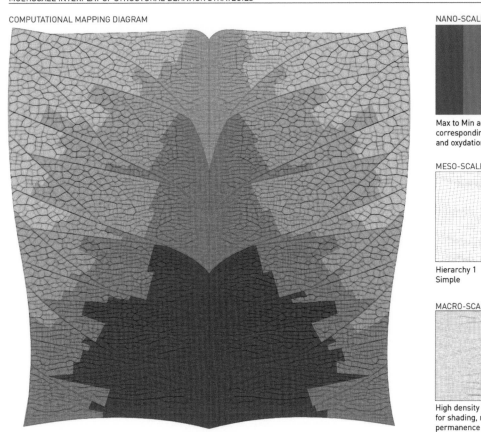

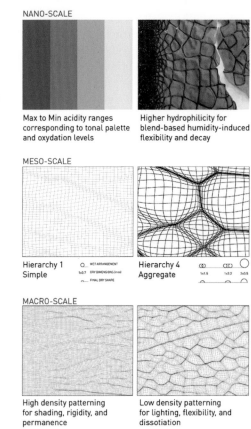

NANO-SCALE

Max to Min acidity ranges corresponding to tonal palette and oxydation levels

Higher hydrophilicity for blend-based humidity-induced flexibility and decay

MESO-SCALE

Hierarchy 1
Simple

WET ARRANGEMENT
DRY DIMENSIONS (mm)
FINAL DRY SHAPE

Hierarchy 4
Aggregate

1x1.5   1x2.2   3x3.5

MACRO-SCALE

High density patterning for shading, rigidity, and permanence

Low density patterning for lighting, flexibility, and dissotiation

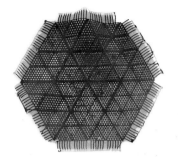  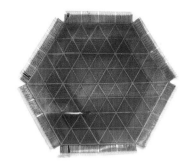 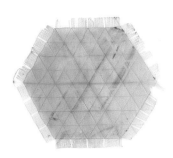

The Hex Series

The Aguahoja I Hex Series includes four hexagonal structures made of pectin, chitosan, and cellulose. Their design and manufacturing processes embody hierarchically informed material and functional tunability.

The panels' relative translucency and viscoelasticity are derived from pectin, contributing to skin-like structural properties. Their rigidity and strength are derived from chitosan and cellulose, contributing to shell-like structural properties. The tradeoffs in dominance between the two structural types – skin and shell – as well as their dissociation constants, are informed by their relative composition, pH, gas permeability, and surface features. Tuning these 'functional knobs' enables adaptive utility and functional gradients that can in turn be parametrically mapped onto a global design at various length scales.

Generative fabrication algorithms have been implemented to enhance the strength of the panels and compensate for their weakness via geometrical and digital fabrication strategies. Those include air pressure modulation and nozzle size variation to tune line diameter, and speed variation to tune resolution and layer alignment. Utilizing these raw ingredients, the four artifacts demonstrate parametric tunability of mechanical, optical, and dissociative properties.

The panels' surface roughness, hydrophilicity, concentration, and pH were modeled and modulated to imbue these biomaterials with mechanical and optical properties that are environmentally responsive, including their dissociation rate (Kd) in water. Surface roughness and hydrophilicity of the panels were controlled through the addition of nanofillers, pH, the relative concentrations of molecular components, and the mixing process. Pectin 'skins' of varying chemical compositions were 3D-printed with our novel water-based digital fabrication platform.

ヘックス・シリーズ

アグアオハIヘックス・シリーズは、ペクチン、キトサン、セルロースでできた4つの六角形の構造物を含んでいる。それらのデザインと製作のプロセスは、階層的に情報が与えられた素材と機能が調整可能なものであることを実際に示している。

パネルの相対的な透過性と粘弾性はペクチンによってもたらされ、皮膚のような構造特性の実現に役立っている。剛性と強度はキトサンとセルロースによってもたらされ、シェルのような構造特性を生みだすことを可能にしている。2つの構造形式——皮膚とシェル——のいずれかが優位になることによるトレードオフ、そしてその解離定数は、素材の配合比率、pH、通気性、表層の特徴から情報が与えられている。逆にこれらの「機能的なノブ」を調整することによって、様々なスケールでデザイン全体にパラメータ的にマッピング可能な、用途と機能の柔軟な配分を実現することができる。

幾何学とデジタル・ファブリケーションによってパネルの強度を高め、それらの弱点を補うために、生成的なファブリケーションのアルゴリズムが導入されている。アルゴリズムには、線の太さを調整するための空気圧の制御とノズル径の変化、解像度とレイヤーの配列を調整するための速度の変化が組み入れられている。4つの制作物は、これらの基本要素を用いることで、機械、視覚、分解に関する特性がパラメータにもとづいて調整可能であることを示している。バイオマテリアルに、水中でのそれぞれの解離定数（Kd）を含む環境に応答する機械的

および視覚的な特性を織り込むために、パネルの表層の粗さ、親水性、濃度、pHがモデル化され、調整されている。パネルの表層の粗さと親水性は、ナノフィルターの付加、pH、分子成分の相対濃度、そして混合のプロセスを通して制御される。様々な化学化合物によるペクチンの「皮膚」は、我々の新たなウォーターベース・デジタル・ファブリケーション・プラットフォームの中で、3D出力されている。　（中田雅章訳）

This page: Close-up perspective showing the regional distribution of aesthetic and mechanical properties derived from geometry and material distribution. Opposite, top: Close-up image of Water-based Robotic Fabrication (WBRF) system printing a flexible skin element. Opposite, bottom: Rigid cellulose-based elements printed onto a flexible skin. All courtesy of The Mediated Matter Group.

本頁：形状および素材組成分布に由来する、美的および機械的特性の局部的分布。右頁、上：軟性スキンを印刷中の水性ロボットファブリケーション（WBRF）システム。右頁、下：軟性スキン上に印刷された硬質セルロースベース要素。

Full unfolded Pavilion／パヴィヴィオン展開図

*Opposite, top: Front view of the
Aguahoja pavilion: A small opening
is designed to enable one person to
immerse him/herself in the multiscale
legibility of both aesthetic and
performative design considerations.
All courtesy of The Mediated Matter
Group.*

左頁、上：アグアオハ・パヴィリオン正面。
小さな開口部が設けられていることによ
り、私たちは作品に集中し、美しさと機能
性を考慮したデザインをマルチスケールに
読みとることができる。

Lattice 1

Dimensions
12.60" x 8.11" x 0.05"

Volume 4.900 in3
Surface Area = 19.176 in2

Composition

Chitosan	8% [w/v]
Cellulose	60% [v/v]
Calcium Carbonate	0% [w/v]
Starch	4% [w/v]
Acetic Acid	4% [v/v]

Effect

Translucency	0.80
Color	0.20
Strength	0.60

Lattice 2

Dimensions
12.60" x 8.11" x 0.05"

Volume 4.900 in3
Surface Area = 19.176 in2

Composition

Chitosan	10% [w/v]
Cellulose	55% [v/v]
Calcium Carbonate	3% [w/v]
Starch	4% [w/v]
Acetic Acid	5% [v/v]

Effect

Translucency	0.75
Color	0.20
Strength	0.80

Lattice 3

Dimensions
12.60" x 8.11" x 0.05"

Volume 4.900 in3
Surface Area = 19.176 in2

Composition

Chitosan	10% [w/v]
Cellulose	60% [v/v]
Calcium Carbonate	5% [w/v]
Starch	3.5% [w/v]
Acetic Acid	5% [v/v]

Effect

Translucency	0.60
Color	0.40
Strength	0.75

Lattice 4

Dimensions
12.60" x 8.11" x 0.05"

Volume 4.900 in3
Surface Area = 19.176 in2

Composition

Chitosan	15% [w/v]
Cellulose	55% [v/v]
Calcium Carbonate	0% [w/v]
Starch	4% [w/v]
Acetic Acid	7.5% [v/v]

Effect

Translucency	0.70
Color	0.30
Strength	0.70

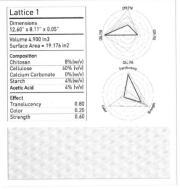

Lattice 5

Dimensions
12.60" x 8.11" x 0.05"

Volume 4.900 in3
Surface Area = 19.176 in2

Composition

Chitosan	15% [w/v]
Cellulose	65% [v/v]
Calcium Carbonate	5% [w/v]
Starch	5% [w/v]
Acetic Acid	7.5% [v/v]

Effect

Translucency	0.90
Color	0.20
Strength	0.90

Lattice 6

Dimensions
12.60" x 8.11" x 0.05"

Volume 4.900 in3
Surface Area = 19.176 in2

Composition

Chitosan	20% [w/v]
Cellulose	50% [v/v]
Calcium Carbonate	0% [w/v]
Starch	4% [w/v]
Acetic Acid	10% [v/v]

Effect

Translucency	0.10
Color	0.90
Strength	0.90

Lattice 7

Dimensions
12.60" x 8.11" x 0.05"

Volume 4.900 in3
Surface Area = 19.176 in2

Composition

Chitosan	20% [w/v]
Cellulose	60% [v/v]
Calcium Carbonate	0% [w/v]
Starch	4% [w/v]
Acetic Acid	10% [v/v]

Effect

Translucency	0.10
Color	0.85
Strength	0.95

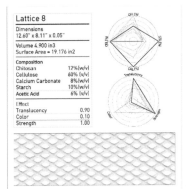

Lattice 8

Dimensions
12.60" x 8.11" x 0.05"

Volume 4.900 in3
Surface Area = 19.176 in2

Composition

Chitosan	12% [w/v]
Cellulose	60% [v/v]
Calcium Carbonate	8% [w/v]
Starch	10% [w/v]
Acetic Acid	6% [v/v]

Effect

Translucency	0.90
Color	0.10
Strength	1.00

Catalog of biopolymer compositions and their corresponding mechanical and optical properties, demonstrating a Parametric Chemistry approach to Fabrication Information Modeling (FIM)／FIMを用いたパラメトリック・ケミストリー手法を示す、バイオポリマー構成と機械的・視覚的特性カタログ

Nexi Oxman and The Mediated Matter Group

Wanderers
Cambridge, U.S.A 2015–

ネリ・オックスマン、メディエイティド・マター・グループ
ワンダラーズ
米国、ケンブリッジ 2015〜

Introduction

The word "planet" comes from the Greek term *planets* meaning "wanderer".

Wanderers is a collection of 3D-printed, biologically augmented "skins" designed to contain and transport microorganisms within spatially differentiated systems of subcutaneous microfluidic channels, folds, pores, and pockets. Each wearable is designed for a specific extreme environment where it transforms elements that are found in the atmosphere to one of the four classical elements supporting life. Design research at the core of this collection lies at the intersection of multi-material 3D printing and in-situ synthetic biology, think of each of the Wanderers as a wearable endosymbiont capable of photosynthesis, a real Material Ecology…

The research we carried out for Wanderers lies at the intersection of design, additive manufacturing and synthetic biology, bringing together digital growth and biological growth. The designs for Wanderers were digitally grown through a computational process capable of producing a wide variety of structures. Inspired by natural growth, the process creates shapes that adapt to an environment. Starting with a "seed form", the process simulates growth by continuously expanding and refining its shape. The wearables are designed to interact with a specific environment characteristic of their destination and generate or grow sufficient quantities of biomass, water, air and light necessary for sustaining life: some will photosynthesize converting daylight into energy, others will bio-mineralize to strengthen and augment human bone, and some will fluoresce to light the way in pitch darkness.

This project is the first of its kind to achieve volumetric translucency gradients in extremely high resolution (a few microns) using a process known as bitmap printing. In this process, material composition is given on voxel resolution and used to fabricate a design object with locally varying properties such as color, rigidity or opacity. Voxel resolution is set by the Stratasys printer's native resolution, making the need for path planning obsolete. Controlling geometry and material property variation at the resolution of the printer provides greater control over structure-property relationships.

Excerpts from "Wanderers – An Astrobiological Exploration", by Neri Oxman

イントロダクション

「惑星（プラネット）」という言葉は、「彷徨い人」を意味するギリシャ語「planets」から来ている。

ワンダラーズは、3Dプリンターによって生物学的に生成された「皮膚」のコレクションで、空間的に皮下の毛細管、ひだ、小孔、ポケットに細分化されたシステムの内部に、微生物をとり込み、運搬するためにデザインされたものである。それぞれのウェアラブルは、大気中に存在するエレメントを、生命をサポートする4つの基本的なエレメントの一つに転換する、特殊な局所環境としてデザインされている。このコレクションのデザイン上の探究の核は、複数の素材による3Dプリンターの出力と生体内での合成生物学が交差する地点にあり、一つ一つのワンダラーズを光合成が可能なウェアラブルな内部共生体、現実のマテリアル・エコロジーとして考えている。

我々がワンダラーズで行った研究は、デザイン、付加製造、合成生物学の交点で、デジタルによる成長と生物学的な成長を一体のものとしている。ワンダラーズのデザインは、様々な構造を生成することができるコンピュータのプロセスを通して、デジタル的に展開している。自然の成長にインスパイアされたこのプロセスは、環境に適応する形態をつくりだしている。「種の形状」から始まるプロセスは連続的に展開し、その形態を洗練することで成長をシミュレートしている。ウエアラブルはそれらが最終的に到達する地点の固有の環境特性に呼応するようにデザインされており、生命を維持するために必要になる十分な量のバイオマス、水、空気、光を生成あるいは成長さ

せている。あるものは太陽の光をエネルギーに転換するために光合成を行い、あるものは人体の骨を強化し、増加させるためにバイオ・ミネラライズを行い、またあるものは漆黒の闇の中でその経路を照らすために発光する。

このプロジェクトは、ビットマップ・プリンティングと呼ばれるプロセスを用いて、立体的な半透明の階調をきわめて高精細（数ミクロン単位）で実現しており、この種のものとしては初である。このプロセスの中で、素材のコンポジションは立体的な解像度をもとに生成され、色彩、剛性、不透明さといった、場所ごとに変動する特性をもったデザイン・オブジェクトをつくりだすために使われている。立体的な解像度はストラタシス社製のプリンターの装置固有の解像度によって規定されており、パス・プランニングはもはやその必要性がなくなっている。プリンターの解像度で形状と素材特性の変動を調整することによって、構造と特性の関係にたいするより緻密な制御が可能になっている。

ネリ・オックスマン『Wanderers, An Astrobiological Exploration』より。

（中田雅章訳）

Opposite: Close-in view of Mushtari filled with chemiluminescent fluid. Photograph by Paula Aguilera and Jonathan Williams.

右頁：化学発光液で満たされたムシュタリの近景。

Credits and Data

Project title: Wanderers
Location: Cambridge, USA
Designer: Neri Oxman
Collaborators: Christoph Bader and Dominik Kolb
Production: Stratasys
Photos: Yoram Reshef

Zuhal: Saturn's Wanderer
The hair-like, fibrous surface is designed to contain bacteria that can convert hydrocarbons to edible matter that can be safely consumed by humans.

ズハル：土星のワンダラー
毛のような繊維性の表面は、炭化水素を食用物質へと変えることができるバクテリアを含むようデザインされている。

Otaared: Mercury's Wanderer
The 3D-printed structure is computationally grown from the scapulae and the sternum outward generating a branched winged exoskeleton. The printed shell is designed to contain calcifying bacteria grown within a wearable Caduceus. The ultimate goal is to grow true bone structures acting as a protective exoskeleton, which, like the bone, integrate living cells with non-living matter to achieve functionalities such as bone regeneration, bone remodeling and self-organization. The complex vein-like system captured within the printed structure represents microfluidic channels that contain and enables the flow of media within and across the structure.

オターレッド：水星のワンダラー
3Dプリントされた構造体は、肩甲骨と胸骨から外側に向けて延びるよう計算され、分岐した羽状の外骨格を形成する。印刷されたシェル構造は着用可能な「ヘルメスの杖」のようにデザインされ、内部で石灰化バクテリアが成長できるようになっている。最終的な目標は、保護用の外骨格の役割をする本物の骨格を生育し、それが実際の骨のように、生きた細胞と非生存物質と統合させ、骨の再生・再構築・自己形成といった機能を獲得することである。印刷された構造物の内部にとり込まれた複雑な血管状のシステムは、内包するマイクロ流体のチャネルを表し、構造の全体に媒質が流れることを可能にする。

Qamar: Luna's Wanderer
This design functions as a wearable surface for generating and storing oxygen. Unlike a wearable biodome, this texture contains spatial spherical pockets for algae-based air-purification and biofuel collection. Photographs on pp. 156–157 by Yoram Reshef, courtesy of Neri Oxman.

カマル：月のワンダラー
このデザインは、酸素を生成し貯蔵する着用可能な表面構造として機能する。着用可能なバイオドームとは異なり、この生地は藻類ベースの空気清浄機能とバイオ燃料収集のための空間的球状ポケットを内包している。

Mushtari: Jupiter's Wanderer
*Designed as a giant single strand
filled with living matter inspired by
the form and function of the human
gastrointestinal tract, this wearable
is conceived of as an organ system
for consuming and digesting biomass,
absorbing nutrients and expelling
waste. The peristaltic movement of
matter within 3D-printed translucent
tracts is designed to support the flow
of cyanobacteria engineered to convert
daylight into consumable sucrose. As
media flows across the tract sucrose is
generated in the form of sugar cubes
contained within each pocket, on
the left and right sides of this corset.
Photograph by Yoram Reshef, courtesy
of Neri Oxman.*

ムシュタリ：木星のワンダラー
人間の胃腸管の形状と機能からインスピ
レーションを得て、生体で満たされた巨大
な単一の撚り糸としてデザインされたこの
着用可能なコルセットは、バイオマスをと
り込んで消化したり、栄養を吸収したり、
廃棄物を排出するための臓器システムとし
て考案された。3Dプリントされた半透明
の器官の内の蠕動運動は、日光を摂取可能
なスクロース（ショ糖）に変換するよう工学
操作された藍藻類（シアノバクテリア）の流
れをサポートするようデザインされた。媒
質が器官系全体を通じて流れると、このコ
ルセットの右側と左側にある各ポケットの
内部にスクロースが角砂糖として生成され
る。

Living Mushtari

We explored these questions through the creation of Mushtari, a 3D printed wearable with 58 meters of internal fluid channels. The wearable is designed to function as a microbial factory that uses synthetic biology to convert sunlight into useful products for the wearer. It does so with a symbiotic relationship between two organisms: a photosynthetic microbe – such as microalgae or cyanobacteria - and compatible microbes – such as baker's yeast and E. coli - that make useful materials. The photosynthetic microbe converts sunlight to sucrose – table sugar – which is then consumed by compatible microbes and converted into materials such as pigments, drugs, food, fuel, and scents. This is a form of microbial symbiosis, a phenomenon commonly found in nature. The wearer would ideally be able to trigger the microbes to produce a particular substance – for example, a scent, a color pigment, or fuel.

The wearable was designed using generative growth algorithms. These computational form generation processes mimic biological growth by generating recursive forms over many iterations of the algorithm.

Mushtari was 3D printed using the Objet Connex3, a color multi-material 3D Printer developed by Stratasys. Printing internal channels required an innovative support solution. Typically, the Objet Connex3 dispenses a gel-like support material into internal channels that cannot be cleared. To overcome this barrier, the Mediated Matter group collaborated with Stratasys to develop an experimental liquid-based support that could be dispensed into the channels during printing and easily cleared afterwards.

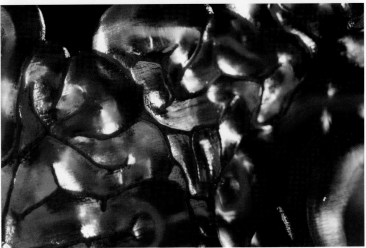

生きたムシュタリ

我々は「ムシュタリ」──58mの循環器管を内包する3Dプリント・ウエアラブル──の制作を通して探求を進めた。このウエアラブルは微生物製造所としてデザインされた。合成生物学を応用し、太陽光を着用者に役立つ物質へと変換する。有用な素材をつくりだすために、光合成微生物（微細藻類や藍藻など）と適合微生物（イースト菌や大腸菌など）、以上2種の有機体同士の共生関係が利用された。光合成微生物が太陽光をショ糖（砂糖）に変換し、ショ糖を吸収した適合微生物がさらに変換を行い、顔料・薬・食物・燃料・香料といった物質が生成される。これらは自然界にもみられる微生物共生の一つのかたちである。理論上、着用者は微生物を刺激し、求めている物質──好みの香り、色、燃料など──を生成させることができる。このウエアラブルは成長生成アルゴリズムを用いてデザインされた。アルゴリズムを何度も繰り返し、反復形状をつくりだすこ

とで生物の成長を模倣する、形態生成コンピューテーショナル・プロセスである。

ムシュタリは、Stratasys社開発のマルチカラーとマルチマテリアルでプリント可能な3Dプリンター、Objet Connex3を用いてプリントされた。しかし導管をウエアラブル内部にプリントするためには新たな手法を開発する必要があった。もともとObjet Connex3では、導管をプリントするためにジェルのような補助素材を用いていたが、この素材は完成後に除去不可能であった。そこでメディエイティド・マター・グループとStratasys社との共同で新素材が開発された。液状のこの実験的素材を用いることで、プリント中は導管を補助し、完成後は容易に除去することが可能となった。

This page, top: Front view of Mushtari filled with chemiluminescent fluid.
This page, bottom: Close-in view of Mushtari filled with chemiluminescent fluid. Photographs by Paula Aguilera and Jonathan Williams.

本頁、上から：化学発光液で満たされたムシュタリの近景。

Credits and Data
Project title: Mushtari and Living Mushtari
Location: Cambridge, USA
Designer: Neri Oxman
Lead Researcher: Will Patrick (Mediated Matter)
Collaborators: Christoph Bader and Dominik Kolb; Prof. Pamela Silver and Stephanie Hays (Harvard Medical School); Dr. James Weaver (Harvard Wyss Institute for Biologically Inspired Engineering); Steven Keating and Sunanda Sharma (Mediated Matter researchers)
Production: Stratasys

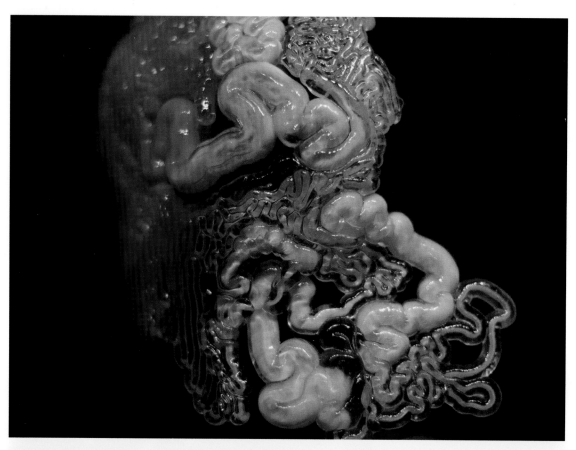

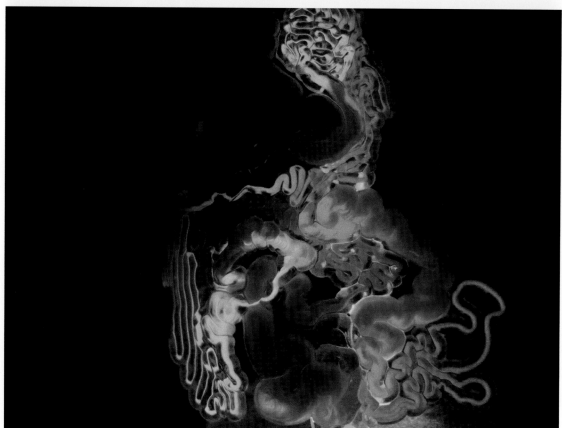

*This page, top and bottom: Time series
of filling a sidepiece of Mushtari with
chemluminescent fluid. Photographs
by Jonathan Williams and Paula
Aguilara.*

本頁、上から：ムシュタリの側面部品を化
学発光液で満たした際の変化。

Fluidics and a syringe pump (center) fabricated using 3D printing. 3D printing enables the manufacturing of micro and millifluidics with complex, 3D geometries. These fluidics were fabricated by The Mediated Matter Group at the MIT Media Lab in collaboration with Dr. David Sun Kong (MIT Lincoln Laboratory), Alec Nielsen (MIT Synthetic Biology Center), Che-Wei Taylor (MIT Media Lab) and Taylor Levy (MIT Media Lab).

3Dプリント技術を使用して製作した流体素子とシリンジポンプ（中央）。3Dプリントにより、複雑な3D幾何形状のマイクロ・ミリ単位の流体素子の製作が可能。これらの流体素子は、MITメディア・ラボのメディエイティド・マター・グループが、MITリンカーン研究所のデヴィッド・サン・コン博士、MIT合成生物学センターのアレック・ニールセン、MITメディアラボのチーウェイ・テイラーとテイラー・レヴィと共同で製作した。

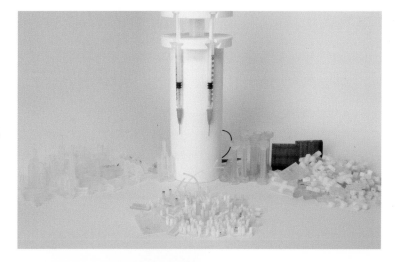

Multi-material fluidic valve 3D-printed using the Connex 500 3D printer (Stratasys). Multi-material 3D printing permits the manufacturing of fluidics with graded material properties, enabling functional fluidic devices such as valves. In the fluidic device above, elasticity of the 3D-printed material is varied to produce a functional proportional valve. Multi-material fluidic channels could be used to control cellular function. For example, the opacity of the channel wall could be varied to change the light radiance experienced by photosynthetic organisms inside the channel. This work was completed by Steven Keating, Maria Isabella Gariboldi, Will Patrick and Dr. Neri Oxman in collaboration with Dr. David Sun Kong.

Connex 500 3Dプリンター（Stratasys社）を用いて3Dプリントされた複数の素材からなる流体バルブ。複数素材の3Dプリントは、類別化された素材特性を備えた流体素子の製作を可能にし、バルブなどの機能的流体装置を可能にする。先述した流体装置の場合、機能的で均整の取れたバルブを製作するためには3D印刷素材の弾性が異なってくる。複数素材の流体チャネルは、細胞機能を制御する目的で使用することが可能である。たとえば、チャネル内の光合成生物が感じる光の輝度を変えるために、チャネル壁の不透明度を変化させることができる。この研究は、スティーブン・キーティング、マリア・イザベラ・ガリバルディ、ウィル・パトリック、ネリ・オックスマン博士と、デヴィッド・サン・コン博士の協働により完成された。

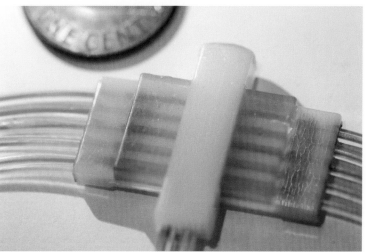

A functional single-material 3D-printed valve. These valves route liquids, such as a culture of synthetic organisms. This work was completed by Steven Keating, Maria Isabella Gariboldi, Will Patrick and Dr. Neri Oxman of the MIT Media Lab Mediated Matter Group in collaboration with Dr. David Sun Kong (MIT Lincoln Laboratory).

3D印刷された、単一素材による機能性バルブ。これらのバルブは、合成生物の培養液などの液体の流路を決定する。この研究は、MITメディアラボのメディエイティド・マター・グループ所属のスティーブン・キーティング、マリア・イザベラ・ガリバルディ、ウィル・パトリック、ネリ・オックスマン博士と、MITリンカーン・ラボラトリーのデヴィッド・サン・コン博士の協働により完成された。

A petri dish containing E.coli, engineered to produce green fluorescent protein. Micro-organisms, such as bacteria and yeast, have been engineered by scientists to fluoresce, bio-illuminate, produce pigments, convert light into fuel, and do many other functions. The Mediated Matter Group aims to use these engineered organisms in wearable products and product design.

緑色蛍光タンパク質を生成するよう操作された大腸菌を培養したペトリ皿。バクテリアやイースト菌のような微生物は、蛍光発光・生物発光・色素の生成・光の燃料への変換、及びその他数多くの機能のために、科学者により工学操作されてきた。メディエイティド・マター・グループは、こうした工学生成された有機体を、着用可能な製品と製品デザインに利用することを目指している。

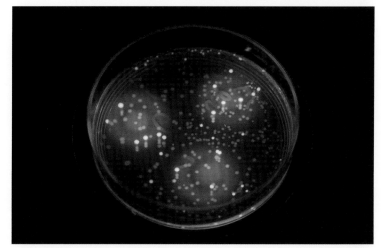

Photographs on this page courtesy of Neri Oxman and The Mediated Matter Group.

Sabin Design Lab
PolyBrick Series
Ithaca, U.S.A.   2014–

セイビン・デザイン・ラボ
ポリブリック・シリーズ
米国、イサカ　2014〜

Credits and Data
Principal Investigator: Jenny E. Sabin
PolyBrick 2.0 is in collaboration with Dr. Christopher J. Hernandez
PolyBrick 3.0 is in collaboration with Dr. Dan Luo
Design, Research and Production:
PolyBrick 1.0: Martin Miller, Nicholas Cassab
PolyBrick 2.0_A: Jingyang Liu Leo, Cameron Nelson, David Rosenwasser
PolyBrick 2.0_B: Eda Begum Birol, Yao Lu, Ege Sekkin, Colby Johnson, David
    Moy, Yaseen Islam
PolyBrick 3.0: David Rosenwasser, Shogo Hamada
PolyBrick H2.0: Viola Zhang, William Qian

PolyBrick interrogates 3D printed nonstandard clay components and digitally steered ceramic bricks and assemblies. Ceramic modules have been used as building blocks for many centuries; ubiquitous bricks and tiles lack recognition as a viable nonstandard building component in contemporary applications of mass customized and digitally fabricated systems. PolyBrick showcases next steps in the integration of complex phenomena through 3D-printed ceramic components and variegated assemblies.

From modular wall assemblies, to bone fragments, to DNA hydrogels, PolyBrick continues to evolve prototypes embedded with behavioral observations and performance. The latest experiment reflects upon new questions of adaptive and live materials in architecture through integration of advanced processes in additive manufacturing. 3D printed ceramic blocks are differentiated via the first architectural component glazed with DNA hydrogel and impregnated with a living signature. Using modified machines, advanced ceramic clay bodies, and high-resolution mold-making processes, our research utilizes 3D printing technology to develop micro-scale forms with customizable wells to produce signatures imbedded with multiple layers of decodable intelligence prescribed through DNA coding.

This system allows for 3D printed parts to exist at a micro-scale in the form of an architectural component, allowing for opportunistic deposition of DNA intelligence. Synthetically designed with advanced bioengineering, these DNA-steered bricks exemplify the future of biologically informed clay and ceramic building blocks in architecture. With unique DNA stamps and glaze, we explore the possibility of live signatures and dynamic surface techniques, coupled with nonstandard bricks in the context of living matter and digital ceramics.

PolyBrick is an ongoing design research project by Sabin Design Lab, Department of Architecture, Cornell University.

ポリブリックは、3Dプリンターで出力されたクレイの非標準部材、そしてデジタル制御によるセラミック煉瓦とその組み立てに関する研究である。基準寸法化されたセラミックの部材は、何世紀にもわたって建設資材として使われてきた。煉瓦やタイルはあらゆる場所で使われているにもかかわらず、細かくカスタマイズされたデジタル製作システムが応用される現代において自由で有用な建設用の部材として認識されることはなかった。ポリブリックは、3Dプリンターによるセラミックの部材と様々な組み立てを通して、複雑な事象を統合する新たな一歩を示している。

モジュール化された壁の構成から骨の細部、そしてDNAハイドロゲルに至るまで、ポリブリックは物質の振る舞いの研究と機能性を織り込んだプロトタイプを進化させ続けている。近年の実験では、3Dプリンターによる最先端の付加製造技術をとり入れ、建築に応用可能なライブ・マテリアルに関する新たな研究にとり組んでいる。DNAハイドロゲルの釉薬が塗られ、生体のシグネチュア（個体識別子）が刻まれたはじめての建築部材を通して、3Dプリンターによるセラミック・ブロックはこれまでとは異なるものになっている。専用の装置と最先端のセラミック・クレイの部材、そして高精度の鋳型加工技術にもとづく我々の研究は、3Dプリントの技術を活用することで、カスタマイズ可能な微細な凹みのマイクロスケールの形態を形成することが可能となり、複数のレイヤーにDNAのコーディングによる読みとり可能情報を埋め込んだシグネチュアが刻まれた。

このシステムは、3Dプリンターによるマイクロスケールのパーツが建築部材として存在し、必要に応じてDNA情報を付加することを可能にしている。最先端のバイオエンジニアリングを融合してデザインされたDNA制御の煉瓦は、生物学的に情報が付加されたクレイやセラミックによる建設資材の未来の可能性を示している。

命ある存在とデジタル・セラミックの関係の中で、固有のDNA型と釉薬を用いて我々が探究しているのは、非標準的な煉瓦に組み込まれた生体のシグネチュアとダイナミックな表層技術の可能性である。

（中田雅章訳）

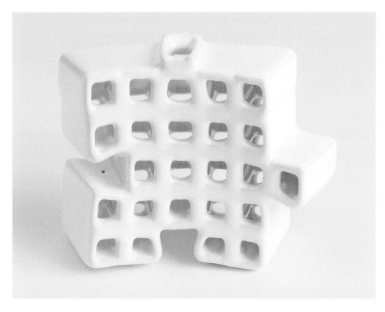

PolyBrick 1.0

PolyBrick showcases the next steps in the integration of complex phenomena towards the design, production, and digital fabrication of ceramic form in the design arts and architecture. This work includes advances in digital technology, three-dimensional (3D) printing, advanced geometry, and material practices in arts, crafts, and design disciplines. PolyBrick makes use of algorithmic design techniques for the digital fabrication and production of nonstandard ceramic brick components for the mortarless assembly and installation of the first fully 3D-printed and fired ceramic brick wall. Using customized digital tools, low-cost printing materials, and component-based aggregations, our research utilizes readily available 3D printing technology to develop large-scale forms through the aggregation of interlocking component based systems.

PolyBrick is an ongoing project in the Sabin Design Lab at Cornell Architecture. Originally on display at the San Francisco Museum of Craft and Design as part of the exhibition, "Data Clay: Digital Strategies For Parsing The Earth". This work is now part of the permanent collection at Centre Pompidou, originally on view as part of the "Mutations-Créations / Imprimer le monde" exhibition.

ポリブリック 1.0

ポリブリックはデザイン手法と建築におけるセラミック形態のデザイン、プロダクション、デジタル・ファブリケーションに向けて複雑な事象を統合する、新たな一歩を示している。この作品は芸術、工芸、デザイン分野でのデジタル・テクノロジー、3Dプリント、最先端の幾何学、そして素材の扱いの進化を包摂している。ポリブリックでは、はじめて完全に3Dプリンターで出力され、焼成されたセラミック煉瓦による壁をモルタルを使わずに組み立てるために、非標準的なセラミック煉瓦のデジタル・ファブリケーションと生産に、アルゴリズムにもとづくデザイン技術を用いている。カスタマイズされたデジタル・ツール、ローコストの出力用素材、そしてコンポーネント単位の組み立てにもとづく我々の研究では、大きなスケールの架構を組み立てる際にも、コンポーネントを基本単位とするシステムを連携させ既存の3Dプリント技術を用いていることが可能となった。

ポリブリックは、コーネル大学建築学部のセイビン・デザイン・ラボで、現在も進められているプロジェクトである。当初は「データ・クレイ：地球を読み解くためのデジタル戦略（Data Clay: Digital Strategies for Parsing the Earth）」展の出展作品として、サンフランシスコのクラフト・アンド・デザイン博物館で公開された。ポンピドゥ・センターでの「ミュータシオン＝クリエイシオン／世界を印刷する（Mutations-Créations / Imprimer le monde）」展で展示された後、現在は同館のパーマネント・コレクションの一つになっている。

（中田雅章訳）

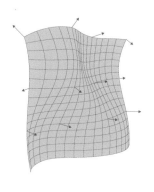
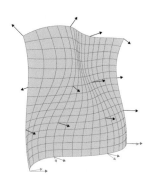
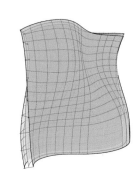

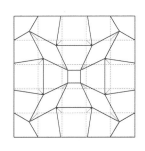
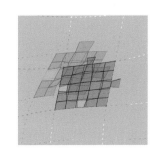
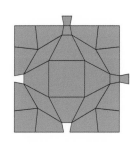
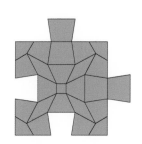

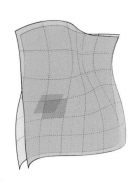
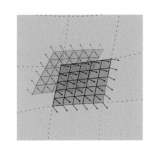
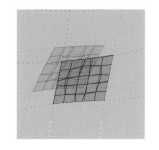
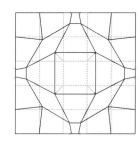

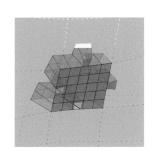
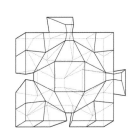
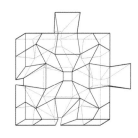
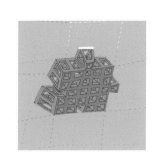

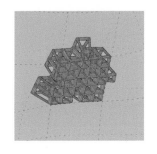
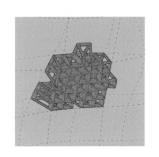

Opposite: Algorithmic design techniques for the digital fabrication and production of nonstandard ceramic brick components were used, enabling a mortarless assembly and the installation of the first fully 3D-printed and fired ceramic brick wall. This page: Diagrams showing the digital generation of the nonstandard bricks. All courtesy of the Sabin Lab.

左頁：非標準セラミック煉瓦構成部材をデジタル製作・生産するためのアルゴリズム・デザインの手法を用いることにより、完全に3Dプリント、焼成されたセラミック煉瓦壁の、モルタルを使用しない組立て・設置がはじめて可能になった。本頁：非標準煉瓦のデジタル生成ダイアグラム。

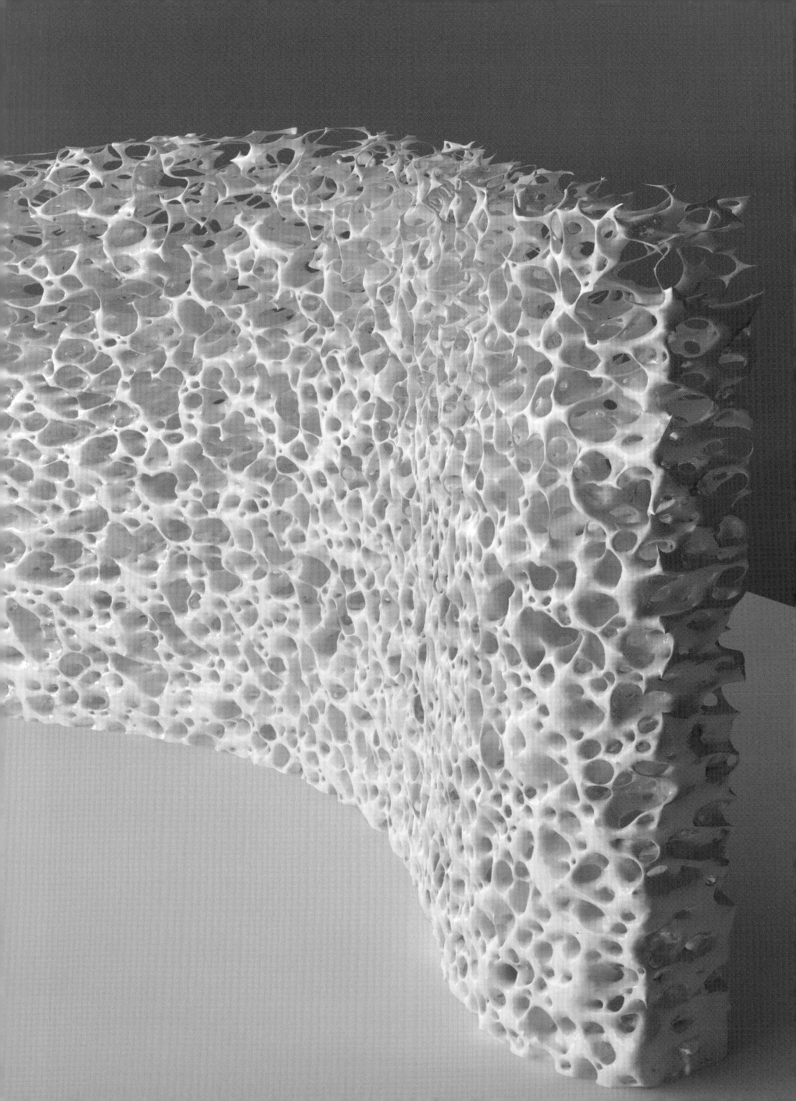

PolyBrick 2.0_A

PolyBrick 2.0 is generated with the rules, principles and behavior of bone formation. This allows for the production of variegated bricks that are light and porous at the top of a given structure and dense at the base to carry load and maintain efficient structural integrity. Using customized digital tools, low-cost printing materials, and component-based aggregations, our research utilizes readily available 3D printing technology to develop large-scale forms through the aggregation of interlocking component based systems. Based upon the principles and rules of bone formation behavior, PolyBrick 2.0 challenges the standardized unit size of a brick and instead proposes, through advances in 3D printing and material craft, the possibility of differentiated brick morphologies.

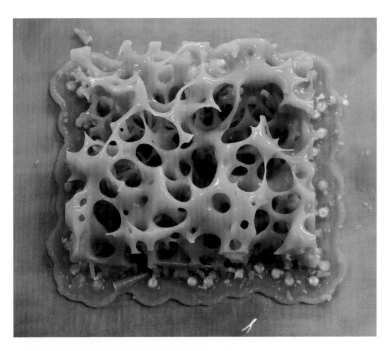

ポリブリック2.0_A

ポリブリック2.0は、骨形成の法則、原理、機序からつくりだされている。これによって、架構の頂部では軽くまばらで、荷重を支え効率的な構造の一体性を維持する足もとでは密度の高い、様々な形状の煉瓦をつくりだすことが可能になっている。カスタマイズされデジタル・ツール、ローコストの出力用素材、コンポーネント単位の組み立てにもとづく我々の研究では、大きなス

ケールの架構を組み立てる際にも、コンポーネントを基本単位とするシステムを連携させ既存の3Dプリント技術を用いていることが可能となった。骨形成の原理と法則にもとづくポリブリック2.0は、煉瓦の規格化されたサイズに疑問を投げでで、それに代わって3Dプリンターと資材製作の進化を活かし、これまでにはない煉瓦の形態的な可能性を示している。 （中田雅章訳）

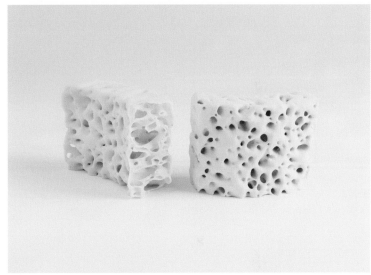

Opposite: Detail of PolyBrick 2.0_A, showing light conditions resulting from variegation. This page: Printing studies generated to emulate the behavior of bone formation, structurally relating to different forces in compression and tension. All courtesy of the Sabin Lab.

左頁：まだら模様から得られる光の様子を表すポリブリック2.0_Aのディテール。本頁：骨形成の挙動を模倣するために作成された3Dプリントのスタディ。構造的には圧縮力と引張力に関連する。

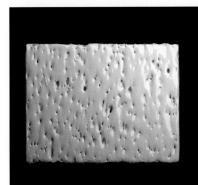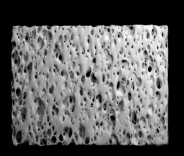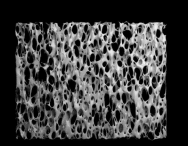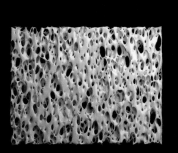

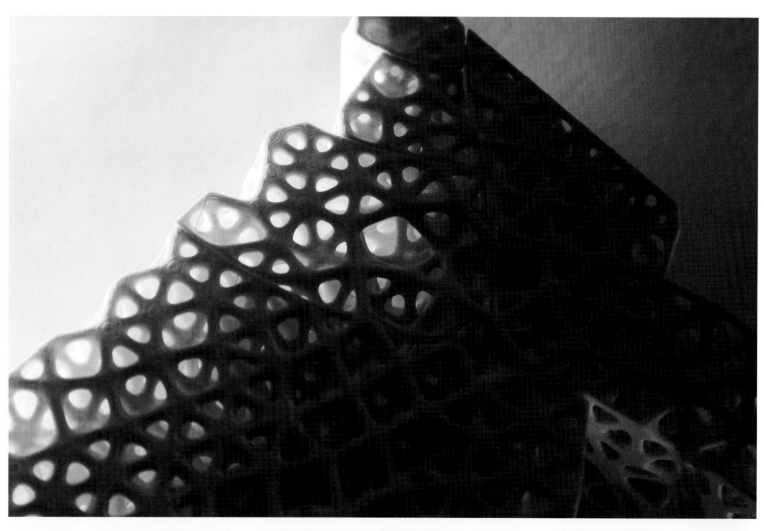

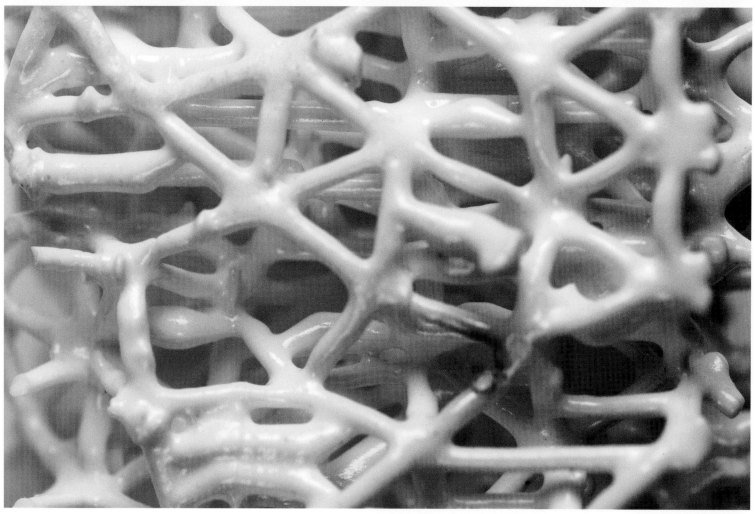

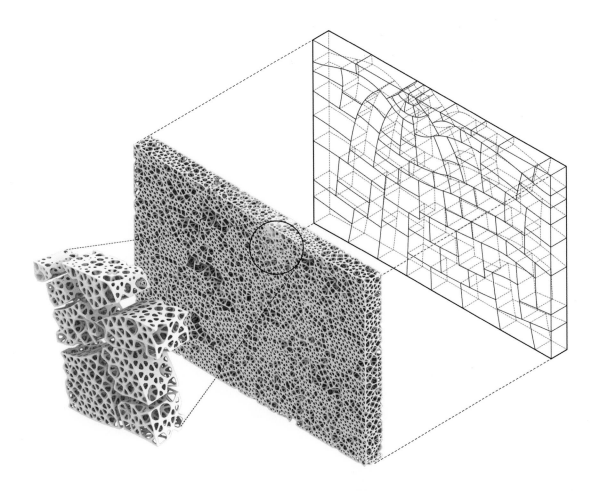

PolyBrick 2.0_B

Natural load bearing structures are characterized by aspects of specialized morphology, lightweight, adaptability, and a regenerative life cycle. PolyBrick 2.0 aims to learn from and apply these characteristics in the pursuit of revitalizing ceramic load bearing structures. For this, algorithmic design processes are employed, whose physical manifestations are realized through available clay/porcelain additive manufacturing technologies (AMTs). As part of the comprehensive workflow novel algorithmic processes are developed, fabrication methods are outlined, prototype performances are evaluated, and architectural applications are envisioned. PolyBrick 2.0 suggests a complete methodology in continuing PolyBrick's ubiquitous aim to "bridge digital processes with the production and design of nonstandard ceramic building blocks in architecture."

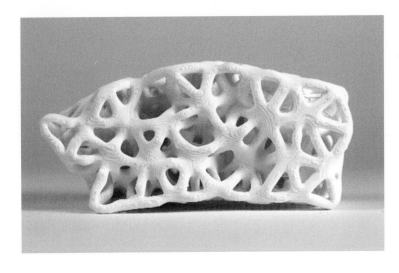

ポリブリック 2.0_B

自然物の荷重支持構造は、固有の形態、軽さ、適応性、そして再生の過程によって特徴づけられる。ポリブリック2.0はこれらの特性から学び、セラミックによる支持構造を改めて活性化するために、その応用を目指している。このため、アルゴリズムにもとづくデザイン・プロセスをとり入れ、このデザインをクレイ／磁器の付加造造技術（ATMs）によって物理的に実現する。広範なワークフローの一部として新たなアルゴリズムの工程が開発され、製作の枠組みが定められ、プロトタイプの性能が評価され、建築への応用が計画されている。ポリブリック2.0は「建築における非標準的なセラミックによる建設資材の製造・デザインとデジタル技術を結ぶ」という、すべてのポリブリックに共通の目的を探究していくうえでの、完全な方法論を示唆している。

（中田雅章訳）

Opposite, top: Detail of PolyBrick 2.0_B, which looks further into natural load-bearing structures. Opposite, bottom: Commercially available clay/porcelain additive manufacturing technologies (AMTs) were employed to work with the algorithmic design processes. The printed result is lightweight and adaptable. This page, top: Diagram showing the use of PolyBrick 2.0_B to constitute a wall assembly. This page, middle: Detail of PolyBrick 2.0_B. All courtesy of the Sabin Lab.

左頁、上：自然の耐力構造をさらに詳しく調べるためのポリブリック2.0_Bのディテール。左頁、下：アルゴリズム・デザイン・プロセスを使い作業するため、市場で入手可能な粘土・磁器の積層造形技術（AMTs）が用いられた。プリントされた成果物は軽量で柔軟性がある。本頁、上：壁の組立構造を構成するためのポリブリック2.0_Bの使用を表すダイアグラム。本頁、中：ポリブリック2.0_Bのディテール。

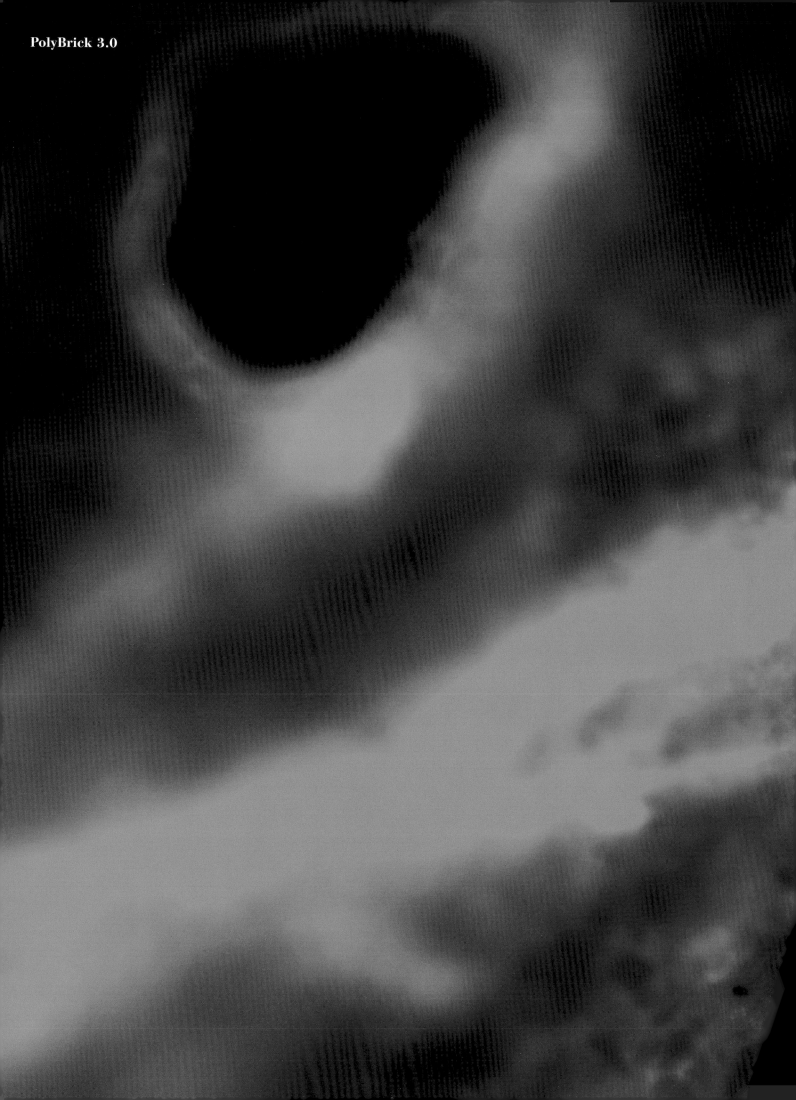

PolyBrick 3.0

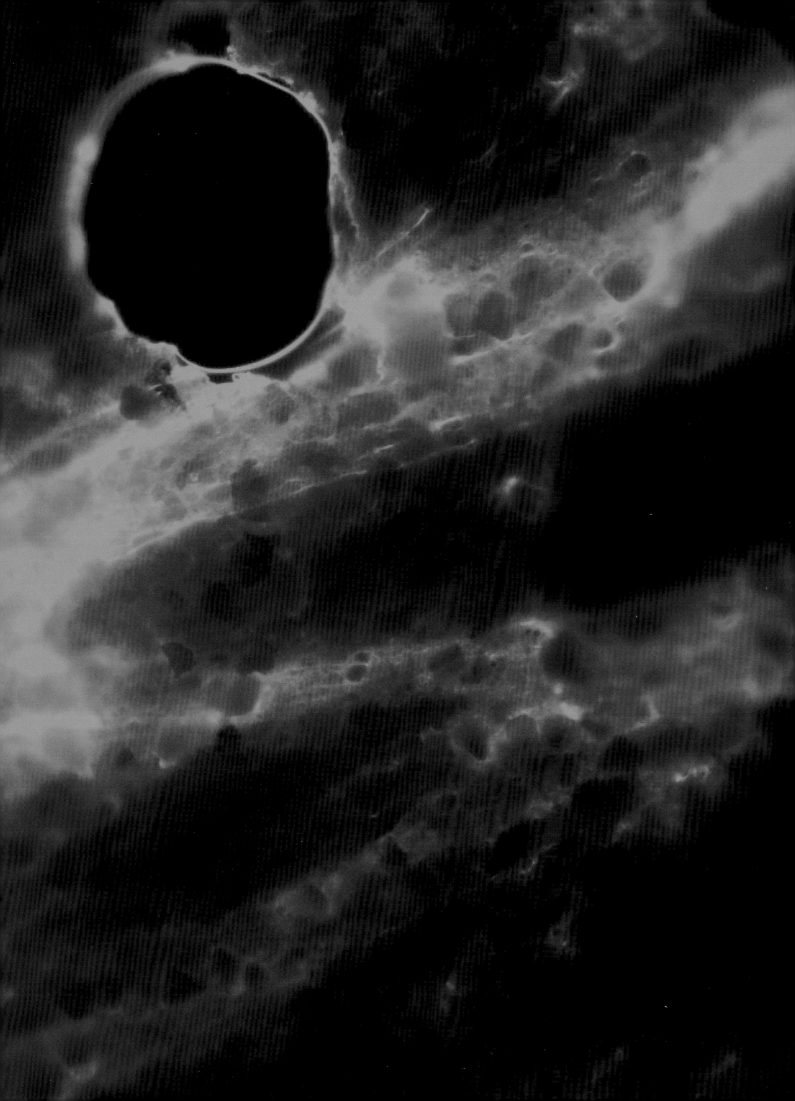

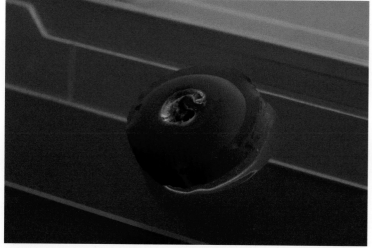

This iteration of PolyBrick reflects upon new questions of material compatibility through integrating advanced processes of additive manufacturing in ceramics with cutting-edge research in DNA hydrogel development. The work engages advances in material science, three-dimensional (3D) printing, micro-scale mold making, DNA hydrogels, and material practices derived from crafts, and computational design disciplines. Polybrick 3.0: Live Signatures Through DNA Hydrogels and Digital Ceramics outlines the use of microscale, three-dimensional printing technologies for the digital fabrication and production of nonstandard and inscribed ceramic block components. 3D-printed ceramic blocks are differentiated via the first architectural component glazed with DNA hydrogel and impregnated with a living signature. Three-dimensional modeling softwares enable precise 3D print resolution, which allows for an iterative feedback loop to be generated based on material constraints as well as performance assessments. Using modified digital fabrication machines, advanced ceramic clay bodies, and high resolution mold-making processes, our research utilizes 3D printing technology available on the consumer market to develop micro-scale forms with customizable wells to produce recognizable signatures imbedded with multiple layers of decodable intelligence prescribed through DNA coding. Operating at a scale that earlier 3D printing technology could not maneuver within, we developed a system of 3D printing molds to cast clay bodies. Eventually, this clay body was 3D-printed to the same effect. We have designed a system that allows for 3D-printed parts to exist at a micro-scale in the form of an architectural component and glaze mold, therefore allowing for the opportunistic deposition of DNA intelligence.

pp. 170–171: Micro-scale detail of a printed architectural component glazed with DNA hydrogel and impregnated with a living signature. This page: PolyBrick 3.0 reflects upon new questions of material compatibility through integrating advanced processes of additive manufacturing in ceramics with cutting-edge research in DNA hydrogel development. Opposite: Detail of PolyBrick H2.0, which adapts bone-based hydraulic networks to the scale of printed micro-textures. All courtesy of the Sabin Lab.

170〜171頁：プリントされた建築構成部材のマイクロスケールのディテール。DNAハイドロゲルが上塗りされ、生きたシグネチュアが埋め込まれている。本頁：ポリブリック3.0は、セラミクスの積層造形の先進的なプロセスをDNAハイドロゲルの開発における最先端の研究と統合することにより、素材の互換性に関する新しい問いを反映したものになっている。右頁：ポリブリックH2.0のディテール。骨をベースにした水力学的ネットワークを、印刷されたマイクロテクスチャーのスケールに適用した。

ポリブリック3.0

続いて進められたポリブリックは、セラミックの最先端の付加製造技術をDNAハイドロゲルを開発する先駆的な研究と融合することで、素材の互換性に関する新たな疑問にとり組んでいる。この研究は材料科学、3Dプリント、マイクロスケールの鋳型加工、DNAハイドロゲル、そして工芸から導かれた素材の扱いの進化とコンピュータによるデザイン制御をとり入れている。「ポリブリック3.0：DNAハイドロゲルとデジタル・セラミックスを通したライブ・シグネチュア」は、デジタル・ファブリケーションのためのマイクロスケールの3Dプリントの技術と、非標準的で刻印を施されたセラミック・ブロックを活用するうえでの基本的な方法を示している。3Dプリントされたセラミック・ブロックにはDNAハイドロゲルの釉薬が塗られ、リヴィング・シグネチュアが刻まれたはじめての建築部材として、これまでとは異なるものになっている。3次元のモデリング・ソフトウェアが3Dプリントによる正確な出力を可能にし、素材の制約

と性能評価にもとづいて持続的なフィードバックのループをもたらしている。専用のデジタル・ファブリケーション装置と最先端のセラミック・クレイの部材、そして高精度の鋳型加工技術にもとづく我々の研究は、市場に公開されている3Dプリントの技術を活用し、カスタマイズ可能な微細な凹みのマイクロスケールの形態を形成することが可能となり、複数のレイヤーにDNAのコーディングによる読みとり可能情報を埋め込んだシグネチュアが刻まれた。これまでの3Dプリント技術では処理できなかったスケールを扱い、我々はクレイの部材を造形するための鋳型の3Dプリント・システムを開発した。最終的にこれらクレイの部材も同品質で3Dプリント出力することが可能となった。我々は3Dプリンターによる部材が、建築の部材として、また表面にコーティングを施された型としてマイクロスケールで存在し、必要に応じてDNAの情報を付加することが可能なシステムをデザインしている。

（中田雅章訳）

PolyBrick H2.0

This project emerged from collaborative trans-disciplinary research between architecture, engineering, biology, and materials science to generate novel applications in microscale 3D-printed ceramics. Specifically, PolyBrick H2.0 adapts internal bone-based hydraulic networks through controlled water flow from 3D-printed micro-textures and surface chemistry. The series is a manifestation of novel digital fabrication techniques, bioinspired design, materials inquiry, and contemporary evolutions of building materials. A new purpose for the brick is explored that is not solely focused on the mechanical constraints necessary for built masonry structures. PolyBrick H2.0 interweaves the intricacies of living systems to create a more responsive and interactive material system. The PolyBrick H2.0 series looks at human bone as a design model for foundational research. PolyBrick H2.0 merges the cortical bone hydraulic network with new functionalities as a water filtration and collection system for self-preservation and conservation as well as passive cooling solutions. It also pushes the ability of 3D printing techniques to the microscale.

ポリブリック H2.0

このプロジェクトは、3Dプリンターによるマイクロスケールのセラミックの新たな応用を実現するための、建築、工学、生物学、材料科学の分野横断的な共同研究から生みだされている。ポリブリックH2.0は特に、3Dプリントによるマイクロスケールのテクスチュアと界面科学にもとづく水の動きの制御を通して、骨内部の水力ネットワークを応用している。このシリーズは、新たなデジタル・ファブリケーション技術、生体に着想を得たデザイン、材料の探求、そして現代の建設材料の進化の結晶である。ここでは、組積造の建物に必要とされる機能だけを考えるのではなく、まったく新しい煉瓦の用途が探求されている。ポリブリックH2.0は、よりレスポンシブでインタラクティブな材料のシステムをつくりだすために、生体がもつ複雑さをとり入れている。

ポリブリックH2.0シリーズの研究の基盤を構築するデザイン・モデルは、人体の骨である。ポリブリックH2.0は、個体の保存と維持、そしてパッシヴな冷却のための水の濾過と貯留のシステムとして、新たな機能に皮質骨の水力ネットワークを組み込んでいる。それはまた、3Dプリント技術をマイクロスケールに拡張している。

（中田雅章訳）

Working with clients that have global reputations for excellence, **Zaha Hadid Architects (ZHA)** is developing transformational projects across six continents. Based in London for 40 years, ZHA has refined architecture for the 21st century with a repertoire of projects that have captured imaginations across the globe. Form and space are woven within the structure of buildings that evolve from their surroundings and tie disparate programs together. Enticingly contextual, each project combines an unwavering optimism for the future with concepts of connectivity and integration. ZHA's architecture is defined by its democratic attitude, offering generous, articulated public spaces inside and out. The ideology embedded within each design is applied with a light touch as well as principled discipline, engaging the city with an act of attraction rather than imposition. Employing **advancements in design, material and construction technologies**, ZHA is a global leader in the application of **Building Information Modeling (BIM)** in the design, construction and operations of buildings to increase efficiencies as well as significantly reduce energy consumption and emissions. Marrying **innovative digital design with ecologically sound materials and sustainable construction practices**, ZHA does not look at the disparate parts, but works to understand them as a whole – delivering practical solutions to the defining challenges of our era. *Photograph by Virgile Simon Bertrand.*

Morphosis is a global architecture and design firm, creating compelling work that is intelligent, pragmatic, and powerful. For more than 40 years, Morphosis has practiced at the intersection of architecture, urbanism, and design, working across a broad range of project types and scales, including civic, academic, cultural, commercial, residential, and mixed-use; urban master plans; and original publications, objects, and art. Committed to the **practice of architecture as a collaborative enterprise**, founder and Pritzker Prize-winning architect Thom Mayne works in tandem with Partners Arne Emerson, Ung-Joo Scott Lee, Brandon Welling, and Eui-Sung Yi, and a team of more than 60 architects and designers in Los Angeles, New York, Shanghai and Seoul.

At the root of all Morphosis projects is a focus on rigorous research and innovation, prioritizing performance-driven design that is environmentally, socially, and economically sustainable. Morphosis has received 29 Progressive Architecture awards, over 120 American Institute of Architects (AIA) awards, and numerous other honors. Morphosis buildings and projects have been published extensively. With Morphosis, Thom Mayne has been the recipient of the highest recognitions in architecture, including the Pritzker Prize (2005) and the AIA Gold Medal (2013). *Portrait by Michael Powers.*

The Living, a first-of-its-kind Autodesk Studio, combines research and practice, exploring new ideas and technologies through prototyping. The studio's work embraces the complexity at the intersection of ideas, technologies, materials, culture, humans, non-humans, and the environment. Focusing on the intersection of biology, computation, and sustainability, the studio has articulated three frameworks for **harnessing living organisms for architecture: bio-computing, bio-sensing, and bio-manufacturing**. The studio welcomes rapid change, embraces design with uncertainty, develops rules rather than forms, and designs with unknowable forces. *Photograph courtesy of The Living.*

Marc Fornes, registered and practicing Architect (DPLG), leads **THEVERYMANY**, a New York-based studio specializing in **large-scale, site-specific structures that unify skin, support, form, and experience into a single system**. Over the last ten years, Marc has designed and built a number of organic, thin-shell constructions that push the limits of form, structure, and space. This body of work is situated between the fields of art and architecture, with a particular focus in the realm of public art. Each public artwork aims to provide a unique spatial experience for its visitors, while also contributing to the visual identity of a place and catalyzing community engagement.

This practice is propelled by Marc's expertise in computational design. THEVERYMANY represents a body of research that continues to advance new parametric outcomes and implement complex techniques in architecture and beyond. Each project evolves previous inquiries and further investigates design though codes and computational protocols, addressing new ways to describe complex curvilinear self-supported surfaces into a series of flat elements for efficient fabrication. *Portrait courtesy of THEVERYMANY.*

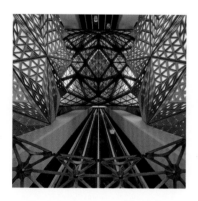

ザハ・ハディド・アーキテクツ (ZHA) は、国際的に著名なクライアントとともに仕事を進め、これまでのあり方を一変させるプロジェクトを世界規模で展開している。ZHAはロンドンを拠点に40年にわたって活動を続け、世界各地のイマジネーションをとらえる様々なプロジェクトで、21世紀の建築をより緻密で高度なものとしている。その作品は、形態と空間を環境に根差した構造に織り込み、多様なプログラムを一つに融合させている。魅力的なコンテクストをもたらすそれぞれのプロジェクトは、コネクティビティとインテグレーションのコンセプトに、揺らぐことのない未来への希望を結び合わせている。ZHAの建築は民主的な姿勢を特徴としており、プロジェクトの内外に、開かれ明確に表現された公共の空間を提供している。それぞれのデザインに込められたイデオロギーは、軽快なタッチと信念に基づく自制心のもとでプロジェクトに表現され、押しつけではなく人々を惹きつける作品を街に織り込んでいる。ZHAは、**デザイン、素材、施工技術の進歩**をとり入れ、効率性を高め、エネルギー消費量や炭素排出量を大幅に低減するために、デザイン、施工、施設運営に**ビルディング・インフォメーション・モデリング (BIM)** を応用しており、この分野での世界的なリーダーである。ZHAは、**革新的なデジタル・デザイン**をエコロジカルな素材とサステナブルな建物に組み合わせることで、パーツを個別に考えるのではなく、それらを全体として理解し、我々の時代の重要な課題にたいする実践的なソリューションをもたらしている。 （中田雅章訳）

モーフォシスは世界的な建築およびデザイン事務所で、知的かつ実用的で力強い、説得力のある作品をつくりだしている。40年以上にわたって建築、アーバニズム、デザインが交わる領域で仕事にとり組み、公共、教育、文化、商業、住居、複合用途など幅広い形式とスケールのプロジェクト、都市のマスター・プラン、そしてオリジナルの出版物、オブジェ、アートなどを幅広く手がけている。事務所は**協働的な組織として建築の実務**にかかわり、創立者でプリツカー賞を受賞した建築家のトム・メインは、パートナーのアルネ・エマーソン、アンジュ・スコット・リー、ブランドン・ウェリング、イ・ウィソンとともに、ロサンゼルス、ニューヨーク、上海、ソウルの60人を超える建築家やデザイナーのチームと協力しつつ仕事を進めている。モーフォシスのすべてのプロジェクトの根源には、徹底した研究とイノベーションにたいする強い意識があり、環境的、社会的、経済的にサステナブルな、パフォーマンスに裏打ちされたデザインを何よりも重視している。モーフォシスは29のプログレッシブ・アーキテクチュア・アワード、120を超えるアメリカ建築家協会賞 (AIAアワード) など様々な賞を受賞し、その作品やプロジェクトは多くのメディアでとり上げられている。トム・メインはモーフォシスとともに、プリツカー賞 (2005年) やAIAゴールド・メダル (2013年) など、建築界で最も栄誉ある賞を受けている。 （中田雅章訳）

ザ・リヴィングは、こうした形式のものとしては世界初となるオートデスク・スタジオで、研究と実践を連携させ、プロトタイプづくりを通して新たなアイディアとテクノロジーを探究している。スタジオの作品は、アイディア、テクノロジー、素材、文化、人間、人間以外の存在、そして環境が交差する場所に生まれる複雑さを内包している。スタジオは、バイオロジー、コンピュテーション、サステナビリティの交点に着目しながら、**生命ある有機体を建築に利用するための3つのフレームワーク、バイオ・コンピューティング、バイオ・センシング、バイオ・マニュファクチュアリング**を確立している。急速な変化を好感とし、不確実さをともなうデザインを受け入れ、形態を決めるのではなくルールを定め、知覚しがたい力でデザインを進めている。 （中田雅章訳）

マルク・フォルネスはフランス登録建築家資格をもつ実務家で、ニューヨークに拠点を置くスタジオ、**ザベリーメニー**を主導し、表層、架構、形態、体験を一つのシステムに織り込む、敷地の特性に根差した大規模な構造物を手がけている。この10年でマルクは、形態、構造、空間の境界を拡張する有機的な薄いシェルの構造物を数多くデザインし、実現している。彼の仕事の根幹は芸術と建築の間にあり、パブリック・アートに特に関心を寄せている。彼のパブリック・アート作品はいずれも、観る者に独特な空間体験をもたらすとともに、場所の視覚的なアイデンティティを強め、コミュニティのかかわりを深めることを目指している。その仕事は、コンピューテーショナル・デザインを活かすマルクの優れた能力によって推進されている。ザベリーメニーは、パラメータにもとづく新たな創作を発展させ、建築やそれ以外の領域に複雑な技術をとり入れていく研究の主体である。それぞれのプロジェクトはこれまでの疑問を発展させ、コード化とコンピューテーショナル・プロトコールによってさらにデザインを探究し、効率的なファブリケーションのために、複雑な曲線からなる自立した表層を平板なエレメントの集合体として描きだす、新たな手法にとり組んでいる。 （中田雅章訳）

The Institute for Computational Design and Construction (ICD) at the University of Stuttgart is dedicated to the teaching and research of integrative computational design and construction processes in architecture. The ICD's goal is to prepare students and researchers for the continuing advancement of computational processes in architecture, as they merge the fields of design, engineering and construction. The interrelation of such topics is exposed as both a technical and intellectual venture of formal, spatial, constructional and ecological potentials. There are two primary research fields at the ICD: the theoretical and practical development of generative computational design processes, and the integral use of robotic fabrication and construction processes. These topics are examined through the development of computational methods which balance the reciprocities of form, material, structure and environment, and integrate technological advancements in manufacturing for the production of performative material and building systems. *Photograph courtesy of ICD.*

Neri Oxman is an architect, designer, inventor, and professor at MIT's Media Lab, where she is the founding director of The Mediated Matter Group, an experimental design practice combining commissioned works with the creation of forward-focused technologies and scientific knowledge. The Group conducts research at the intersection of computational modeling, digital fabrication, materials science, and synthetic biology, and applies that knowledge to design across disciplines from the microscale to the building scale.

Oxman pioneered the field of Material Ecology, which studies relationships and interactions between designed objects and the natural environment. Her work – documented in over 150 scientific publications and inventions – is in the permanent collections of MoMA, SFMOMA, Centre Pompidou, the Museum of Fine Arts in Boston, Cooper Hewitt, and the Smithsonian Design Museum, among others.

Since 2005, Oxman and her team have won numerous awards and have grown in international scope and acclaim. Among her awards are the London Design Innovation Medal (2018), and the Cooper Hewitt National Design Award (2018). Most recently, Oxman was the recipient of an Honorary Fellowship by the Royal Institute of British Architects (2019). *Photograph courtesy of The Mediated Matter Group.*

With strong links to the Sabin Lab at Cornell AAP, Jenny Sabin Studio is an experimental architecture studio based in Ithaca, NY. The studio investigates the intersections of architecture and science, and applies insights and theories from biology and mathematics to the design, fabrication, and production of material structures and spatial interventions. We collaborate with scientists and engineers and employ architects, designers, and artists to interrogate the space between disciplines. Our applied projects are diverse and operate across multiple length scales including adaptive materials, building facades, installations, pavilions, tapestries, rugs, and architectural interventions. Our portfolio is equally diverse including clients such as Microsoft, the Museum of Modern Art, Nike Inc., Cooper Hewitt Design Museum, the American Philosophical Society Museum, the Exploratorium, and the Frac Centre. *Photograph courtesy of Jenny Sabin Studio.*

Sabin Lab, Department of Architecture, Cornell University at Cornell AAP is a trans-disciplinary design research lab with specialization in computational design, data visualization and digital fabrication. We investigate the intersections of architecture and science, and apply insights and theories from biology, robotics, computer science, mathematics, materials science, physics, fiber science, and engineering to the design, fabrication, and production of responsive material structures and systems. Our research including bioinspired adaptive materials, DNA 3D printed bricks, robotic fabrication, and 3D Kirigami assemblies has been funded substantially by the National Science Foundation, Autodesk, the Grainger Foundation, and the National Academy of Engineering. *Photograph courtesy of Sabin Lab.*

コンピュテーショナル・デザインおよび建設研究所（ICD）は、シュトゥットガルト大学内の建築における統合的なコンピュータを用いたデザインと建設プロセスの教育・研究機関である。ICDの目的は、コンピュータによる工程を建築の世界でさらに展開していくために、学生と研究者を、デザイン、エンジニアリング、建設の各分野をまとめるうえで必要な能力を備えた人材とすることである。それらのテーマのかかわりは、形態、空間、建設、エコロジーの可能性の、技術と知の両面での冒険として姿を現してくる。ICDには2つの基本的な研究領域がある。一つは生成的なコンピュータによるデザイン・プロセスの理論的および実践的な開発、もう一つはロボット製造と建設プロセスの一体的な活用である。これらのテーマは、形態、素材、構造、環境をバランスさせ、有効な素材と建設システムをつくりだすための、生産における技術の進化を統合する、コンピュータを用いた手法の開発を通して探求されている。

（中田雅章訳）

ネリ・オックスマンは建築家、デザイナー、発明家。MITメディア・ラボの教授で、作品づくりを未来志向のテクノロジーと科学的な知識と組み合わせる実験的なデザインを実践するメディエイティド・マター・グループをラボ内に創設し、ディレクターを務めている。グループは、コンピュテーショナル・モデリング、デジタル・ファブリケーション、マテリアル・サイエンス、合成生物学が交差する領域で研究にとり組み、その知見をマイクロスケールから建物のスケールに至るまで、幅広い分野のデザインに適応している。

（中田雅章訳）

ジェニー・セイビン・スタジオは、ニューヨーク州イサカに拠点を置く実験的な建築スタジオであり、コーネル大学建築・芸術・都市計画学部（AAP）のセイビン研究室と強いつながりをもつ。スタジオは建築と科学の交差点を追求しており、生物学と数学からの洞察や理論を、材料組織と空間的介入のデザイン、製作、製造に応用する。科学者やエンジニアと協力し、建築家、デザイナー、アーティストを雇用し、専門分野間の空間について問いかけを行っている。応用的なプロジェクトは多岐に渡り、適応材料、建物のファサード、インスタレーション、展示館、タペストリー、ラグマット、建築的介入を含む複数範囲の規模で稼働している。クライアントには、マイクロソフト社、ニューヨーク近代美術館、ナイキ社、クーパー・ヒューイット国立デザイン博物館、アメリカ哲学会博物館、エクスプロラトリアム、Fracセンターなどが含まれ、ポートフォリオもまた多様である。

（松本晴子訳）

コーネル大学建築・芸術・計画学部（AAP）のセイビン・ラボは、コンピュテーショナル・デザイン、データの視覚化、デジタル・ファブリケーションにとり組む分野横断的なデザイン・リサーチ・ラボである。建築と科学が交差する地平を探究し、生物学、ロボット工学、コンピュータ・サイエンス、数学、材料科学、物理学、繊維科学、そしてエンジニアリングから導かれた知見と理論を、レスポンシヴな材料による構造とシステムのデザイン、製作、生産にとり入れている。生体に着想を得た応用可能な材料、3Dプリンターで出力されDNAが刻まれた煉瓦、ロボティック・ファブリケーション、そして3次元の切り紙細工などの研究は、アメリカ国立科学財団、オートデスク、グレインジャー財団、アメリカ国立技術アカデミーから多くの研究資金を得ている。

（中田雅章訳）

a+u Digital Issues

2019年12月号

OFFICE Kersten Geers David Van Severen

オフィス・ケルステン・ゲース・ダヴィド・ファン・セーヴェレン

2019年11月号

Contemporary Sri Lanka on Geoffrey Bawa's 100th

スリランカの現在──ジェフリー・バ100周年

2019年10月号

Drawings from the Kenzo Tange Archive–National Gymnasiums for Tokyo Olympics

丹下健三アーカイヴのドローイング──国立屋内総合競技場

2019年9月号

Heinz Bienefeld – Drawing Collection

ハインツ・ビーネフェルト──ドローイング・コレクション

2019年8月号

Arabic Context and Culture–3 Projects by Jean Nouvel Recent Projects

アラビアの文化とコンテクスト・ヌーヴェルの3作品最新作品

2019年7月号

Transit Oriented "Development and Management"

35都市のTODM──持的なまちづくりのマネジメント

2019年6月号

Diller Scofidio + Renfro

ディラー・スコフィディオ＋レンフロ

2019年5月号

Mid-century Modern Houses in New Canaan

ニューケイナンのミッドセンチュリー・モダン・ハウス

2019年4月号

Coussée and Goris

クセー・アンド・ゴリス

2019年3月号

Álvaro Siza and Eduardo Souto de Moura

アルヴァロ・シザとエドゥアルド・ソウト・デ・モウラ

2019年2月号

The Thinking Hand – Takenaka Corporation and Takenaka Carpentry Tools Museum

手わざと建築──竹中工務店と竹中大工道具館

2019年1月号

Re: Swiss Emerging Architects Under 45 in Switzerland

Re:スイスの建築家 U-45

発行：(株)エー・アンド・ユー
〒100-6017　東京都千代田区霞が関三丁目2番5号　霞が関ビルディング17階
TEL：03-6205-4384 | FAX：03-6205-4387